SACRAMENTO PUBLIC LIBRARY
828 "I" Street
Sacramento, CA 95814
04/12

THE UNFINISHED
REVOLUTION

D0058962

THE UNFINISHED
REVOLUTION

VOICES FROM THE GLOBAL FIGHT
FOR WOMEN'S RIGHTS

EDITED BY MINKY WORDEN

Seven Stories Press
NEW YORK

Copyright © 2012 by Minky Worden
Individual chapters © 2012 by each author

A Seven Stories Press First Edition

All rights reserved. No part of this book may be reproduced, stored in a retrieval system, or transmitted in any form or by any means, including mechanical, electric, photocopying, recording, or otherwise, without the prior written permission of the publisher.

Seven Stories Press
140 Watts Street
New York, NY 10013
www.sevenstories.com

Library of Congress Cataloging-in-Publication Data

The unfinished revolution : voices from the global fight for women's rights / edited by Minky Worden.
    p. cm.
Includes bibliographical references and index.
ISBN 978-1-60980-387-2 (pbk.)
  1. Women's rights. I. Worden, Minky.
HQ1236.U49 2012
305.42--dc23
                                        2011052738

College professors may order examination copies of Seven Stories Press titles for a free six-month trial period. To order, visit http://www.sevenstories.com/textbook or send a fax on school letterhead to (212) 226-1411.

Book design by Jon Gilbert

Printed in the USA.

9 8 7 6 5 4 3 2 1

For Cynthia Brown,

who pushed the human rights movement to recognize and defend women's rights,

who never succumbed to the professional temptations of convention and convenience,

and whose fierce intellect, golden pen, and wise ways inspire us all.

Contents

PART 4

THE ECONOMIES OF RIGHTS: EDUCATION, WORK, AND PROPERTY

Dorothy Q. Thomas
The Revolution Continues

LIST OF ACRONYMS USED IN THIS BOOK

ACLU   American Civil Liberties Union

CARMMA   Campaign on Accelerated Reduction of Maternal
                   Mortality

CEDAW   Convention on the Elimination of All Forms of
                   Discrimination Against Women

CSW   Commission on the Status of Women

FDLR   Democratic Forces for the Liberation of Rwanda

FGM   female genital mutilation

ICEUS   Immigration and Customs Enforcement

ICCPR   International Covenant on Civil and Political Rights

ICERD   International Convention on the Elimination of all
                   Forms of Racial Discrimination

ICESR   International Covenant on Economic, Social, and
                   Cultural Rights

ICRC   International Committee for the Red Cross

ICRW   International Center for Research on Women

ILO   International Labor Organization

LGBT   lesbian, gay, bisexual, and transgender community

MDG   Millennium Development Goals

NGO   non-governmental organization

NSHR   National Society for Human Rights

PRC   People's Republic of China

UDHR   Universal Declaration of Human Rights

UNAMA   United Nations Assistance Mission in Afghanistan

UNDP   United Nations Development Program

UNESCO   United Nations Educational, Scientific, and Cultural Organization

UNFPA   United Nations Population Fund

UNHCR   United Nations High Commissioner for Refugees

UNICEF   United Nations Children's Fund

UNIFEM   United Nations Development Fund for Women

WHO   World Health Organization

WRD   Women's Rights Division at Human Rights Watch

A Historic Moment for Women's Rights

Christiane Amanpour

To the one who makes the lonely feel they are not alone, who satisfies those who hunger and thirst for justice, who makes the oppressor feel as bad as the oppressed. . . . may her example multiply,
May she still have difficult days ahead, so that she can do whatever she needs to do, so that the next generation will not have to strive for what has already been accomplished.

—Brazilian author Paulo Coelho, from his poem "To Shirin Ebadi," read at the Nobel Peace Prize concert in 2003

In October 2011, the Norwegian Nobel Committee named three women winners of the Nobel Peace Prize—an award won by only a dozen women since 1901. Liberian President Ellen Johnson Sirleaf, her compatriot Leymah Gbowee, and Yemeni activist Tawakkol Karman were honored "for their nonviolent struggle for the safety of women and for women's rights," in a declaration that was clearly intended to send the message that the moment for women and girls to achieve basic rights had arrived.

The Peace Prize citation proclaimed, "We cannot achieve democ-

Christiane Amanpour is the anchor of ABC's Sunday morning news program, This Week with Christiane Amanpour. Chief International Correspondent at CNN from 1992 to 2010, she joined CNN in 1983. Amanpour has reported on and from the world's major hot spots including Afghanistan, the Balkans, Iran, Iraq, Rwanda, and Somalia, and has won every major broadcast award—including nine Emmys, four George Foster Peabody Awards, two George Polk Awards, and the Courage in Journalism Award.

racy and lasting peace in the world unless women obtain the same opportunities as men to influence developments at all levels of society." As the Nobel Committee emphasized, this moment is as dramatic as any in recent decades for women and girls.

I have been a foreign correspondent for almost three decades in just about every war zone there is. I have made my living in an overwhelmingly male profession, bearing witness to some of the most horrific events of the end of the last century. In this time, we have seen enormous changes in law and practice, with measurable progress in women's ability to get an education, to work, and to make decisions about their own bodies.

Yet as this book seeks to explain, in much of the world, basic rights such as control over their lives and access to health care remain far out of reach for millions of women and girls.

In India, some state governments can't be bothered to count the number of women dying from preventable causes in pregnancy and childbirth. In the United States, rape victims are denied justice through bureaucratic inertia. In Somalia, warlords and famine—yet again—threaten women's lives and families. In some European countries, women fleeing domestic violence are sent home to "work it out" with their abusive spouses. In Saudi Arabia, women of all ages live under a male guardianship system, preventing them from working, studying, marrying, driving, or traveling abroad without the permission of a male guardian—a father, husband, brother, or even a son.

China is a country of contradictions that has lowered infant and maternal mortality rates, and raised education standards, while still imposing a one-child policy that often leads to major abuses of women, including forced abortions. Indeed, in many countries, the picture is mixed, with progress in education and maternal mortality paired with escalating health threats such as HIV/AIDS and barriers to participation in public life.

In several places, including Iraq and Afghanistan, women are losing ground, facing violent insurgencies that threaten and attack women who are active in public life or work outside their homes. As Rachel Reid writes in this anthology, a common form of threat in Afghanistan is the "night letter" left at a house or girls' school, such as this ominous letter sent to a female government employee: "We Taliban warn you to stop working for the government, otherwise we will take your life away. We will kill you in such a harsh way that no woman has so far been killed in that manner. This will be a good lesson for those women like you who are working."

With societies from Tunisia and Egypt to Libya in political transition from repressive dictatorships, fundamental questions remain about whether women will indeed benefit from the overthrowing of tyrants. It is not yet clear whether they will be allowed to participate in the new political systems in the Middle East, or whether their rights will be protected under the region's new constitutions.

This book is designed to spotlight these and other pressing problems for women and girls in the world today, and to give a road map to solutions that can work. In these pages you will meet tenacious women human rights defenders. You will hear in their own voices from women and girls who have faced unimaginable terror and grief. And you can decide for yourself whether so-called "traditional practices" such as early marriage or female genital mutilation are just harmful practices that have no rightful place in the world today.

Human Rights Watch was one of the first international organizations to treat domestic violence as a human rights issue. In war-torn Bosnia and Rwanda, researchers documented systematic rape and other forms of violence against women as a "weapon" in war, laying the groundwork for courts to later prosecute sexual violence as a crime against humanity. The organization's experts, such as Nadya Khalife, who writes movingly about her work to end female genital mutilation in Iraq, show us how it should be possible at this historic moment for women's rights activists to expand local campaigns and achieve truly global impact.

In some cases, as when Eleanor Roosevelt championed the Universal Declaration of Human Rights, change for women can come at the stroke of a pen; in other cases, change takes generations. In Libya and states now building institutions from the ground up, addressing rights and protections for women is not yet at the top of priority lists. However, as the US State Department's Ambassador-at-Large for Global Women's Issues Melanne Verveer points out, this is a shortsighted and dangerous approach because "the vibrancy of these potential democracies will depend on the participation of women."

When women are fully empowered, there is clear evidence that previously unthinkable opportunities develop, for them—and also for their families, communities, and countries. The effectiveness of women as peace negotiators in conflict zones led the United Nations Security Council to adopt Resolution 1325, which recognized "the important role of women in the prevention and resolution of conflicts and in peace-building," as well as "the need to increase their role in decision-making with regard to conflict prevention and resolution." The selection of Leymah Gbowee as a laureate of the 2011 Nobel Peace Prize was based largely on her tireless activities as a peace negotiator in Liberia.

In September 2011, just before the Nobel committee announced its award recognizing the vital work of women, the world lost one of its few female Nobel laureates. Wangari Maathai, the first African woman to be awarded the Nobel Peace Prize, was a pioneering professor who led an environmental revolution in her native Kenya. Her key to success, she often said, was empowering women "to create a society that respects democracy, decency, adherence to the rule of law, human rights, and the rights of women."

It is a time of change in the world, with dictators toppling and new opportunities arising, but any revolution that doesn't create equality for women will be incomplete. The time has come to realize the full potential of half the world's population.

Revolutions and Rights

Minky Worden

A round the world today, enormous strides for women's rights have been made on many fronts: domestic violence legislation, girls' education, recognition of the value of women's work, and the dynamic growth of the women's rights movement. Yet women and girls are still being married as children, trafficked into forced labor and sex slavery, trapped in conflict zones where rape is a weapon of war, prevented from attending school, and prevented from making even deeply personal choices in their private lives.

The Unfinished Revolution tells the story of the ongoing global struggle on many fronts to secure basic rights for women and girls around the world, including in the Middle East where the Arab Spring has raised high hopes—but where it is already clear that these political revolutions alone will not be enough to secure rights for women, and might even lead to the weakening of key rights protections. At this time of global unrest and change, how women fare is a key test of other human rights and freedoms, which makes it all the more important

As Human Rights Watch's director of global initiatives, Minky Worden develops and implements international outreach and advocacy campaigns. She previously served as Human Rights Watch's media director, helping journalists cover rights abuses in some ninety countries worldwide. Before joining Human Rights Watch in 1998, she served as an adviser to Democratic Party Chairman Martin Lee in Hong Kong, and as a speechwriter for the US attorney general in Washington, D.C. She is the editor of China's Great Leap: The Beijing Games and Olympian Human Rights Challenges *(Seven Stories, 2008) and the coeditor of* Torture *(New Press, 2005).*

that women have a seat at the table when decisions impacting their lives are made.

In 2011, the archipelago of dictatorships across the Middle East and North Africa was swept by popular tsunamis ousting Tunisia's Zine El Abidine Ben Ali, Egypt's Hosni Mubarak, and Libya's Muammar Gaddafi. These revolutions—and demonstrations in Bahrain, Syria, Yemen, Iraq, and other countries—were all different in their demands but had a common factor: women were often visible on the frontlines of the protests in countries where the treatment of women had long been a barometer of societies badly in need of reform.

One of the indelible images of the Arab Spring was that of female protesters wearing headscarves or the full black abaya—or just in jeans and T-shirts—carrying banners, marching on government offices, sleeping in tents. Women brought their babies to city squares to participate in the historic changes; female journalists and social media organizers tweeted, filmed, and reported the revolutions. Women demonstrators were harassed, detained, shot by snipers, and teargassed. Female human rights activists, including my Human Rights Watch colleague Heba Morayef in Cairo, went from morgue to morgue documenting the human toll of the government crackdowns. Laila Marzouq and Zahraa Said Kassem, the mother and sister of twenty-eight-year-old Khaled Said, refused to be silent about his violent death at the hands of police in Alexandria and participated in a number of anti-torture protests before, during, and after Mubarak's ouster. Indeed, it was their vocal fight for justice that helped ignite the revolution in Egypt.

During Mubarak's three decades of rule in Egypt, women joined protests demanding civil liberties and were harassed, tortured, and imprisoned alongside men. Despite—or perhaps because of—the repressive atmosphere, Egypt developed a vibrant civil society, with the founding of many women's rights and human rights groups, such as the El-Nadim Center for Rehabilitation of Victims of Violence, headed by the powerful female anti-torture advocates Aida Seif El Dawla and Magda Adly. Veteran women's rights groups, such as the New Woman Foundation and the Center for Egyptian Women's Legal Aid, spent decades educating and organizing to bring about equality for women and girls.

In Tunisia, following the fall of Ben Ali, women's rights activists fought for and won key electoral and legal protections for women. The government took early steps to consolidate women's rights, including becoming the first Arab country to lift most reservations on CEDAW, the treaty that aims to eliminate all forms of discrimination against women. In April 2011, Tunisia's electoral commission backed a gender parity law requiring each party to run an equal number of male and female candidates in the Constituent Assembly elections. The 217-seat assembly was elected on October 23, 2011, and was tasked with writing Tunisia's next constitution.

Tunisia already had a robust civil society network of women and the most progressive personal status code in the region, banning polygamy, allowing abortion, and giving women equal rights with regard to marriage and divorce. Nadya Khalife, who monitors women's rights in the Middle East for Human Rights Watch, is cautiously optimistic: "The increased representation of women is no guarantee that a new constitution will protect women's rights and advance gender equality. But the gender parity law recognizes the importance of fair representation in politics and in the decision-making processes that will help shape Tunisia's future."

Arab Spring, Women's Winter?

But there are also clear signs that political revolutions alone will not be enough to secure fundamental rights for women. In post-revolution Egypt, the same women lawyers and opposition leaders who helped crack the foundation of Mubarak's rule found themselves almost immediately excluded from the post-revolution committee that was set up to change the constitution. In March 2011, male and female protesters were hauled off Cairo's Tahrir Square by military forces, with seven of the female protesters subjected to sexual violence—forced "virginity testing." A solidarity march on March 8, 2011, for International Women's Day was disrupted by men who assaulted and insulted female participants. The Supreme Council of the Armed Forces, the governing transitional military authority put in place after Mubarak was toppled, included no women (indeed, there are no women in the Egyptian military).

Countries in the Middle East that have ostensible democratic institutions are not much better at protecting women's rights. Human Rights Watch's Iraq researcher Samer Muscati describes how conditions for women and girls have actually deteriorated since Saddam Hussein's ouster. At a protest in Baghdad's own Tahrir Square in June 2011, groups of government-backed thugs armed with wooden planks, knives, iron pipes, and other weapons beat and stabbed peaceful protesters and sexually molested female demonstrators. During the attack, the assailants groped female demonstrators, and in some cases attempted to remove their clothing, calling them whores and other sexually degrading terms.

Another cautionary tale comes from Iran's recent history. In 1979, a young lawyer named Shirin Ebadi was on the frontlines of the Islamist revolution. Three decades and one Nobel Peace Prize later, she writes in this volume that Iran's revolution led to the enactment of numerous laws that discriminate against women and hamper their ability to participate in public life to this day.

Will the women who supported and participated in the 2011 revolutions be pushed aside by military, Islamist, or other leaders, or will they be allowed to take part in governing, in the judiciary, and in making autonomous decisions about their own lives?

Just as Tunisia's overthrow of Ben Ali set off a chain reaction of political revolts in the region, there are hopes that the openings in Tunisia, Egypt, and Libya could herald a regional tipping point for rights for women and girls. As Christoph Wilcke explains in his chapter, women are even forcing change in calcified Saudi Arabia, where the so-called guardianship system requires them to obtain permission from a male relative to travel, work, study, or take part in public life. In a surprise move in September 2011, Saudi Arabia's King Abdullah bin Abd al-Aziz announced that women would be allowed to participate in the 2015 municipal elections and become full voting members of the advisory Shura Council. Yet the vast majority of Saudi women—who are still banned from driving and who have seen past promises of electoral participation unfulfilled—are still waiting for their "Arab Spring."

There are reasons for caution and for redoubling efforts to ensure that women's rights are not sacrificed in the horse trading that takes place during political transitions. This book's two chapters on Afghanistan, by Rachel Reid and Georgette Gagnon, show the grim reality of life for women and girls whose lives are threatened by extremists, deeply entrenched and long-standing norms, and a lack of political will.

Abuses Start Young

Around the world, millions of women and girls begin life hampered by personal status laws that claim to protect women but in fact restrict their choices in life—including whom and when to marry and divorce, decisions that affect health for a lifetime, and their role in the family and society.

"I was sold twice," seventeen-year-old Samira told Georgette Gagnon in a juvenile correction center in Kunduz province, Afghanistan. Engaged at age two, married at thirteen, and beaten regularly, she was later sold again by her husband to a stranger who raped her, before she ended up in jail for her own "protection."

Child marriage is a harmful traditional practice that affects some 10 million girls a year—as many as 100 million girls over the next decade if nothing is done to stop it. Graça Machel and Mary Robinson are members of the "Elders"—a group of former heads of state and international rights advocates founded by Nelson Mandela—who have built a global coalition to end the practice. As they explain, early marriage is both a product of and a cause of poverty, and has been embedded in the social customs of Asia, Africa, the Middle East, and in some communities in Europe and the Americas for thousands of years. Families marry off girls young because of poverty, to settle debts, and to protect "honor," since sex before marriage is seen as shameful. Thus, instead of marriage being a moment of joy, the reality of life for most child brides is forced marriage, forced sex, an end to education, and few choices about their future.

The Elders' "Girls Not Brides" campaign is designed to promote a revolution in thinking about the value of girls to the world. Success will be achieved once this practice initially viewed as honorable is in time widely recognized as harmful, as Princeton University scholar

Kwame Anthony Appiah writes in his 2010 book *The Honor Code: How Moral Revolutions Happen*.[1]

Women who are forced into marriage as children often face dire health consequences later on, including fistulas and death in childbirth. Mumbai-based expert Aruna Kashyap writes of India's maternal mortality crisis, and how simple steps could prevent needless deaths of women in childbirth. Agnes Odhiambo writes of the anguish caused by fistulas, a preventable health crisis for women, which is often associated with marrying young. Marianne Mollmann outlines the stark and often fatal consequences for women who are denied contraception and abortion in Latin America.

In 1972, the Egyptian feminist writer Nawal el Saadawi published a bold exposé of female genital mutilation, known as FGM, which she herself had experienced as a child. As a medical official with the government, she had also seen countless girls maimed by this painful procedure. This widespread practice has deep roots in the notion that women are the gatekeepers of family honor. It should shame us that, four decades later, FGM is still practiced around the world today and that so many cultures believe girls' sexual desires must be controlled early to prevent immorality. Nadya Khalife's chapter details the lasting physical and psychological wounds caused by cutting girls' sexual organs, but also outlines a road map for rolling back the practice, describing how Human Rights Watch worked to get a religious fatwa to fight FGM in Iraqi Kurdistan.

Education and Opportunity

Sharing information and education can also help to eradicate harmful traditional practices. As journalist Sheridan Prasso writes, at the beginning of the last century, girls across China had their feet bound to make them more attractive to men. Today, within a few generations, that harmful, traditional, and literally crippling practice is forever ended. In their book *Half the Sky: Turning Oppression into Opportunity for Women Worldwide*, Nicholas D. Kristof and Sheryl WuDunn— whose grandmother had bound feet—describe how this practice was "embedded in traditional Chinese culture" before being largely eradicated by the mid-twentieth century.[2]

In her chapter, Isobel Coleman of the Council on Foreign Relations sets out how education and a "quiet revolution" driven by new technologies can improve family health, boost incomes, and enhance security in conflict zones. From computers to contraceptives to cell phones, technology can be harnessed to reduce women's workload, enhance their health, improve their educational opportunities, and increase both their access to ideas and their ability to share their thoughts with one another.

Education is also a key element of the One Million Signatures Campaign, a tenacious domestic campaign to overturn the laws that make an Iranian woman or girl's life legally worth half that of a man's. One of the campaign's organizers, Sussan Tahmasebi, describes how the campaign uses technology as well as humor and a grassroots approach to educate the people of Iran about these discriminatory laws. The campaign's hallmark is that it seeks to involve all generations of women—mothers, grandmothers, wives, daughters, and sisters—to lobby the men in their families in the fight for equal rights for women. Tahmasebi is convinced that solidarity and learning from other women's groups across the Middle East can make it harder to isolate and marginalize women, and will bolster prospects for durable reform.

Education can play an important role in eradicating harmful practices and empowering women to protect their health. Meena Seshu, the founder of the Indian non-governmental organization Sampada Gramin Mahila Sanstha (SANGRAM), is an example of a human rights defender who has used education in her organization's efforts to prevent HIV/AIDS in the provinces of Maharashtra and northern Karnataka, particularly among sex workers who have a relatively high risk of contracting the disease. Education can also serve to protect rights endangered by policies rooted in prejudices or ignorance. Judith Sunderland, a senior researcher on Western Europe for Human Rights Watch, points out that the ban on burqas or other forms of religious dress violates women's rights to freedom from discrimination, religious expression, and personal autonomy; yet many support this ban because they mistakenly believe that such garments always represent a type of forced veiling, even in cases when it is entirely voluntary.

Violence Against Women

One of the most pernicious types of abuse covered by this book is violence against women, which knows no borders and occurs in many forms. In October 2000, the UN Security Council adopted Resolution 1325, which sought to make violence against women in armed conflict an international security issue. Yet the crisis of violence against women remains. Anneke Van Woudenberg describes in her chapter the use of rape as a weapon of war in the Democratic Republic of Congo. Jody Williams, who in 1997 was awarded the Nobel Peace Prize for her work on the campaign to ban landmines, details the lasting harm suffered by women and girls in conflict zones.

Gauri van Gulik lifts the veil on the domestic violence that all too often takes place behind closed doors in Turkey and many European countries. Sarah Tofte, who directs advocacy efforts at the Joyful Heart Foundation, an organization dedicated to helping victims of sexual assault, highlights the hundreds of thousands of cases in the United States in which rape victims endure evidence collection but their rape kits go untested and unused in the justice system, compounding victims' suffering for years and even decades after the crime.

Liesl Gerntholtz explains that global efforts to end violence against women, including the campaign launched by UN Secretary General Ban Ki-moon in 2008, are encouraging. Ultimately, however, according to Gerntholtz, "real progress in preventing violence requires changing deeply entrenched social norms and challenging cultural, traditional and religious stereotypes about women, their role in society, and their relationships with men."

Some forms of violence against women are rooted in economic factors. Ambassador Mark Lagon, who headed the US Department of State's Office to Monitor and Combat Trafficking in Persons, outlines the supply-and-demand model of criminal networks, corruption, lack of education, and misinformation about employment opportunities that make women and girls vulnerable to trafficking. Elaine Pearson, deputy director of Human Rights Watch's Asia division, explains the complex challenges of helping trafficking victims without compounding the abuses they face.

The exploitation of domestic migrant workers is also driven by economic factors, particularly against Asian women and girls who have fled poverty or strife in their native countries and sought to support their families abroad. Nisha Varia tells the story of these workers in her chapter, and the hope generated by the new convention adopted by the International Labor Organization in June 2011, thanks in part to her own tireless advocacy efforts. Meghan Rhoad highlights the impossible choices immigrant women in the United States too often must make.

The Power of an Idea

The power of human rights resides in the idea that all people are born equal in dignity and rights. But it's an idea that doesn't have an enormous army behind it. It's an idea whose effectiveness depends on people themselves believing in it, taking it up, and being willing to defend it.

—Dorothy Q. Thomas, founder of Human Rights Watch's Women's Rights division

The beginnings of the unfinished revolution date to earlier generations of women who fought for their rights in inhospitable climates, from the suffragettes and equal rights movement in the United States to generations of activists seeking basic rights and freedoms in many countries around the world. In this book you will find important perspectives from more contemporary women's rights activists, who examine emerging challenges such as property rights for women, rape in wartime, the impact of armed conflict on girls and women, violence against immigrant women, and a new global movement to protect domestic workers' rights. We also examine the modern roots of the global women's rights movement and the international human rights discourse as well as recent decades of both progress and setbacks for women and girls around the world.

Ellen Chesler, in her chapter, writes about Eleanor Roosevelt, who chaired the first UN Commission on the Status of Women and helped give birth to a foundational document for human rights work, the Universal Declaration of Human Rights (UDHR). Charlotte Bunch, a strategic advocate and leader at dozens of landmark UN conferences (who brought the phrase "women's rights are human rights" into popular use well before Hillary Clinton), writes about their successful battles in the corridors of power to build an international legal framework to protect women and girls. Gara LaMarche draws on his long experience as a donor to human rights causes to set out benchmarks for making the best use of philanthropic resources to build and support local networks for women.

Dorothy Thomas, the trailblazing researcher and first director of the Women's Rights Division of Human Rights Watch, gave the women's rights movement a grounding in fact finding that continues to guide us today. We give her the last word.

A "Global Spring" for Women's Rights?

The images from the Arab Spring of 2011—women wearing gas masks and tweeting from cell phones—are inspiring. But overthrowing repressive governments via street protests may yet prove to have been the easy part. The harder part of any revolution is building a new society that truly recognizes and protects the human rights of all its members, upends long-standing inequalities, and incorporates mechanisms for redress and justice when things go wrong. Revolutions in the name of political freedoms have far too often failed to end the marginalization of women and girls.

The long-term struggle for women's rights in the Middle East and around the world will include the participation and leadership of women in political processes, campaigning for candidates who will back women's rights in new committees tasked with rewriting constitutions, pushing clerics for progressive interpretations of Islamic law to give girls choices in health and marriage, shaping national legislation to guarantee opportunities for women, and changing attitudes in the mosques and in the media.

In April 2011, I found myself eight months pregnant in Cairo, interviewing human rights activists, women's rights veterans, and organizers of the Tahrir Square protests. I spoke with Mohammed Abbas, a leader of the youth wing of the Muslim Brotherhood, alongside Sally Moore, a Coptic Christian youth leader. They had shared common political cause and worked closely together week after week on Tahrir Square. They jointly drafted a "birth certificate of a free Egypt" on a piece of cardboard.

I interviewed them together, and Moore pointed out that when the demonstrations began, Abbas would not shake her hand because she is female. On the day Mubarak was ousted, "I remember him actually saying, 'Okay, forgive me, but I'm going to do it!' So he did it and now he does it a lot," she said. "I was translating it [the birth certificate] into English very quickly for PBS . . . and the most interesting thing is that when he was writing the birth certificate, in the first paragraph—coming from Muslim Brotherhood—it was talking about tolerance, about citizenship. He was talking about equality."

Will the heady and exciting days of solidarity and regime change translate into more progressive changes in attitudes? Tahmasebi, the One Million Signatures Campaign activist, reminds us that the transitions set into motion by the Arab Spring protests mark a fresh opportunity for the UN and other institutions to insist that the many qualified women have a real role in shaping post-transition institutions. The Arab Spring was a reminder that the movement for women's rights that has changed lives fundamentally over the past generation in many parts of the world such as North America and Europe had not yet truly become a global revolution. As Egyptian women's rights advocate Esraa Abdel Fattah explains in her chapter, political changes in the Middle East must be watched closely for their longer-term impact on women. No measure will be more important than whether the unfinished revolution for women's rights in the region is permitted to take hold and flower.

This book presents the opinions, ideas, and commitments of many writers. Some are current or former colleagues from Human Rights Watch. Others are longtime activists and advocates working from a range of diverse contexts, from grassroots organizing to government. They all share a deep dedication to defending women's rights. The writers who are not Human Rights Watch experts represent their own perspectives and experiences, but not necessarily the institutional positions of Human Rights Watch.

As Graça Machel and Mary Robinson believe, once a fundamental change is made, it can be irreversible. Once families stop marrying daughters young, and once those girls have a chance to go to school and wed later, they will not in turn be likely to impose early marriage on their own daughters. The same model may be applied to rights for women worldwide. As internally displaced women seek shelter at Dr. Hawa Abdi's women-run hospital and haven in war-torn Somalia, their daughters and sons become educated about maternal health and equality, at the same time they are protected from militias. The women who shared political goals and tear-gas masks with their male compatriots in Egypt have every reason to insist on a place at the table when the next constitution is being drawn up, and the men who fought with them to oust a dictator should be convinced to give them space.

We must all take a page from the playbooks of these activists, who have worked for women's rights for decades. They know that the best resources are women and girls themselves, and that in our work to support women's rights, we must take our cues from them.

Many of the women's rights activists I met in Cairo in the spring of 2011 had been fighting for decades to end the emergency law and other tools of state repression. However, the euphoria of bringing a thirty-year dictatorship to an end was giving way to certainty that the revolution itself will be insufficient to protect and advance women's rights in Egypt.

Mozn Hassan, the executive director of Nazra for Feminist Studies, told me: "I do think that the struggle for women's rights is an unfinished battle. We are in the process of a social revolution, and respect for women's rights can only be developed over the long term. That is because we first have to create more space for discourse over our society's socially conservative approach. This is about the definition of women's rights—if we see it as only women's rights in the private sphere without real involvement in the public space and changing societies, we will lose out. But if we see this as a long-term process of having women be active and have a say in decision making in a society where women's rights are mainstreamed, we will be able to see this result in a generation."

Hassan captures the risks, hope, and possible turning point that this moment represents for women across the world. Bolstered by a new generation of women and girls who participated in their own revolutions, they have learned communications skills and political tenacity. They believe they at last have a chance to shape their own destinies and societies. Now that is a revolution worth completing.

PART 1

A REVOLUTION IN THINKING
WOMEN'S RIGHTS ARE HUMAN RIGHTS

CHAPTER 1

The Shoulders We Stand On
Eleanor Roosevelt and Roots of the Women's Rights Revolution

Ellen Chesler

Preparing to celebrate the tenth anniversary of the United Nations' Universal Declaration of Human Rights, Eleanor Roosevelt made her way to the organization's imposing new headquarters on Manhattan's East Side.[1] The occasion on March 27, 1958, was a small, scarcely noticed ceremony to release a guide for community-based action on human rights. There, in the hope of rekindling interest in the landmark document that had been forged under her skillful leadership, she uttered several sentences that have become among her most famous:

> Where after all do human rights begin? In small places, close to home—so close and so small that they do not appear on any map of the world. Yet they are the world of the individual person: The neighborhood he lives in; the school or college he attends; the factory, farm, or office where he works. Such are the places where every man, woman, and child seeks

Ellen Chesler, PhD, is a senior fellow at the Roosevelt Institute and a member of the Advisory Committee of the Women's Rights Division at Human Rights Watch. Among other works, she is coeditor with Wendy Chavkin, MD, of Where Human Rights Begin: Health, Sexuality and Women in the New Millennium *(Rutgers University Press, 2005). This essay on the historical foundations of women's human rights draws on Chesler's introduction to that volume.*

equal justice, equal opportunity, equal dignity without discrimination. Unless these rights have meaning there, they will
have little meaning anywhere. Without concerted citizen
action to uphold them close to home, we shall look in vain for
progress in the larger world.[2]

Mrs. Roosevelt's remarks tacitly acknowledged that the once bold
vision she and others had put forth for a postwar world governed by
collective security arrangements and grounded in a doctrine of universal human rights transcending the sovereignty of nation states was
in trouble, a casualty of Cold War politics. If she quietly despaired of
state recognition and enforcement of international human rights, however, her conviction that progress could be made instead among
families and local communities, where habits of tolerance and of democratic citizenship are first imbued, was not just born of idealism. Even
as the mainstream human rights agenda appeared to founder in the
years following World War II, incremental steps were taken by the
United Nations to broaden accepted definitions of how rights are constituted and codified in communities around the world—especially
with respect to the rights of women, a matter in which Mrs. Roosevelt
had long taken special interest. In this still formative but potentially
significant dimension of the human rights revolution, Mrs. Roosevelt
had good reason to feel some encouragement.

Women's rights first came to be understood as fundamental human
rights through the determined efforts of a small group of women from
around the world who came together at the dawn of the United
Nations and insisted that sex discrimination be part of the conversation. Uncovering these developments is a necessary corrective to a still
nascent historiography of the larger human rights enterprise that has
so far, by and large, ignored them.

Birth of the Modern Human Rights Movement

In August 1941, months before Pearl Harbor and America's formal declaration of war, Franklin Roosevelt and Winston Churchill met
secretly at sea and produced the Atlantic Charter, with its fateful

proclamation that all people deserve the right to "live out their lives in freedom from fear and want." Within a year, four more countries had joined in the formal Declaration of the United Nations and entered the fight against fascism. Growing recognition of Hitler's heinous crimes against humanity strengthened American and international resolve for a peace that would be secured not only militarily but also morally. Enthusiasm also came from individual crusaders such as H. G. Wells, then arguably the most famous writer in the English language and a friend of the Roosevelts, whose provocative 1941 book-length essay *The Rights of Man or What Are We Fighting For?* was translated widely and distributed in forty-eight countries, sparking extensive discussion and debate about non-Western human rights traditions, as well as those born of the European Enlightenment.

In the formal practice of diplomacy, however, this new way of thinking required nothing short of an intellectual revolution. The conduct of international relations had long taken the state as its exclusive subject and relegated all else to peripheral roles. Even as Allied forces dropped copies of the Wells book behind enemy lines, tensions developed between human rights advocates and professional diplomats, especially in the United States, where a postwar planning committee authorized to advise on the formation of the United Nations could not agree on how to balance concern about rights for individuals with a meaningful mechanism for enforcement.

In San Francisco, where the United Nations Charter was drawn in April 1945 just weeks after Franklin Roosevelt's death, the will of the major powers prevailed with the formation of a Security Council they would permanently control and whose actions any one member may veto. Equal representation of all nations was guaranteed through the General Assembly, however, which was responsible for establishing the conditions for respect of rights and for the advancement of higher standards of living to help secure them.

In London the following year, when the recently widowed Eleanor Roosevelt joined the five-member US delegation to the first meeting of the United Nations as President Truman's appointee, she was shuffled off to the Social, Humanitarian and Cultural Committee of the General Assembly. Popularly called Committee III, it was considered a relatively insignificant and safe berth by her US government colleagues, whose attention was drawn to what they saw as the tougher issues of economic reconstruction, atomic diplomacy, and the like. Committee III, however, authorized a Commission on Human Rights that unanimously elected Mrs. Roosevelt as its chair and authorized the drafting of a human rights declaration. For three years she presided patiently over contentious debate, earning widespread respect as a diplomat from the US foreign policy establishment though never any meaningful enthusiasm for human rights as foreign policy.

A Historic Declaration

Bearing the unmistakable stamp of Mrs. Roosevelt's good will and genial temperament, the Universal Declaration of Human Rights (UDHR) begins with the bold conviction that "recognition of the inherent dignity and of the equal and inalienable rights of all members of the human family is the foundation of freedom, justice and peace in the world."[3] It encourages all peoples and nations to adopt its specific provisions as "a common standard of achievement" and obliges citizens to accept ultimate responsibility as individuals for the enforcement of rights, but it contains no sanctions for state violations.

Most significantly, the UDHR moves beyond traditional civil claims involving the personal liberties and political safeguards of individual freedom to an expanded definition of social citizenship requiring state investment in education, employment, health care, housing, safety, and social security as necessary foundations for productive citizenship. For Mrs. Roosevelt, these commitments realized a firm conviction she shared with her husband that totalitarianism had taken root in the economic convulsions, social dislocations, and fears of the twentieth century—that poverty, hunger, illiteracy, and disease are not conditions in which democracy is likely to flourish. It fulfilled the promise of Franklin Roosevelt's 1944 State of the Union address, where he called for a "second Bill of Rights," guaranteeing US Constitutional protection to minimum standards of social and economic well-being.

The UDHR's commitment to social, economic, and cultural rights also served as a practical bid for support from Russia and its satellites, who in the end rejected the declaration because of its civil and political rights provisions, but in doing so, chose to abstain, rather than vote no, and permitted the General Assembly to reward Mrs. Roosevelt with a unanimous endorsement of the declaration. Even so, many Americans in both political parties saw its social and economic provisions as a menacing back door to Communism and an affront to classic liberal principles. By 1951, the Human Rights Commission had drafted a Covenant on Human Rights, converting the declaration's general provisions into a binding treaty, but it quickly fell victim to intensifying Cold War politics, with the Americans objecting to the inclusion of all rights under the same heading, and with the Soviets scuttling Mrs. Roosevelt's effort to broker a compromise by drafting two separate covenants.[4]

On taking office in 1953, Republican President Dwight David Eisenhower announced to a shocked world that the US would not be party to any human rights treaties and that Mrs. Roosevelt would not be reappointed when her term at the Human Rights Commission ended, despite a commitment to non-partisanship at the UN. She then resigned immediately. Until her death, she traveled widely, fervently promoting human rights against its many detractors and encouraging citizen education and involvement.

The completion of UN covenants on human rights reached a stalemate until 1965, when indignation over the apartheid policies in South Africa led to the adoption of the groundbreaking International Convention on the Elimination of all Forms of Racial Discrimination (ICERD). The US, in the throes of its own civil rights revolution signed the treaty, and the logjam was broken. Within a year, agreement was reached on the terms of two separate covenants, as Mrs. Roosevelt had long ago suggested, one for Civil and Political Rights (ICCPR), which the Russians refused to ratify, and a second for Social, Economic, and Cultural Rights (ICESR), which the American government to this day has refused to sign. Still, an enforceable and enduring system of international law was put in place, and the door was opened for human rights instruments to gain broader acceptance and for its doctrines to become, in the words of the UN, "the common language of humanity."[5]

Women's Rights as Human Rights

All the while—beneath the radar screen of cold warriors—efforts to address the human rights of women quietly gained traction. Eleanor Roosevelt was one of only seventeen female delegates from eleven countries in London in 1946, but their influence was amplified by a large and vocal non-governmental contingent of women who came from around the world, establishing a historic precedent for official recognition of lobbyists that has since been widely celebrated for its positive impact on UN deliberations.

These delegates issued a manifesto calling for women to engage in public affairs—to come forward and share in the work of peace and reconstruction, as they had done in the war itself. They also argued for the creation of a Commission on the Status of Women (CSW), independent from the Human Rights Commission, a move Mrs. Roosevelt first opposed on the grounds that a separate body was not likely to be equal in resources or influence.[6] But with nearly unanimous support for the view that women would benefit from focused attention, she changed her mind and had the US delegation introduce the resolution to create the commission, which then played a major role in drafting the UDHR, insisting on gender-neutral language that guaranteed rights to "all human beings," not just to men. Mrs. Roosevelt later quoted the women of Committee III as insisting, "If it says *all men*, when we go home it will be all men."[7]

By the end of World War II, substantial numbers of women around the world were educated, working for formal wages and experiencing an unprecedented degree of freedom. The war itself had accelerated change, with many women entering the civilian workforce to fill critical jobs, while others directly supported military operations as office personnel, nurses and volunteers. Women in Europe joined movements of resistance, and in the colonial world women rose to leadership positions in movements of national liberation and independence. Everywhere, the rights of women were violated as they became civilian victims of conflict, enduring rape, prostitution, forced migration, and other tragedies. These incontrovertible facts contradict common allegations in recent years that the modern women's rights agenda has largely been a product of Western feminism.

So too, as human rights scholar Felice Gaer has explained, the development of a women's human rights movement required more than a population of women eager to be recognized. First, the principle that individuals of either sex had rights to assert against the state needed to be established. This process actually began long before World War II through treaties forged to abolish human slavery; provide victims of war with standing to seek redress; resolve conflicts in national law on basic citizenship rights affecting, marriage, divorce, and inheritance; and prohibit trafficking in persons.

Second, women had to assert rights of their own—independent of those they had traditionally derived from men—by claiming their individual sovereignty; by demanding for themselves traditional obligations of citizenship, such as voting and holding office and serving on juries; and by rejecting laws that accorded women protected but inferior status. Finally, they had to demand that issues of equal protection and nondiscrimination be applied to women not only in term of their status as citizens, but in all aspects of life, including education, employment, and family relationships.

Pioneering Efforts in the Twentieth Century

Many of these concerns had first been brought to the attention of an international body in the late 1920s, when Latin American and Caribbean women petitioned the League of Nations to undertake an analysis of women's status around the word, an undertaking disrupted by the Great Depression and World War II. Such formidable women as Bodil Begtrup of Denmark, who pushed that agenda at the League, later returned as delegates to the UN, providing important continuity and bringing hard data to bear on their demand that discrimination against women be viewed as a necessary and appropriate matter of international concern, not as a category privileged and protected by local sovereignty or by local customary or religious practices governing marriage and family relations.

The United Nations thus became the first international body to recognize that women oppressed in private places cannot realistically claim their legitimate rights as human beings. To advance women's rights, each state must address personal spheres of conduct and eliminate everyday forms of discrimination. To these ends the UDHR establishes broad protections for women as citizens and workers and stakes a landmark claim on still contested matters of family law, including full consent to marriage and divorce and the right to resources to care for children when divorced, widowed, or abandoned. In these respects, it anticipates and establishes a precedent for the later extension of rights to govern other aspects of women's lives including sexuality and reproduction.

During the 1950s the Commission on the Status of Women managed to document the challenges continuing to face women in many places around the world as part of the process of drafting and negotiating the adoption of legally binding treaties governing women's political rights, nationality rights, age of consent and minimum age of marriage, property rights, educational opportunities, and labor standards. In the years following, landmark studies were conducted on family planning, housing, health, and human services, leading to a new emphasis on the responsibility to provide women not just legal protections but also the benefits of development assistance.

In 1967, capping years of careful draftsmanship by the Commission under its Mexican chair, Maria Lavella Urbina, the UN adopted a formal Declaration on the Elimination of Discrimination Against Women. According to Arvonne Fraser, who later became a US Ambassador to the Commission, this declaration was written with the active participation of women from Afghanistan, who in one of history's great ironies, introduced the concept that pervasive discrimination against women warrants the granting of special privileges as amends, privileges since known as "temporary special measures" at the UN, but an equivalent to the American legal doctrine of affirmative action.[8]

The following year the UN marked the twentieth anniversary of the UHDR with a special conference on human rights in Tehran, where women's rights provided a rare arena of agreement between Russians eager to call attention to the educational and employment opportunities their government had granted women, and Americans, for whom these issues were gaining momentum as a result of an emerging second wave of feminism. The conference adopted resolutions encouraging support for a legal rights project to address gender discrimination and development assistance targeted to women, especially in agriculturally based economies in the developing world based largely on women's labor.

Most significantly, the conference identified family planning as a basic human right and paved the way for the establishment of a UN fund for population. Between 1975 and 1995, the UN sponsored four international conferences on women, all of which drafted wildly optimistic blueprints for the achievement of concrete gains by women, which have been dismissed by some as lacking both focus and practical strategies for implementation, while others insist that however often they may still be honored in the breach, these plans of action have raised awareness, shaped aspirations, and in countless significant and concrete ways helped change laws and reshape behaviors.

A Visionary Women's Bill of Rights

In 1979, following two decades of documentation and deliberation, the UN Declaration on Women was codified and adopted as the binding Convention on the Elimination of All Forms of Discrimination Against Women, commonly known as CEDAW. This visionary international women's bill of rights, while cautiously acknowledging the importance of traditional obligations to the family, establishes new norms for participation by women in all dimensions of life.

As one of the five major pillars on which international human rights implementation now stands—along with prior treaties on civil and political rights, social and economic rights, race, and torture—CEDAW gives precise definition and actionable protection to a broad range of women's rights in marriage and family relations, including property and inheritance and access to health care, with an explicit mention of family planning. It establishes the principle of equal protection for women as citizens in their own right entitled to suffrage, political representation, and other legal benefits; to education, including elementary and secondary schooling that provides professional and vocational training free of gender stereotypes and segregation; and to formal employment, deserving of equal pay, social security benefits, and protection from sexual harassment and workplace discrimination on the grounds of marriage or maternity.[9]

In this respect, according to human rights theorist Rebecca Cook, CEDAW moves beyond prior agreements employing a sex-neutral norm requiring equal treatment of men and women measured by a male standard, to one that acknowledges the pervasive and systemic discrimination against women in all forms as worthy of legal and public policy response.[10]

In 1992, CEDAW was expanded so that gender-based violence is also formally identified as a fundamental violation of human rights, and governments are obliged to take action.[11] This breakthrough was made possible by the pioneering work of Charlotte Bunch and feminist colleagues from around the world who joined the Center for Women's Global Leadership at Rutgers University in New Jersey to document evidence of demonstrable abuses of women including "torture, starvation, terrorism, and even murder" that continue to be routinely accepted without legal recourse in many places. "Crimes such as these against any group other than women would be recognized as a civil and political emergency as well as a gross violation of the victim's humanity," Bunch wrote in a pathbreaking 1990 article in *Human Rights Quarterly*.[12] In 1993, at the Vienna Conference on Human Rights, drawing on a slogan that originated with a grassroots women's coalition in the Philippines, Bunch first popularized the claim later trumpeted around the world and given resonance by Hillary Clinton, who declared at the fourth UN Conference on Women in Beijing in 1995 that "women's rights are human rights."

Today the human rights of women are enshrined in international law and in the constitutions and case law of many countries. Lawyers all over the world regularly call on provisions of the treaty when petitioning for further reforms. A robust UN CEDAW committee meets regularly to review the progress of the 186 UN member states that have ratified are making to address violations of the treaty's provisions. An optional protocol permits petition to that committee by individual parties who have not been able to redress their grievances locally, and, most significantly, the International Criminal Court recently agreed to try perpetrators of rape as war criminals, establishing the important precedent that violations of women have legal as well as moral consequences. Finally, while many CEDAW signatories originally exercised their UN permitted right to reserve on aspects of the agreement not to their liking, especially Article 16, which contains its family law provisions, the trend of recent years, even in historically conservative Muslim countries such as Morocco and Tunisia, has been to remove these reservations altogether.

Improving the status of women is today, as never before, widely recognized not just as a moral imperative but also a necessary condition to sustaining democratic institutions, building the conditions for peace and security, and promoting economic progress. Still, universal standards for women's human rights offer no sure cure for violations that persist with uncanny fortitude and, in many instances, with unimaginable cruelty. With harsh fundamentalism resurgent in many countries, women and girls are especially vulnerable: their rights remain an arena of intense political conflict as a perhaps predictable response to the social dislocations that result from changing gender roles, and to the larger assaults on traditional cultures from both the real and the perceived injustices of modernization and globalization.

Even in the United States today, decades of substantial progress by women have fueled a fierce backlash, so much so that America continues to reside in the unlikely company of Iran, Sudan, Somalia, and a few Pacific Island nations as the only UN member states that have failed to ratify CEDAW, much as we remain the only industrialized nation in the world that provides women no formal constitutional guarantee of equal rights under our own laws. President Jimmy Carter signed the treaty shortly before leaving office in 1979 and sent it to the Senate for ratification, where it has remained in limbo for more than three decades, held hostage by three obstacles: the high bar of sixty-seven votes needed for US ratification of international treaties; the hostility of conservatives to multilateralism; and, of course, their historic contempt for women's rights agreements of any stripe.

President Barack Obama and Secretary of State Hillary Clinton have both endorsed ratification of CEDAW, but without unlikely changes in the composition of the Senate to make room for more progressives, immediate prospects are not promising. Especially in the United States, therefore, this enhances the obligation of determined and courageous non-governmental advocates like the Women's Rights Division of Human Rights Watch, now marking twenty years of innovative work in the field, to continue to raise public awareness of women's human rights and to expose violations here at home and abroad.

Today's advocates of women's rights stand on the shoulders of Eleanor Roosevelt and other pioneers, realizing their once revolutionary vision and carrying it forward with rigor and reliability in countless new and innovative and directions that are having practical impact around the world.

CHAPTER 2

How Women's Rights Became Recognized as Human Rights

Charlotte Bunch

I first remember hearing the expression "women's rights are human rights" as the name of a campaign launched in 1988 in the Philippines by GABRIELA, a women's coalition that emerged from the anti-Marcos struggles. It immediately clicked as a succinct way of expressing what many of us were saying. This short phrase was catchy and proactive, and made the case for women's rights in terms of human rights law, concepts, and practices—instead of asking permission from others to include us.

Of course, adopting an effective tagline was the easy part. Making a slogan reality for billons of women turns out to be much harder.

The first mobilizing tool for what became the Global Campaign for Women's Human Rights was a short but groundbreaking 1991 petition to the United Nations World Conference on Human Rights to be held in Vienna in 1993, that asserted, "Violence against women violates human rights," and went on to read:

Charlotte Bunch is the founding director and senior scholar at the Center for Women's Global Leadership at Rutgers University. She is the author of numerous works on women's rights, including Passionate Politics: Feminist Theory in Action *(St. Martin's Press, 1987). A recipient of several honors including the 1999 Eleanor Roosevelt Award for Human Rights, Charlotte Bunch served on the Advisory Committee for the United Nations Secretary General's 2006 Report to the General Assembly on Violence Against Women. She is on the Board of the Global Fund for Women and is a member of the Advisory Committee for the Women's Rights Division at Human Rights Watch.*

The Universal Declaration of Human Rights protects everyone "without distinction of any kind such as race, colour, sex, language . . . or other status" (art 2). Furthermore, everyone has the right to life, liberty, security of person (art. 3) and "no one shall be subject to torture or to cruel, inhuman or degrading treatment or punishment" (art 5). Therefore, we the undersigned call upon the 1993 UN World Conference on Human Rights to comprehensively address women's human rights at every level of its proceedings. We demand that gender violence, a universal phenomenon which takes many forms across culture, race and class, be recognized as a violation of human rights requiring immediate action.[1]

These simple but powerful words touched a nerve and helped to spark a movement that was revolutionary in its consequences for women. When the agenda for the Vienna conference was first drawn up, women and gender were nowhere to be found on it, and violence against women was not contemplated as a human rights concern. But by the time the petition was presented on the floor at the world conference less than two years later, women's rights had become a central theme. The petition had been translated into twenty-three languages, was sponsored by more than a thousand organizations in 124 countries, and had garnered half a million signatures, including thumbprints from illiterate women—bearing witness to the truth it spoke.

In a pre-Internet era, the rapid movement of the petition by hand, letter, or—for a privileged few—sparkling new fax machine reflected the emergence of the women's movement as a global political force. However, the petition was not just to be signed. It was an organizing tool for feminists to provoke a discussion of why human rights were not already systematically seen as including women's rights, in particular the issue of gender-based violence, as well as to mobilize women around the world to make their voices heard.

Global Feminism Meets Human Rights

Framing women's rights in terms of human rights, as expressed by the phrase "women's rights are human rights," was an idea and a movement whose time had come. Like many good ideas, it came simultaneously from more than one source, but it began to bubble to the surface in the context of the global feminist movement of the 1980s. This was a formative time for me and many other feminists in our development as women's *human* rights activists.

During the United Nations Second World Conference on Women in Copenhagen in 1980, I organized a small section of the NGO Forum on International Feminist Networking, sponsored by the International Women's Tribune Centre and ISIS International. While the Copenhagen conference became known for its heated exchanges between women from the North and South, most of our sessions on violence against women led to eagerly exchanged stories, tears, and laughter, with participants intently listening and learning across these divides. Violence against women existed everywhere—no country was really "developed" when it came to this question, and neither did activists from various nations think they had all the answers. The similarity in the problems, social attitudes and feminist strategies was striking— even while the manifestations of violence varied as they intersected with the particulars of culture, race, class, and other factors.

Beginning with this experience in Copenhagen, I came to see violence against women as a cross-cultural issue that women from different countries could work on together, and soon after, I co-organized a global feminist workshop on traffic in women in the Netherlands in 1983. While discussing what could be done about the traffic in women from Asia to Europe and the United States for various forms of sexual slavery, we asked why they could not obtain refugee status in the countries where they landed.

Why had Bangladeshi women who had been raped in the independence war with Pakistan in the 1970s not been offered asylum elsewhere? An insightful paper presented by Ximena Bunster, a Chilean anthropologist, on the sexual torture of female political prisoners in the "dirty wars" of Latin America asked why this abuse had not been visible as part of the dynamic human rights struggle there. We began to see the gendered exclusion of women's experiences from the human rights agenda as part of the answer.

The Nairobi Conference

By the Third UN World Conference on Women in Nairobi in 1985, many issues of gender-based persecution and violence against women were raised at both the governmental conference and the NGO Forum. Domestic violence, sex tourism, forced prostitution, and female genital mutilation, among others, were discussed but not yet presented as matters of human rights. The Nairobi conference was particularly important as the place where feminists from the global South became more visible as leaders of the women's movement and began to exert more influence over its direction.

Regional women's conferences and organizations flowered as did international feminist networking in the 1980s around a number of issues—from women in development to health, trafficking, and violence. In Latin America and parts of Asia that had known significant national human rights struggles, feminists began to try to link women's rights with other human rights issues.

From stuffy UN meeting rooms to peace tents and regional gatherings in classrooms, feminists were looking for ways to hold governments more responsible for the plight of women, as well as for more effective mechanisms to lift violations of women out of the shadows of the private and community spheres. Turning toward human rights as a framework for thinking about this, and seeking to work with human rights groups as allies, came naturally for many who had come from or supported other rights struggles. The urgency of framing women's rights as human rights issues grew into a determination among us to apply feminist theory to human rights. We also challenged mainstream human rights organizations to address women's rights and violence against women in particular.

A deeper exploration of this became possible for me at Rutgers University in 1987 when, as a visiting scholar, I led a seminar on global feminism and human rights. I came in contact with activists and scholars from around the world who were eager to talk, or indeed already were talking, about human rights in relation to women's issues. For example, one women's organization in the United Kingdom had published a provocative version of the UDHR using female pronouns.

When I cofounded the Center for Women's Global Leadership at Rutgers University in 1989, we decided to further develop and popularize this approach. Women's leadership for and feminist perspectives on human rights and violence against women became the themes of our Women's Global Leadership Institutes that launched in 1991.

In the early 1990s, a number of events, campaigns, and articles looking at women's human rights emerged in academic and human rights contexts, as well as among feminist groups. Women's caucuses formed within human rights organizations like Amnesty International, and Human Rights Watch established its own Women's Rights Division to research global abuses against women and girls in the context of international law.

Such activities laid the groundwork for women's organizing around the Second World Conference on Human Rights in Vienna in 1993. Held soon after the end of the Cold War, the conference took place at a time when new thinking about human rights outside that box became possible, and it proved to be the turning point in global acceptance of women's rights as human rights. Women from the global South and North organized together for Vienna and also worked across sectors—our caucuses included not only women from the feminist movement but also women working inside human rights organizations, in UN bodies and on government delegations.

The Vienna Conference

The petition calling on the Vienna conference to address women's rights circulated widely among feminists and became a vehicle for informing women about the conference and the preparatory activities for it. Women activists at the local and regional level met to define issues they wanted on the agenda in Vienna, lobbying both governments and mainstream human rights groups nationally and at the UN regional preparatory meetings in Tunis, San Jose, and Bangkok. For example, Latin American feminists held a parallel event ("La Nuestra") just before the regional meeting, where they prepared a nineteen-point advocacy agenda. The organization Women in Law and Development Africa set up a series of subregional meetings where participants contributed to a regional women's paper for the preparatory meeting in Tunis. Similarly, women caucused and lobbied both governments and NGOs at the international preparatory meetings, drafting texts to ensure inclusion of women's rights and to address violence specifically.

Building on the human rights tradition of giving testimony on violations, those of us in the Global Campaign for Women's Human Rights organized a Global Tribunal on Violations of Women's Human Rights as part of the civil society activities in Vienna. Feminist organizations in each region selected the cases they wanted to highlight, and the tribunal included testimony from thirty-three women from all over the globe. It covered a wide range of issues from domestic violence to rape in war, from trafficking to bodily integrity, and the abuse of migrant women to political persecution of lesbians. This riveting daylong event exposed concrete and vivid personal examples of the consequences of the violation of women's rights, demonstrating in graphic terms that being female can be life threatening and often constitutes not only inhuman and degrading treatment but also torture, terrorism, and slavery. It provided substance to the language women sought to introduce in the official document.

The intergovernmental conference negotiations in Vienna often divided North and South and broke down completely several times— particularly over development and socioeconomic rights. Meanwhile, the issue of women's rights which had been brought to governments by women from within their own countries, and at all the regional meetings emerged as an area where there were few disagreements by region. Therefore, the text on women came to the conference almost free of brackets, to the surprise of some men in human rights organizations where the issue was still seen as marginal, if about human rights at all. Underestimating the issue, one comment heard was that women had "hijacked" the conference.

Language adopted in the Vienna declaration affirmed "the human rights of women and of the girl-child are an inalienable, integral and indivisible part of universal human rights" and went on to name gender-based violence as an abuse to be eliminated. It may sound logical—even undeniable—today, but the change in conceptual and policy direction this represented was enormous. The far-reaching implications of these changes were probably only barely imagined by the governments who adopted the declaration and not even fully by those of us advocating for it at the time.

The Global Campaign for Women's Human Rights continued after the Vienna conference, organizing human rights caucuses and global hearings at both the International Conference on Population and Development in Cairo in 1994 and at the UN World Summit for Social Development in Copenhagen in 1995. The language adopted in Vienna contributed to framing women's health, reproductive, and sexual rights as human rights in Cairo. This shift in the United Nation's work on population put women at the center of the discussion and continues to guide the efforts not only of this global body but also of other players, funders, and governments in this arena. It has also attracted some of the most heated controversies and determined backlash against women's rights.

Moving Forward: Beijing and Gender Integration

Perhaps most important for broadening and advancing women's rights as human rights was the Fourth UN World Conference on Women held in 1995 in Beijing. We in the Global Campaign organized another tribunal at the NGO Forum there and continued to circulate the Vienna petition—this time asking the United Nations to report on its efforts to advance women's rights as human rights since Vienna, and aimed at bringing this framework to all the issues of the Beijing conference.

First Lady Hillary Clinton's adoption and promotion of the phrase "women's rights are human rights" in Beijing also legitimized it and galvanized media attention to the issue. The Platform for Action adopted by governments in Beijing included a chapter on human rights and one on violence against women, but it also served as a manifesto of women's human rights in a wide range of areas from health to poverty, and education to equality in political participation.

Framing women's rights as human rights emerged from Vienna, Cairo, and Bejing to become the prevailing global approach to women's issues and empowerment, particularly in the context of the

United Nations. This energized the feminist movement and connected it more to the global human rights movement as well as to the United Nations and governments. Human rights abuses of women and girls moved from being seen as lamentable (read: "inevitable") problems to being the responsibility of governments who would be held to account for redressing them.

An explosion of activity followed in the 1990s as women's groups and human rights organizations began to document abuses and demand changes on a wide range of issues, such as those covered in this book. It also led donors, the media, governments, the United Nations, and other international agencies to respond with greater resources, new laws and mechanisms, and more attention to women's concerns.

Greater interest from the women's human rights movement also revitalized the Convention on the Elimination of All Forms of Discrimination Against Women and its treaty-monitoring committee as the legal instruments spelling out those rights and what governments should do to realize them. Civil society organizations sought to use CEDAW more legally and to do shadow reports that monitored government's accountability to it. Efforts to set standards on women's human rights intensified, and new instruments for addressing them were created, from the UN Declaration on the Elimination of Violence Against Women to the establishment of a new position, the Special Rapporteur on Violence Against Women, Its Causes and Consequences. These steps were soon followed by the creation of similar positions of regional rapporteurs and the drafting of measures on women's rights in various countries.

The Vienna, Cairo, and Beijing processes also spawned a commitment from the United Nations, some governments and many human rights organizations to the objective of "gender integration" into the rest of their work. While the experience of gender "mainstreaming" remains incomplete and even controversial, especially when it is done superficially, it is a critical process for integrating gender and the concerns of women into all fields. In human rights, this has led to an ever-expanding body of work on gender in areas including refugees and asylum, socioeconomic rights, torture, armed conflict, and transitional justice.

Among the most significant successes of gender integration was the inclusion of gender-based persecution and sexual violence—as well as other gender-specific procedures—in the Rome Statute that created the International Criminal Court (ICC). This resulted in new opportunities to prosecute crimes such as rape in war as well as the ICC becoming the only global judicial body with gender parity among its judges. In 2000, the UN Security Council adopted its first resolution specifically on women: Resolution 1325 on Women, Peace and Security, addressing violence against women in armed conflict and the role of women in peacekeeping.

The New Century

After a decade of considerable progress on recognition and adoption of measures around women's human rights, the new century brought ever-growing signs of backlash against these gains. As advocates sought to realize and make concrete the United Nations agreements on women's rights, the problem of implementing them in the face of long-standing patriarchal structures and attitudes proved challenging. At the United Nations' five-year review of the Beijing Platform for Action in 2000, some governments sought to weaken its clarion call on women's rights as human rights, especially around women's sexual and reproductive rights. This effort did not succeed, but it detracted attention from movement forward on the difficult task of implementation.

The backlash was fueled by religious fundamentalism in various regions that grew stronger as a result of uncertainty caused by rapid gender changes and the dislocations of globalization. Fundamentalist groups often center on controlling women, partly by using cultural arguments against women's rights. The terrorist attack on September 11, 2001, and the US government's pursuit of war in the Middle East, with undertones of the "clash of civilizations," increased polarization in the global geopolitical context, including at the United Nations. This has often made it more difficult to advance women's human rights claims.

Nevertheless, an impressive array of global reports and policy recommendations from the World Bank and other key actors highlight evidence of the centrality of women's issues to development and social stability. A country's prosperity seems clearly to rest on improvements in women's status—an often noted fact, yet one that few governments have taken seriously in terms of real economic investment and political will. One significant advance in this direction in 2010 was the creation of UN Women, a stronger consolidated United Nations body headed by former Chilean President Michelle Bachelet and meant to serve as an international vehicle for greater efforts to advance gender equity and women's empowerment as key to global progress. Yet for all its potential and the attention given its creation, donors have thus far failed to respond with the kind of investment needed to make it a success.

Addressing the growing gap between women whose economic and personal status has improved as a result of gains for women and those who have been left behind is another urgent challenge today. The gap between rich and poor, connected and powerless, has widened over the past two decades among men as well as women, but the gap between women has grown more dramatically as some have advanced and others become even more marginal to the world economy. UN Women's 2011 Report on Progress of the World's Women, focused on access to justice, which is essential to realizing human rights, shows clearly that justice is still a distant dream for most women. When it comes to violence against women in particular, impunity is still rampant and justice is often denied.

Defending the Defenders

Major, even revolutionary, advances have been made in awareness, recognition, and standard setting around women's rights as human rights; yet, all too often over the past decade, women's advocates have found themselves needing to focus on defending previous gains rather than advancing on the difficult tasks of implementing these rights. One central issue that has emerged out of this decade is the backlash and violence experienced by women human rights defenders—women working on any issue of human rights as well as women and men who advocate for women's and sexual rights in particular.

Women defenders often face gender-specific abuse in addition to the threats all defenders face, especially if they are seen as defying societal norms. This can take many forms: sexual violence and harassment, familial pressures and threats to their children, name calling and sexuality baiting, or other attacks on their reputation in the community or work place. Increasing numbers of women activists have been murdered or driven out of their communities for their defense of women's rights from Colombia to Nepal to South Africa and Mexico. Measures to combat these violations include documentation of gender-specific forms of abuse; attention to why women activists are often invisible internationally; awards and educational efforts to make them visible; monitoring trials and other conflict situations; legal, medical, and psychosocial counseling; safe houses and hotlines; protective accompaniment; relocation programs that take account of children; and demands imposed on state and nonstate actors doing the violating.[2]

Despite all of the remaining challenges, women keep showing extraordinary, and often unexpected, courage and creativity in demanding their rights and seeking to create a better world. From the veiled women demonstrating against their government in the streets of Yemen during the Arab Spring of 2011 to topless Ukrainian feminists in bridal veils protesting in the snow against the mail-order bride business, to Mexican women standing up to drug kingpins, women are bravely responding to the new challenges of the day.

New technologies have spread ideas of change rapidly, and young women have played key roles in the recent revolutions in the Middle East. These women—connected to each other and women in the rest of the world—are poised to be key actors and potential leaders in movements for change as well as governments in the near future. For a field that has only really existed for two decades, the spirit and vitality of women's human rights is alive. As the chapters in this book attest, many problems still remain, but there is also an ever-widening number of actors—men as well as women—seeking state and global accountability for women's human rights. This engagement of new players, seeking new remedies to both ancient and fresher challenges, should lead to another decade of discovery and recognition in the work for women's rights as human rights and the realization of human rights for all.

CHAPTER 3

Technology's Quiet Revolution for Women

Isobel Coleman

On the eve of Egypt's January 2011 revolution, I happened to be in Cairo, having dinner with Gamila Ismail, a longtime Egyptian political activist who had spent decades opposing the Mubarak regime. "What will happen tomorrow?" I asked her, referring to the public demonstration planned for the next day in Tahrir Square. "It will be the huge," she insisted, monitoring Twitter and Facebook feeds on her cell phone. Gamila and a young assistant had spent weeks helping to organize the demonstration through social media. "We think hundreds of thousands of people could join the protest. This could finally be our moment for real change." Indeed.

Much has been made of the role of social media in the Arab uprisings, in particular how it has given voice to youth and women in unprecedented ways. But social media is just the latest in a long line of technologies that have been driving profound changes in civil society for centuries. From the first notions of community developed

Isobel Coleman, a senior fellow at the Council on Foreign Relations, is the Director of the Council's Civil Society, Markets, and Democracy Initiative and CFR's Women and Foreign Policy Program. She is the author of Paradise Beneath Her Feet: How Women Are Transforming the Middle East *(Random House, 2010) and a contributing author to* Restoring the Balance: A Middle East Strategy for the Next President *(Brookings Institution Press, 2008). She has also served as a track leader for the Girls and Women Action Area at the Clinton Global Initiative. In 2011,* Newsweek *named her as one of "150 Women Who Shake the World."*

around the earliest campfires to the rise of social organizations aided by the printing press, to the revolutionary role of radio and then television, technologies have shaped ideas, forged movements, and driven social and political activism. The spread of new technologies across much of the developed world in the past century has also helped drive a revolution in women's empowerment and rights.

Now, a new generation of technologies is spreading to the developing world with a similar effect. Technological advancements are making contraceptives accessible to millions of poor women in developing countries, giving them more control over birth spacing and family size. Time-saving devices are freeing women from nonproductive chores, allowing them to engage in a wide range of economic, social, and political activities; new communication tools are giving women access to ideas, education, and learning. New media are encouraging women's mobilization. Across the developing world, a quiet revolution is taking place for women, aided by technology in many ways.

Transforming Daily Lives

Some years ago, I was in a small village outside of Herat in western Afghanistan, sitting in on a workshop teaching women how to start a small business. The room was filled with *burqa*-clad figures fidgeting restlessly in the heat. As the session wore on, a woman in the back shouted out something in Dari, starting a commotion. I asked the translator what she was saying. He was embarrassed, but explained that the woman was demanding to know about birth control. "What's the point of learning how to start a business if we don't have access to birth control?" she repeated, with other women in the room nodding in agreement. This consensus was not surprising. Not only does Afghanistan have one of the highest fertility rates in the world, with women on average having more than six children, but it also has one of the highest rates of maternal mortality, with one out of eleven women likely to die from childbirth.

Increasing access to modern contraceptives is one of the most significant changes under way for women in many developing countries.

While various forms of birth control methods have been around since ancient times, new advancements are making contraceptives more effective and more accessible to millions of women living in rural areas. However, there are still 215 million women who would like to be using contraception to avoid or delay pregnancy but have no access to birth control. Of the forty highest-fertility countries in the world, 90 percent are in sub-Saharan Africa. Accessing contraception often requires a trip to a distant health care provider every several months to receive a shot or refill a prescription, an insurmountable barrier in terms of time and expense for many women who live in countries without adequate health care infrastructure.

Today, new delivery methods and products are improving on older contraceptives to make them more affordable and longer lasting, and allow safe distribution by community health workers instead of doctors. Already, more than one third of women in sub-Saharan Africa using modern contraceptives use an injectable form (usually Depo-Provera). Advances in injectables, long-lasting implants, and self-administered insertable forms of contraception will give women who want to use birth control more access to it. Declines in fertility from five or more live births per woman (the rate for the majority of women today in sub-Saharan Africa) to two to three live births (or fewer) have a transformative impact on women's lives. As in other countries that have already gone through the demographic transition, reduced childbearing and child-rearing responsibilities allow more time for women to pursue education, earn an income, and become more involved in civil society.

In addition to child-rearing, rural women in less developed economies spend significant time collecting the basic necessities of life: water and cooking fuel. They walk for miles with impossibly heavy jugs balanced carefully on their heads, often with loads of bulky kindling strapped to their backs. In arid stretches of sub-Saharan Africa and South Asia, women and girls can spend upward of half their waking hours on these back-breaking chores, leaving little time for more productive activities such as going to school and tending crops. Worse still, much of the water they carry is unsanitary, resulting in the diarrhea and dysentery that kill thousands of young children every day.

Gathering firewood for cooking denudes forests, depletes soil, and leads to flooding. When burned, the firewood fills unventilated homes with dirty soot, a major source of respiratory illnesses that cause 1.6 million deaths a year, more than malaria.

New technologies like small-scale, solar-powered devices that can filter water, solar-powered cook stoves that mitigate the need for firewood, and solar-powered lights that can replace dirty, dangerous kerosene and extend the workday, hold the promise of significant health improvements and time savings for women and girls. Just as washing machines, refrigerators, and other household appliances liberated women in industrialized countries from hours of daily chores, new technologies can free up the time of rural women and girls in developing countries. The heavy burden of chores at home is a large part of the reason that two thirds of school-age children who are not in school are girls. Lifting that burden is an essential component of women's empowerment. Cost-effective, sustainable technologies can help compensate for the lack of public infrastructure that hinders many less developed economies and lighten women's workload.

This is particularly true in agriculture. Today, the bulk of food crops in sub-Saharan Africa and South Asia are produced by women. New technologies that improve women's productivity in the field are essential not only for feeding the world's expanding population, but also for reducing poverty and allowing millions of women to move beyond basic survival in their daily lives. With less than 5 percent of land under irrigation in Africa, drought-resistant seeds and sustainable irrigation techniques are critical for the next green revolution. For example, affordable hand-operated and foot-operated pumps that are light enough for women to use can add to their income stream and free up their time for other activities. Yet, numerous studies show that men have been the primary adopters and shapers of agricultural technologies in developing countries, and agricultural innovations have been designed specifically for men's use.[1] Women's economic empowerment depends on closing this gap.

Accessing the World

Labor-saving technologies are a necessary but insufficient factor for women's empowerment. Even as women become more productive, they still face significant cultural, social, and religious barriers to their full participation in public and civic activities. The spread of modern communications around the world, even to remote areas, is playing a role in breaking down these barriers. For decades, radio has been the most effective medium for bringing information to largely illiterate rural populations. Battery-operated radios have connected thousands of villages in remote regions of Africa, Asia, and Latin America to more urban areas. Women's groups have long used radio to impart not only training and education, but also messages about women's rights and empowerment. In Pakistan, for example, NGOs like the Aurat Foundation produced radio soap operas in the 1990s to influence people's ideas on contentious issues such as child marriage, girls' education, and women's mobility.

With generator-powered satellite dishes spreading from village to village, messages of women's empowerment are migrating from radio to television. In Afghanistan, nearly 60 percent of the population watches Tolo TV. Founder Saad Mohseni is using the power of his network's popular television shows like *Afghan Star* (a talent show with Afghan men and women competing side by side) and *The Secrets of This House* (a provocative soap opera) to challenge entrenched mores and change opinions. Female characters on his soap operas refuse arranged marriages, decide not to wear the *burqa*, have opinions and education, and work outside the home. Tolo TV also broadcasts Indian soap operas featuring uncovered women. Mohseni himself has been denounced by fundamentalists as going against Islam.

Across the Arab world, one of the most popular television shows in recent years has been a Turkish soap opera called *Noor* ("light" in Arabic) that depicts a modern marriage between the dashing male lead, Muhannad, and his beautiful wife, Noor. He supports her career as a fashion designer and includes her in important family decisions; some of the female characters do not wear headscarves, and the show airs controversial subjects such as abortion, premarital sex, and abusive mothers-in-law. Saudi clerics found the messages of *Noor* so subversive that they issued fatwas against watching the show. Still, when the final episode aired in 2010, more than 85 million Arabs tuned in to watch, and now a feature-length film is in the works.

The Power of Cell Phones

For millions of women, their newest tool of empowerment is the increasingly ubiquitous cell phone, connecting them to information and opportunities in unprecedented ways. Today, more than 90 percent of the world's population has access to a mobile network. Women now use cell phones not only to stay connected with loved ones, but also to access banking services such as making payments or transfers and saving money. They receive important health information—about vaccinations, nutrition, and sanitation—via text messages.

In Ghana, for example, the Mobile Technology Community Health Initiative (MoTeCH) is improving maternal health through its "mobile midwife" application that allows nurses to monitor pregnant patients from afar. In Ethiopia, "fistula ambassadors" are identifying fistula patients in the field, and using mobile money transfers to provide bus fare for them to travel to fistula hospitals for surgery, increasing fistula operations by 65 percent a month. In Afghanistan, village leaders use mobile phones to call for an emergency vehicle in remote areas to help women reach care during life-threatening deliveries. Mobile phones are also being used to deliver distance learning to girls and women. In May 2011, UNESCO launched a new initiative, "Better Life, Better Future," to scale up women's literacy programs through mobile phone applications in partnership with corporate players like Nokia and Microsoft.

According to a 2010 study by the Cherie Blair Foundation, mobile phone ownership provides multiple benefits to women: 90 percent of women report feeling safer, and 85 percent report feeling more independent, because of their mobile phone, while more than 50 percent of women business owners say that this device helps them earn additional income.[2]

Of course, mobile phone access benefits men greatly, too, but women face specific cultural barriers to mobility and access to income-generating opportunities, not to mention security concerns, that mobile phones help address. Yet, in Africa women are 23 percent less likely to own a phone than men; in the Middle East they are 24 percent less likely, and in South Asia they are 37 percent less likely. In some conservative societies, men deny their wives a phone precisely because it translates into greater freedom for women, and women risk beatings to sneak phones into the home. Closing the gender gap in mobile phone access would bring the benefits of the technology to an additional 300 million women worldwide.[3]

Mobilizing for Change

Women are using new technologies not only to increase productivity, enhance their economic opportunities, and access education, but also to expose injustices around them. In another chapter in this book, Dr. Hawa Abdi describes how she used her cell phone to alert international media when her Somali hospital was besieged by Islamic radicals. The international attention helped save her life and the lives of many women who had found refuge in her hospital. Around the world, atrocities are now regularly captured on mobile phones and uploaded to the Internet for millions to view. Cell phones and the Internet are exposing oppression and extending a lifeline to women worldwide. They are also enabling women to mobilize for change.

In Saudi Arabia, one of the most conservative and oppressive countries for women, activists launched the Women2Drive campaign on the Internet. Using Facebook and YouTube, the organizers have posted videos of themselves driving, resulting in their arrests and detentions and forcing a national debate on this divisive issue. One of the leaders, Manal al-Sharif, was quickly dubbed the "Rosa Parks of Saudi Arabia" by bloggers after her arrest. In Afghanistan women have been using social media to bring attention to a number of sensitive topics, including domestic violence and honor crimes. In countries like these, where women have few other avenues for public protest, the Internet is opening important new channels of scrutiny and dissent.

Of course, new technologies are not a panacea for women's problems around the world. Cultural norms that put a low value on the lives of women and girls are one of the roots of these problems. New technologies can help change those dynamics—but also entrench them in other ways. The spread of inexpensive sonogram technology, for example, is driving an epidemic of sex-selective abortion across China and India that is resulting in millions of "missing" baby girls, with negative long-term demographic consequences for both countries. In this case, technology is part of the problem, not the solution.

When it comes to social media, progressive voices do not have a monopoly. Saudi critics, for example, have mocked the Women2Drive campaign and disparaged its leaders. A dueling Facebook site called Iqal— the Arabic word for the cord that holds in place the headdress that men in the Gulf region traditionally wear—urged men to beat women with the cord if they dared to drive. The site was taken off Facebook for inciting violence, but not before thousands of visitors "liked" it. Saudi clerics also use social media to speak out against reforms, and some well-known conservatives have tens of thousands of followers on Facebook and Twitter.[4]

Closing the Digital Divide for Women and Girls

To the extent that technology can be harnessed to reduce women's workload, enhance their health, improve their educational opportunities, and increase their access to ideas and learning, it is playing a crucial role in women's empowerment. Narrowing the digital divide between men and women, particularly in cell phone and Internet access, will help speed up the revolution in women's empowerment already under way. But understanding and addressing the cultural constraints that inhibit women's access to new technologies are also critical.

The good news is that the gender gap in technology is beginning to catch the attention of the marketplace. Technology vendors increasingly see women as an untapped business segment that needs special attention, one that potentially offers high returns. With women now constituting a majority of farm labor in parts of Africa and South Asia, they are increasingly recognized as important decision makers in purchasing new agricultural inputs, such as seeds and irrigation devices. Likewise, women are the end users of clean cookstoves and many solar devices. Those manufacturers who address women's needs in designing products are likely to achieve higher market penetration rates.

The opportunity presented by women's growing ownership of mobile phones is of particular interest to vendors. According to the Cherie Blair Foundation, closing the mobile gender gap by adding 300 million women subscribers in low- and middle-income countries represents an incremental $13 billion revenue gain to mobile operators. Over the next five years, two-thirds of new subscribers around the world are likely to be women.[5]

Roshan, Afghanistan's largest mobile operator, is among the companies already targeting this market, with positive results. In 2009, after a study showed that only 6 percent of its subscribers were women, Roshan launched a new product and marketing campaign targeted specifically at women. It used the culturally acceptable theme of family and addressed much of its messaging to men, as the traditional decision makers, to encourage them to allow their wives and daughters to own cell phones.

"With the advertising and education that we're doing to the men directly, we've seen that women today will go out and buy phones themselves whereas four years ago they wouldn't," explains Karim Khoja, the CEO of Roshan.[6] Although research shows that Roshan's female customers spend only 80 percent of what men spend each month, they have higher retention rates and therefore end up being more profitable to the company.[7] By targeting women, Roshan enjoys the double bottom line of benefiting the most marginalized in society while also making money.

Women will undoubtedly continue to face cultural constraints in accessing new technologies, and gender gaps will persist. But smart product development that includes women in the design phase—and marketing efforts that target them as customers and address the specific barriers they face—will narrow those gaps. Explaining how new technologies can improve family health, boost incomes, and enhance safety are winning arguments that will help drive this quiet revolution.

PART 2
REVOLUTIONS AND TRANSITIONS

CHAPTER 4

Islamic Law and the Revolution Against Women

Shirin Ebadi

Although the 1979 revolution in Iran is often called an Islamic revolution, it can actually be said to be a revolution of men against women. It led to the enactment of numerous discriminatory laws against women, which effectively took us backward in time.

When I first read the Islamic Penal Code instituted after the revolution, I couldn't believe my eyes. I thought I had read it mistakenly. When I read it the second time, I thought maybe I did not understand it perfectly, or maybe it was just poorly written, and the drafters meant something else. So I read it a third time, and then it dawned on me: the drafters of this document had truly taken us many years back in time—some 1,400 years. I became very angry, and developed a bad migraine. Since that day, the migraine has often recurred, especially when I think of the Islamic Penal Code and its nefarious consequences for women.

When I went to law school, women's rights were recognized to some extent. Of course, they were not fully recognized, but the situa-

Dr. Shirin Ebadi, one of Iran's leading lawyers and human rights activists, is the winner of the 2003 Nobel Peace Prize—the first Iranian and the first Muslim woman to do so. A lawyer, author, and former judge, she was forced into exile in June 2009. She has written more than a dozen books, including her memoir, Iran Awakening: A Memoir of Revolution and Hope *(2006), and* The Golden Cage: Three Brothers, Three Choices, One Destiny *(2011). In this chapter she describes the heavy price women in Iran have paid in the wake of the country's 1979 revolution, and outlines why the Middle East will advance only once women and girls are able to participate in government and exercise basic rights.*

tion was better than after the revolution. During the shah's reign, a few good laws were passed, such as the law of the protection of the family. However, after the revolution—before even the drafting of a new constitution or establishment of a parliament—the revolutionary councils changed the laws and permitted men to marry four wives. This legalization of polygamy is just one reason why this was, in my view, a revolution of men against women.

Prior to the revolution, I had enjoyed being a judge. I was successful, and even became a presiding judge. When the revolution broke out in 1979, I was initially on the side of the revolutionaries and I believed in their cause. However, I was shocked and pained when soon after their success, the revolutionaries decided that women could no longer hold positions such as judges and had to instead take administrative positions. I was demoted to secretary—while many of my male colleagues, who were not as professionally qualified for the job as I, were appointed judges. Worse still, several male clerics who had not even attended law school arrived at the Ministry of Justice and took up positions as judicial officials.

This was both painful and discouraging for me, but I found another way to advocate for rights: I turned to writing. I wrote fourteen books, and dedicated myself to legal and human rights work.

On the day in 2003 when I won the Nobel Peace Prize, the news was broadcast all over the world and people could watch it via satellite everywhere, even in my own country, Iran. During the ceremony I imagined the head of the judiciary might at that moment be ruefully thinking, *I should have kept Ebadi as a judge because then this would be my judge receiving the Nobel Peace Prize.*

Not Yet an "Arab Spring"

I do not agree with the phrase "Arab Spring," as coined by the global media. This is because the overthrow of dictatorships is not itself sufficient. Only when these repressive governments are replaced by democracies can we consider the popular uprisings in the Middle East to be a meaningful "spring." In 1979, when the Iranian people succeeded in overthrowing the shah, our political system was not replaced with democracy. Instead, a religious dictatorship took its place.

Since women make up half of the region's population, any democratic developments must also result in the improvement of the social and legal status of women in the Arab world. As of this writing, it appears that Tunisian society has strong civil institutions, and there is much hope that democracy can indeed take hold there. But in Egypt, unfortunately, many political actors are talking about returning to Islamic law, which could result in similar regression of rights for women and girls as we experienced in Iran.

I hope that in the Arab countries, where people have risen against dictatorships and overthrown them, they will reflect and learn from what happened to us in Iran in 1979. My recommendation to Arab women is to focus on strengthening civil society institutions and to familiarize themselves with religious discourse so that they can demonstrate that leaders who rely on religious dogma eroding women's rights are doing so to consolidate power.

There are interpretations of Sharia law that allow one to be a Muslim and enjoy equal gender rights at the same time, rights that we can exercise while participating in a genuinely democratic political system. Sharia law and women's rights do not have to be mutually exclusive.

It is essential for women to master religious discourse because patriarchal culture is usually protected and strengthened in the name of Sharia law, and by political forces who exploit Muslims' ignorance of various interpretations. Instead of acquiescing to these interpretations, women's rights activists must arm themselves with religious discourse so that they can stand up to and debate the reactionaries who want to trample on women's rights in the name of religion. They must be ready to show that injustice and discrimination against women is the result of skewed and wrong interpretations.

Thus, in my view, the true Arab Spring will dawn only when democracy takes root in countries that have ousted their dictatorships, and when women in those countries are allowed to take part in civic life.

Half a Man's Value

In the "green movement" protests that took place after June 2009's disputed presidential elections, the world witnessed how many Iranian women were on the streets, and how strong our feminist movement is. More than 65 percent of university students are women, many university professors are women, and women are present in most important and sensitive social positions.

However, the law that is being enforced in Iran today does not consider women to be full human beings.

Instead, it ascribes to women a value half that of a man. If a man and woman are injured in an accident, the compensation paid to the woman for the same injury is half the amount paid to the man. Under current Iranian law, the testimony of two women in court equals the testimony of one man. If a woman kills a man and the man's family does not forgive her, she will be executed. But if a man kills a woman, it is different: if the woman's family does not forgive him and he is executed, the woman's family will have to pay half his "blood money"—since executing a man is executing a "full human being" as opposed to "half" a human being.

A man can marry four wives and can divorce a wife at will, but initiating divorce can be very difficult for a woman. A married woman even needs the written consent of her husband to travel.

Such discriminatory and misogynistic laws are not Islamic and cannot be found in the Koran. In Iran, women from all walks of life are opposed to these laws and this is one reason why women are on the front lines of every protest against the government.

Indeed, Islam can be interpreted in different ways, and could actually be used to defend women's rights rather than trample on them. For example, Islam prohibits female genital mutilation, and can therefore be used as a tool to end this shameful practice in countries where girls are cut.

Another example is that stoning is a medieval punishment, but the government of Iran unfortunately insists on carrying it out. The world was horrified by the case of Sakineh Mohammadi Ashtiani, an Iranian woman who was sentenced to death by stoning for allegedly committing adultery, and whom I defended. Sadly, there are many similar cases that people outside Iran do not even know about. For the past twenty-five years, I have lent my voice to campaigns by women's rights

advocates, lawyers, and other activists seeking to ban corporal punishments such as stoning, flogging, or cutting off the hands of thieves.
Our efforts have not been successful so far, but we will not give up.

Many Iranian religious authorities are against these laws and state
that they have to be changed. Yet the fundamentalists in power,
because they belong to a patriarchal culture where women are not considered real human beings, insist on enforcing them. Today Iranian
women are doubly oppressed, both by discriminatory laws enforced
by fundamentalist Iranians in power who deprive women of their
rights, and by unjust traditions.

Women are victims of the patriarchal culture, but in a sense they
also perpetuate it when raising their sons. Patriarchal culture is comparable to a disease like hemophilia, where the defective gene is
transferred by the mother to her son but not to her daughter. Sons in
Iran and similar societies usually grow up to be patriarchal, whereas
their daughters may not. In order to disrupt this pattern, we have to
educate women about how patriarchy works so that they know how to
fight it. Patriarchal culture exists in all cultures to varying degrees,
even in America. A scantily clad woman who appears in a toothpaste
commercial also reflects a patriarchal culture, to a certain degree.

Education's Ripple Effects

Education is one key to the future of Iranian women, and women
around the world. They must become aware of their rights—those
rights which have been taken away from them. In 2001, I cofounded the
Center for the Defense of Human Rights in Tehran. One of our first
actions was the publication of pamphlets on women's rights, which we
distributed freely to Iranian women. Every year the center published
100,000 of these brochures, which played a key educational role.

Education was also the centerpiece of the "One Million Signatures"
campaign which we launched in 2006 with the aim of ending gender
discrimination in Iran. The campaign's actions included theater per-
formances in the street, which attracted crowds and helped us collect
thousands of signatures. The campaign was like a small stone thrown
in a still pond—it created many waves. I am convinced that educated

women will ultimately form the backbone of a revitalized civil society in Iran.

Another key to ending discrimination against women in Iran is using all the legal tools at our disposal, such as the International Covenant on Civil and Political Rights, to which Iran is a signatory. The international community can play an important role in urging Iran to ratify the Convention on the Elimination of All Forms of Discrimination Against Women (CEDAW). Today Iran is one of only six countries that have not yet ratified this crucial convention. When President Mahmoud Ahmadinejad said last year, "We will never accept CEDAW," this simple sentence provided a chilling insight into the obstacles we still face in seeking to advance women's rights in Iran.

I have paid a high personal price, as has my family, for my involvement in the struggle for human rights in Iran, and women's rights in particular. As a result of these activities and the ensuing threats and harassment to which I was subjected in Iran, I have been living in forced exile since June 2009. I am separated from my husband, who is still in Iran, where he has been imprisoned and tortured to force him to speak out against me. My sister has also been imprisoned, and other family members are regularly harassed and threatened. They are summoned to interrogations at least once a month.

My family is far from being a unique case. All human rights defenders and civil rights activists in Iran are in the same situation. In May 2010, five political prisoners were executed in Iran despite their absence of guilt. They had merely participated in peaceful demonstrations and demanded the respect of their civil rights. After they were executed, the Iranian government even refused to hand over their bodies to their families. This clearly shows the determination of the regime to crush opposition as well as the scale of the challenge facing all rights activists in Iran.

President Ahmadinejad has claimed several times that Iran is the freest country in the world, that women in Iran have no problems, and indeed that women from other parts of the world should view Iranian women as their role models. But when Iranian women actually speak up to demand their rights, or merely voice their opposition to polygamy, the government accuses them of threatening national security and, in some cases, imprisons them. In January 2011, for example, Nasrin Sotoudeh, a prominent human rights lawyer and women's rights defender, was sentenced to eleven years in prison on spurious charges of endangering national security. She has a four-year-old son and an eleven-year-old daughter. Although they are both very young and miss their mother, they appreciate Nasrin's sacrifice. The main reason I am glad I was awarded the Nobel Peace Prize is that this honor enables me to speak with a louder voice on behalf of unjustly jailed women such as Nasrin, to ensure they are not forgotten in prison.

My message to the Iranian government is that in the long term, violence and oppression do not work. Iran is like fire under the ashes.

For each woman who is jailed, another will take her place and swell the ranks of the women's movement. One day, Iran will shed once and for all its medieval shackles and women will again proudly resume their rightful place in a modern and rights-respecting society.

CHAPTER 5

A Civil Society-Led Revolution?
Promoting Civil Society and Women's Rights in the Middle East

Sussan Tahmasebi

When we started the One Million Signatures campaign in Iran in 2006, we were aware that demanding a change to laws that discriminate against women in an Islamic state could result in a backlash.

The goal of the One Million Signatures campaign is modest and straightforward: to press for reform, from inside Iran, to the laws that make an Iranian woman or girl's life legally worth half that of a man's.

We set out to do so by educating the people of Iran, because we knew that both culture and law had to be changed in order to achieve equal rights for women. We engaged in face-to-face discussions with the public about these discriminatory laws, and encouraged Iranians to join us—their mothers, wives, daughters, and sisters—in this struggle. We then asked members of the public to sign a petition addressed to the Iranian Parliament asking for the reform of laws that discriminated against women.

Sussan Tahmasebi is an Iranian women's rights activist who has worked to strengthen civil society with a focus on gender issues and women's rights. She is a founding member of the award-winning One Million Signatures campaign, which seeks an end to Iran's gender-biased laws. Tahmasebi, who has been harassed by Iranian security forces and was banned from traveling abroad for over two years because of her work, is a 2011 recipient of Human Rights Watch's Alison Des Forges Award for Extraordinary Activism. Tahmasebi is currently working to promoting women's rights, peace, and security in the Middle East.

We fully anticipated accusations that our demands contradicted Sharia, or Islamic, law and that we were "promoting a Western agenda." For that reason, we made an effort to explain in our materials and during our discussions with the public that our demands for change and equality did not in fact contradict Islam, and instead helped promote progress in Iran.

We built our case to ordinary Iranian people by explaining that Islamic scholars offered various interpretations to Sharia law when it came to women's rights. We referred to the cultural advancement of Iranian society and the social achievements of Iranian women, and explained the negative impact of legal discrimination on the lives of women, the structure of the family, and society as a whole.

We discussed—but eventually decided not to tackle directly—the issue of the hijab, the Islamic dress code for women, which we felt should be voluntary rather than compulsory—because we realized it was an ideologically charged issue and could hijack the overall goal of pressing for improvements in many other areas that affect women's everyday lives. Thus, we generally referred to imposed veiling as a form of legal discrimination in our literature, but did not highlight it as one of our main petition demands. These were some of the strategies we chose to pursue in order to minimize the possible negative backlash we would receive for making such a bold and public demand for women's equality in Iran.

A Dangerous Petition

As it happens, the authorities never accused us of promoting an agenda in contradiction to Islam, and our critics only accused us of promoting a Western agenda in passing. To our surprise and dismay, however, our efforts to engage with the public elicited a violent response from Iranian authorities, and security forces began arresting our members as soon as they set out to collect signatures.[1] The authorities formally charged our members with alleged crimes such as "endangering the national security" and spreading propaganda against the state. They not only prevented us from reaching out to the public, but also disrupted our efforts to hold public or private meetings to advance our campaign.

In June 2006, several months before the official launch of our campaign, women's rights activists planned a public protest in Haft-e Tir Square in Tehran to demand equality for women. The protest turned violent. Security forces arrested seventy protesters, and the authorities charged many of them with security crimes. The Iranian government had drawn a line in the sand: public protests constituted a threat and would not be tolerated.

So we changed our tactics and decided to rely solely on collecting signatures and engaging with the public through dialogue. We assumed that the peaceful and transparent strategy of holding face-to-face discussions with Iranians and collecting signatures in support of a petition to the parliament would be tolerated by the authorities.

We were wrong.

This was our wake-up call. To the Iranian government, ensuring control over its population was paramount. It didn't matter how reasonable our campaign goals were. The reality is that when you work in a politically closed environment, any form of organizing, any effort to build networks and to connect individuals, is viewed by the state as a security threat. When that organizing takes place around women's rights, the situation becomes that much more complicated.

Today, women in Islamic countries—especially politically closed or transitioning societies—have to contend with an entirely different set of challenges than women activists elsewhere. These challenges require increased cooperation, collaboration, sharing of strategies, and solidarity of women's movements throughout the region. In this way, not only can women build on and learn from one another's experiences, they can speak for one another when political and fundamentalist forces make it too dangerous to speak inside a given country. In so doing, they can drive home the point that the demand for women's rights is in fact an indigenous one, echoed and bolstered by progressive voices across the region. The specific challenges women face after 2011's mass movements for democracy in the region make the formation of such a solidarity network even more imperative.

Religion and Culture Versus Human Rights

Too often when women in Islamic countries work for equal rights, their efforts are dismissed in their own countries as "Western demands." The argument used for justifying continued discrimination against women is often a religious one based on a conservative interpretation of Sharia law. This is the case in Iran. Supporters of this conservative interpretation claim women and men have complementary but different roles and responsibilities in Islam. Therefore they should also enjoy different rights.

This argument ignores the more progressive interpretations of Sharia law, which have been used in places such as Morocco and were instrumental in reforming the *Moudawana*, or the family code. Instead, authorities often rely on interpretations of Sharia law that reflect existing cultural practices that are often rooted in patriarchal beliefs or cultural traditions that reinforce the notion of women's primary roles as mothers and wives. These interpretations of Sharia law are, in turn, viewed as sacred and immutable.

Around the world, those seeking to reform religious laws (regardless of the religion) are often met with reprisals and sometimes accused of heresy. They endure threats, arrests, and even assaults and attempts on their lives. In Egypt, for example, Coptic Christians are not allowed to seek divorce. In order to get a divorce, some Copts have converted to Islam, where limited divorce rights are granted to women. This practice has contributed to sectarian tensions and even violence between Copts and Muslims. Even in countries with more progressive gender laws, challenging the validity of religiously based legislation poses many difficulties.

Despite these dangers, brave women activists and Islamic scholars in countries as diverse as Bahrain, Iran, Morocco, and Malaysia are promoting more progressive interpretations of Sharia law. This is a long and arduous struggle. Unlike conservative or fundamentalist forces that often have access to mainstream media outlets to spread their message, reformists often work in isolation and have limited access to mainstream media. Progressive scholars are even viewed as a threat to the status quo and are often targeted by both their critics and authorities.

One consequence of this imbalance is the somewhat surprising complacence of Western and international policymakers when it comes to speaking out on women's rights. We are often surprised, if not shocked, to see some Western observers and policymakers relying on cultural relativism arguments to justify discrimination against women in Islamic countries. From Afghanistan to Iraq and beyond, where the West has on occasion stepped in by military force or through other means, to "ensure democracy and human rights," the most negotiable item is often women's rights. This is, in part, because of the harsh backlash by indigenous political leaders and religious conservatives in the region, who have often chosen to draw a red line when it comes to the "imposition of Western ideals" with respect to women's rights. The fact is that women's rights are not Western but rather universal human rights, guaranteed by numerous UN declarations, conventions, and treaties.

The complacency of some international policymakers leaves women activists in the Middle East wondering, would the international community be as accommodating to conservative forces if the targets of discrimination were ethnic or religious groups and not women and girls?

What After the Revolution?

Many Western observers in the region believe that democracy in countries that have recently experienced popular uprising or revolution will look different from what we see in Western democracies because it will have to be based, at least in part, on Sharia law. In fact, the concept of "Islamic democracy"—what it will look like and how it will function—is is still quite vague, with many questions unanswered. Whose interpretation of Sharia law will be used? Will Sharia laws apply to religious minorities, such as Christians and Jews, or will religious minorities have their own religiously based civil code? Will the penal code adopted in these new democracies include punishments authorized by certain interpretations of Sharia law such as flogging and stoning? Will the new judicial system rely on interpretations of Sharia law that limit women's personal status rights?

These questions help us to identify the real challenges that await the countries and societies that are currently experiencing transitions resulting from the "Arab Spring." That challenge is to make it clear that women's rights may not be sacrificed or bargained away by anyone, whether protesters, democracy activists in the region, or the international community.

Unfortunately, the voices of progressive women are often completely excluded from discussions regarding the future of these transitioning nations at the international and regional levels, and absent or muffled at the national and local levels. This despite the fact that the changes set into motion by the Arab Spring provide an invaluable opportunity for the UN and other key actors to insist that women have a seat and a voice at the negotiating table when it comes to determining the future of their nations. After all, millions of women joined, and were on the front lines of the revolutions that have shaken and shaped the Middle East and North Africa.

It is no small irony that when you work to advance women's rights in politically closed systems, democracy advocates who should be your staunchest allies are often the ones working against you. We are often assured by these advocates that when democracy is achieved, then women's rights too will be realized. We are cautioned that demanding gender equality early on would be divisive and that we would be better off focusing our energy on the demand for broader democracy. But often this is not the case, and once the revolution has toppled the old regime, discrimination against women not only continues, but is promoted and justified by religious and cultural norms by the very same "democracy activists" who have now assumed the reins of power.

We saw this in Iran during after the Islamic Revolution of 1979. And then again later, when women played a key in electing President Mohammad Khatami in 1997, a reformist who ran on a platform of promoting civil society and citizen participation. During his eight years in office, reformist politicians often cautioned women and other rights groups not to publicly criticize the government of Khatami, then under fire by conservative political groups. Women's groups largely gave in to this demand, hoping that reformists would push for major change in women's rights once they consolidated power. But women's rights reforms were never a top priority. As a result, reformists and women's groups failed to build successful alliances based on mutual respect, which could have transformed demands for equality into legal reform.

By the 2005 elections, women's groups in Iran came to realize that the only way they could advocate for women's rights was to do forge a new path free from political alignments and considerations. This strategy was instrumental in elevating the voice of Iranian women activists and their demands to the national level. They sought to ensure that their movement was strong and independent, and that their ideals were not held hostage to the whims of political parties and their leaders.

Today, across the Arab Spring countries, we are witnessing similar demands by "democracy activists" who are urging women's rights advocates to remain silent and hold off on their legitimate demands for equality. Again, women are being told that when the task of building of democracy is complete, their demands will naturally be met.

The toppling of dictators and dictatorships does not guarantee the advancement of women's rights. In post-revolution Egypt and Tunisia, some women's rights activists have come under attack for having allegedly been aligned with dictators. Others are accused of advocating a Western agenda not in line with Sharia law. This is in part because in pre-revolution Tunisia and Egypt (and even Iran), women's rights had been used as indicators of progress toward democratization—without there being a genuine or substantive effort toward broad-based democracy and institution building. After the revolutions, a backlash toward these gains took shape, and the demands of women's rights activists were not always viewed as responsive to real social needs. As a result many pro-democracy activists who should otherwise be natural supporters of gender equality now see the inclusion of women in the democratic process as peripheral or nonessential at best.

To subordinate women's rights is a mistake. If women's equality is not viewed as a prerequisite to achieving democracy, the prospects of realizing a true democracy later will be all the more difficult if not impossible.

A New Paradigm for Women's Rights

During the coverage of public protests in Iran in 2009 and across the Arab world in 2011, I noticed that many observers were surprised, if not shocked, at the active participation of women. These images helped dispel many of the myths surrounding Muslim women—that they are subservient and passive by nature. Instead, many viewers began to realize, perhaps for the first time, that women in Muslim societies were both politically and socially engaged and were often on the front lines of the push toward change.

I visited both Egypt and Tunisia shortly after their respective revolutions and met countless women's rights activists who were working to ensure that women's voices were included during the transition toward democracy. Their ideas and approaches were varied, but they all valued the importance of raising cultural awareness through education, advocating for legislative reform, and participating in the elections as both voters and candidates. One women's rights activist in Egypt told me that it was important for women to be present in all aspects of social life, and to speak about issues beyond women's rights, so that the Egyptian population views them as capable of advocating for all of the population on a range of issues, as opposed to just the family code.

Yet the challenges for political transitions across the region are immense, including facing increased militarism and fundamentalism from both state and non-state actors, and rebuilding critical institutions like the judiciary. While citizens in some countries in the region are moving toward democracy, others are faced with increased conflict and repression. These developments have posed even greater challenges for women's rights.

In Morocco, where rapid reforms on women's rights have been introduced and women have proposed language in the constitution guaranteeing equality, major barriers to women's equal participation remain and the women's rights reforms are viewed negatively or with suspicion by an increasingly conservative public.

In countries that experienced revolutions, political space has opened up for the general public, but women are facing challenges they had not faced before. In Tunisia, for example, there is greater scrutiny of women, who are targeted for their dress and activism, and are pressured to conform to "Islamic" ideals. At one stage a hit list targeting progressive activists, including women's rights advocates, circulated on the Internet in Tunisia. One positive sign was the government's decision in August 2011 to lift key reservations to the Convention on the Elimination of All Forms of Discrimination Against Women, known as CEDAW, but women's equal participation in decision making still faces great challenges and women are grossly underrepresented in public and political life. In Egypt, hard-won gains such as (limited) divorce rights for women are being threatened.

Despite upcoming elections in Tunisia, Egypt, and Libya, existing barriers to democracy and women's equal participation and representation in the social and political spheres make it difficult for them to ensure their voices are taken seriously. As a result of decades of political repression, liberal groups are less organized than many of their more conservative counterparts—some of whom promote a regressive vision of women's rights. The progressive groups also benefit from less funding and support and do not enjoy strong community networks. At the same time, women face serious barriers even within progressive parties.

In Tunisia, where a proportional system is in place, despite not being listed at the top of party ballots for the Constituent Assembly elections in October 2011, women managed to win 24 percent of the vote, or 49 seats.[2] With 37 percent of the vote, or 90 seats out of 217, Ennahda, the Islamist party, managed to win the largest percentage of votes in Tunisia's first free elections after the revolution.[3] Ennahda candidates stressed tolerance generally and respect for women's rights specifically, including the upholding of women's legal gains. But following the elections, Ennahda's spokeswoman, Souad Abderrahim, made headlines by claiming that "single women were a disgrace to Tunisia and did not have the right to exist."[4] Her statements exemplify the often uncertain and complex environment women face in postrevolutionary Tunisia.

In Egypt, proposed quotas for women's representation in political office have been criticized by feminists as insufficient, and few qualified women have been willing to take up the challenge of political life.

In Iran, there is greater repression after the protests following the disputed presidential elections in 2009. Women are being targeted in ways unprecedented since the early days of the 1979 revolution. Increased control of women's dress not only serves misogynistic ideals but allows police presence on the streets to control the public at large. Syria, Libya, Bahrain, Iraq, Afghanistan, and Yemen are facing increased or chronic conflicts—conflicts that seriously undermine the ability of women to advance their political and social agendas. In Iraq, women will for the first time enjoy fewer rights and freedoms and will be less educated than the generation of women that preceded them.

In some countries, women's rights activists are grappling with the question of Sharia law for the first time. Islamist women who have been denied public presence and the opportunity to participate in politics now have the opportunity to engage more fully in advocating for an Islamic state. As a consequence, secular feminists are under attack more than ever. Those who survived or created some semblance of public space to advocate their agenda before the periods of transition are now feeling more isolated and threatened than ever.

One strategy utilized by some women's rights advocates in the region is inclusion in the political process—as candidates, members of political parties, and voters. But considerable training is needed for women candidates to be able to speak to issues beyond women's rights. Outreach to voters—especially women—is critical to ensure that women themselves vote for progressive agendas, yet civil society groups are less organized and not as well funded as established forces like the Muslim Brotherhood in Egypt.

Women's groups have also been unable to bridge their practical gaps with the general public. Many younger activists are expressing a need to learn how to build movements on and about women's rights. Some younger feminists in Egypt are focusing more on the cultural challenges at hand and do not see much of a discrepancy between cultural norms and Sharia law. They are instead choosing to focus their energies on building a culture of equality rather than fighting to ensure the adoption of civil over religious laws. But more experienced Egyptian feminists insist that the focus should be two-fold: to include both legislation and adherence to international standards, as well as cultural education. They view family laws, along with other restricting laws, as major barriers to women's equality. But often their focus on laws and regulations that affect women is working against them, because work on family law and women's rights issues has historically been viewed as a "soft issue" not worthy of consideration by "serious politicians" concerned with more broad-based issues concerning democracy.

Women's Equality and Participation: An Indigenous Demand from Muslim Women

Women's rights activists across the Middle East face similar questions. How can we best promote women's rights in an Islamic context? How can we reach out to the public? Who are our most likely allies? How do we stay true to our ideals and values, while respecting the culture of the communities in which we work? To answer these fundamental questions, we need to learn from one another and draw on multiple experiences in the region. Only then will we be able to craft sustainable rights-based solutions to the specific problems faced by women in the Middle East, North Africa, and other Muslim-majority societies.

As women's rights come under fire on a daily basis, or women's rights advocates are pressured, threatened, targeted, or arrested, strong statements of solidarity from regional women's movements along with international leaders are essential to providing support to rights activists and pressuring rights violators. Regional cohesion and collaboration among women's groups will also force political players at the national and regional levels to take the demands of these groups more seriously.

Of course, women in the Middle East cannot do this alone. We need support from international women's movements, human rights organizations, and nontraditional actors at the national and regional levels. We need better access to national and international media, in order to successfully engage with the public, influence culture and thinking, and share messages and visions of equality.

Perhaps most important, women's rights defenders need to support and learn from one another and be advocates, first and foremost, for themselves. Through regional solidarity, they will finally be able to hold national, regional, and international policymakers and actors to a higher standard of inclusion and gender equality.

We must systematically and relentlessly drive home the point that democracy will not be realized and stabilized without ensuring rights for half of the population.

CHAPTER 6

After the Arab Spring, Mobilizing for Change in Egypt

Esraa Abdel Fattah with Sarah J. Robbins

When I was young, my mother told me that the most courageous Egyptian women were in history books—she admired the courage and leadership of early feminists like Hoda Sharawy, but she said that those were the old days, when women had no voice at all. As an English literature major at Cairo's Ain Shams University and later, as I started my career as a human resources specialist, I followed the news and discussed political life with friends. I never thought that I would become an activist myself.

Then, in 2005, I joined the liberal, secular Al-Ghad party. It was my first political "school," alongside a diverse group of people, some as young as sixteen. I was swept up in the Egyptian Movement for Change because I believed that its slogan *kefaya*—"enough"—gave voice to something long inside the hearts of Egyptians who chafed under the repressive rule of President Hosni Mubarak since 1981. I went to

Esraa Abdel Fattah is an Egyptian blogger who gained worldwide fame as "Facebook Girl" for her live Internet updates on the revolution that toppled President Hosni Mubarak. She earned her nickname in 2008, when the Facebook group she started with the "April 6" youth movement to support a textile workers' strike attracted seventy-seven thousand followers—and eventually landed her in jail. In November 2011, she was honored as one of Glamour *magazine's "Women of the Year." Abdel Fattah is media director of the Egyptian Democratic Academy and a member of Vital Voices Global Partnership's Policy Advocates program, which is working to ensure that women keep and expand their rights in the new Egypt. In 2010 she co-founded the group Free Egyptian Women, to train women to become political leaders. This chapter was co-written with author Sarah J. Robbins.*

demonstrations and to the streets to hear the speeches of Dr. Ayman Nour, the only one serious in his candidacy against Mubarak. And I began to take a leadership role, fundraising, running trainings and seminars, and encouraging the youth to speak out against corruption and military rule.

When I told my mother that I was working with the political party, she expressed concern. "They will be silent, you will be alone out there," she cautioned. "There is no hope for a change in Egypt."

If change was to come, I told her, it would be from the Egyptian people's own hands. Indeed, at this time, social media helped us mobilize more and more, and I started a Facebook group that called for people to stay at home for a nationwide workers' strike on April 6, 2008. That day, on my way to a demonstration in Tahrir Square, police arrested me for calling the strike. For more than two weeks I was held in Al-Qanater prison, sometimes interrogated for hours, until I felt like dying. Those eighteen days were difficult and discouraging, but meeting with fellow activists inside the prison convinced me that I should be prepared to sacrifice for what I believed in.

For the first 24 twenty-four hours after my arrest, my mother didn't know where I was. Frustrated, angry, and afraid, she contacted lawyers and journalists. "These are my daughter's words, right and fair, against a dictator," she said.

After my release, I did my best to calm her. Though it was very hard for me, I stayed away from activism, focusing on my job and my personal life. But I couldn't be silent about the injustice and corruption I saw. Step by step, I tried to convince my mother that my work as an activist was not only for me, but for my future children, and for the children of my brother and sister. I appealed to her sense of morality: "We can't sit idly by as these people are suffering," I said.

Miracle at Tahrir Square

In January 2011, we saw six years of work miraculously come together in Tahrir Square. Although I agree with my colleague, Ahmed Maher, who tweeted, "The revolution is not a sudden event from the 25th of January," it was a moment of achieving our hopes and dreams. In the square alone there were two hundred thousand people; across the country millions more were using social media, broadcasting our own fight with our own hands. We saw people standing together, unafraid to raise their voices for freedom, justice, and democracy. Facebook and Twitter gave us credibility. We could publish what was right and what was wrong in messages, in photos, and in videos; across the world, people saw the power of ordinary Egyptian people.

More than anyone else, my mother encouraged me to stay at the Tahrir demonstrations. "Mubarak will leave," she told me on the phone one day, when I was in the square. "Don't worry. Continue." Now my mother is even more politically engaged than I am—more up-to-date on the news, the talk shows and debates. She and her friends respect my work for the Egyptian Democratic Academy, a nonprofit organization I helped establish to promote the development of democracy, human rights, and political participation of all citizens, including women, in Egypt. Women's new mentality toward political engagement is a positive sign for Egypt, since here, mothers are the main source of power in the family. Now, when I share my struggles with my mother, she advises me to be patient. "Egypt will take a long time to change," she says.

The first stage of elections took place in November 2011, when voters elected 168 members—roughly one third—of Egypt's 498-seat lower house of parliament. The results were disappointing: only three women earned seats in parliament, out of 212 female candidates running for the available 168 seats.[1] Sadly, we didn't expect much: although our election rules said that each party should have at least one woman on the list, they did not say what position the woman should take. Since all parties listed women in the last positions, this was the logical result.

The quotas for women in parliament were unfair before the revolution—their goal was only to strengthen the National Democratic Party, and the women they chose were not well-equipped to lead. It will take time to shift society's mentality so that women are seen as leaders and decision-makers chosen for their qualifications, not their gender.

Change Through Education

In 2010 some of my friends and I started the Free Egyptian Women group, with a goal of bringing well-known, well-educated, and well-qualified women into parliament. Now we're training about one hundred women, ages twenty-five to thirty-one, in five of the country's twenty-seven governorates. We're teaching them about political participation and elections, and we're helping them join campaign staffs, so they can gain the experience to make them good candidates one day. As half of the society, we need to participate as much as men in any negotiation about the future of Egypt.

It's a new generation for activism; we've joined together with the long-established groups to insist that without the rights of women, without representation at all levels, there can be no justice. We know we cannot change laws without convincing the people. By participating in Vital Voices' Policy Advocates program's Egypt delegation, I'm helping to develop a women's rights platform to share with every sphere of influence, including civil society, politicians, the media. We're a diverse team, with different strengths, so we can reach a wide range of people with our message.

Today we need to mobilize using all the same tools, the same network, that we employed during the revolution. Now, as we await the selection of a hundred-member assembly to draft our post-Mubarak constitution, I think we need to have at least ten women on that committee—a small number, but it's a start. For the first time, Egyptians will have a first free and fair constitution; above all, it must protect the rights of all citizens, regardless of gender, age, or religion.

My mother cried for the youth who were killed in the Tahrir uprisings. Still, she tells me, "Tahrir is waiting for you." It is a complicated time, but after so many years without dignity, only dialogue will help our differences and close our generation gap. Older Egyptians need to help the younger generation, encourage them and believe in us. They can't fear their sons and daughters to the extent they prevent us from playing a part to change their country.

And we must listen to their advice: we cannot change decades of wide, deep corruption in five minutes—change can only be brought about through education. Now is our time to develop women's roles, support them in leadership positions, and encourage their work. This transition period may be years of ups and downs, and we may see more violence and violations of human rights. Yes, we must be patient, but unlike my mother's generation, we can't afford to wait 30 years. We must use our strengths, and our networks, to reach the civil society, the politicians, and the media with our message: We cannot say we have democracy in Egypt without achieving women's rights.

CHAPTER 7

Women in Iraq
Losing Ground

Samer Muscati

Two months after US-led troops invaded Iraq on March 19, 2003, a group of armed men abducted fifteen-year-old Muna B. and her two sisters while they were walking to a market near their home in the port city of Basra. The men jumped out of a taxi next to the three sisters, covered the eyes and mouths of the terrified girls, and whisked them away.

Muna later told Johanna Bjorken, a researcher for Human Rights Watch, that the men held her and her sisters, ages eleven and sixteen, at a house with seven other young children, ages six to fourteen. On the first day of the girls' arrival, one of the men whipped the children with a plastic hose to punish them for crying. The next day, the men separated Muna from her sisters and put her in a room alone. It was during this time she heard them rape her older sister. "They did bad things to my sister," she later recalled. "They beat her, and they did bad things. One night, I heard her shouting, and then a week later, they brought her to me, but only for one hour. She told me that they had

Samer Muscati is a researcher for Human Rights Watch's Middle East and North Africa Division and a former journalist, whose work focuses on Iraq and on the United Arab Emirates. He is the author of two reports on Iraq, At a Crossroads *(2011) and* On Vulnerable Ground *(2009). Before joining Human Rights Watch in 2009, he worked in Baghdad as an Iraqi government adviser. Muscati, who holds a law degree from the University of Toronto, also photographed Iraqi women demonstrators for the cover of this book.*

slept with her; she was crying. She only told me about that one night, but she said that all [four men] did it."

On several occasions, the men brought other people who looked the children over, the way one might examine a cow at a cattle market. Muna believed them to be traffickers who were going to bid on children:

"They brought in people they wanted to sell us to. They would bring men, they would look at us, and then bargain, negotiate a price. One was a fat woman wearing a veil, and another time two men came. They bargained and negotiated the prices, they would talk and laugh but not let us know, the [buyers] would ask how much, and then [the captors] would wink their eyes and say, 'Don't talk now, in front of them.' . . . Then they would talk to us, saying, 'Don't worry, we'll make you happy, we'll give you a happy life, don't worry, don't cry.' . . . I think they wanted us to be dancers or something like that, they told us that."

The last "buyer" came in early June 2003. He returned the following day with another man. Convinced that she and her sisters would be sold to these men, Muna managed to escape when her captors left to get food for breakfast. She ran through fields for about fifteen minutes until she reached a road, then flagged down a car that took her to Baghdad, where she eventually made her way to US soldiers who took her to a police station. When Human Rights Watch spoke to Muna on June 13, she had not seen her sisters since her escape and feared that they were still in captivity or that they had been sold.

Although Muna managed to escape her captors, there would be no fleeing the trauma and stigma of her abduction. For the women and girls caught in the wave of sexual violence and abductions that spread through Iraq in the months after the invasion, informing a male family member about an attack could have potentially exposed them to additional violence as punishment for their "transgression." The war meant there was limited access to adequate health care. Even with the assistance of US military police officers who tried for two days to organize medical attention for Muna, three hospitals refused to examine her. She wanted a forensic examination to document her assertion that she had not been raped, because she feared that her family might kill her if she returned home without proof that her virginity was still intact. In Iraq, such "honor killings" were not uncommon.

The complete breakdown in the policing and security system as a result of the invasion created additional hardship for girls and women brave enough to buck cultural norms and turn to the authorities for protection. Overwhelmed and undertrained police and security officers frequently did not appear to recognize, or purposefully downplayed, the seriousness of allegations of sexual violence and abductions in the months following the invasion. When Human Rights Watch inquired about Muna's case, Iraqi police at the station referred to her as "the girl who ran away from home." Muna said that while Iraqi police and USU military police were present when she gave her statement, the Iraqi police did not seem interested in her case. "The Iraqis didn't write anything down. The Iraqis said, 'It is not up to us, we have nothing to do with your case.' They said that the 'Americans are handling it.'" Police officers at the station confirmed that they did not open an investigation, claiming that it was not within their geographical jurisdiction; however, they failed to refer the case to Iraqi police officers in the relevant district.

Although Saddam Hussein's official army had been easily defeated by the US-led forces in 2003, on the streets of Iraq a series of conflicts was still unfolding, including one that would be waged against women and their rights for years to come. The resulting chaos of the US invasion, followed by sectarian strife that engulfed the country, has exacted an enormous toll on Iraqi women and girls, who are now still worse off, in many respects, than before 2003.

The collapse of Iraq's security promoted a rise in tribal customs and religiously inflected political extremism, which have had a deleterious effect on women's rights, both inside and outside their homes. In the decades prior to the first Gulf War of 1990-91, Iraqi women surprisingly enjoyed some of the highest levels of rights protection and social participation in the region. For these women, the steady erosion of this status has been a heavy blow.

"They Tried to Kill Me Because I'm a Political Woman"

As a result of the invasion and subsequent lack of security, armed groups proliferated across Iraq and continue to this day to target female political and community leaders and activists. The threat of violence has had a debilitating impact on the daily lives of women and girls, and has reduced their participation in public life. It has also adversely affected their professional lives, as many female doctors, journalists, activists, engineers, politicians, teachers, and civil servants have quit their jobs out of fear for their safety.

In the spring of 2010, while conducting research for a Human Rights Watch report on the eight-year anniversary of the 2003 US-led invasion, I interviewed a women's rights activist who led public campaigns against domestic violence and other women's issues in the city of Najaf, south of Baghdad. She told me she had started to receive numerous death threats via text messages starting in August 2007. The messages were variations on the same theme: "Oh, you bitch, stop your work or we will kill you." This activist was well known because she published articles in her own name. In September 2007, assailants bombed her house, damaging it and twelve others in the neighborhood. She continued to receive threats in the weeks following the explosion.

This woman explained that the police took some photos of the wreckage but did not follow up with a proper investigation, so she tried to pursue the case on her own by hiring a private investigator to determine who was sending her the threatening text messages. She described her predicament: "The police did not do anything to help us or investigate the attack because the perpetrators were extremists and they were afraid. All the police would tell us is, 'You're lucky to still be alive.'"

On November 12, 2009, an assailant shot Safa 'Abd al-Amir, the principal of a girls' school in Baghdad, four times. The attack happened shortly after she announced that she was running in the national elections as a Communist Party candidate. After al-Amir left her school in the al-Ghadir district at about 1:30 p.m., a maroon-colored BMW approached her vehicle from behind to the side; an assailant shot her three times in the face and once in the arm. She did not immediately realize what had happened to her because the gunman used a silencer. Despite her injuries, al-Amir managed to leave her car and walk barefoot for about sixty feet. When police arrived at the scene, they initially feared she was a suicide bomber because she was drenched in blood. "I couldn't answer the questions because they had shot my mouth—I just kept pointing to my mouth," al-Amir later related to me.

After numerous operations, including one to reconstruct her jaw, she was still undergoing treatment when I met her in April 2010. "They tried to kill me because I'm a political woman," she said. "According to the extremists' beliefs, an unveiled progressive woman running for political office sets a bad example for other women." She said the police conducted a superficial investigation, which comprised only obtaining her statement in response to a few questions and no follow-up. She said the police either did not care or were afraid to investigate. Authorities have made no arrests in the case.

As the Arab Spring unfolded across the Middle East in early 2011, protesters and activists in Iraq, including women, were increasingly targeted as they took to the streets calling for an end to a chronic lack of basic services and widespread corruption. Even though Iraq was by then considered to be a democracy, its leaders still reacted to these protests in much the same way as their despotic counterparts around the region: with violence and repression. Security forces and their proxies were equal-opportunity abusers in dealing with protesters; however, armed assailants used particularly degrading methods to silence some women who dared to speak out.

At a protest in Baghdad's Tahrir Square on June 10, 2011, groups of government-backed thugs armed with wooden planks, knives, iron pipes, and other weapons beat and stabbed peaceful protesters. During the attack, the assailants beat and groped female demonstrators, and in some cases attempted to remove their clothing. They taunted them, calling the women whores and other sexually degrading terms.

Among the female demonstrators who were sexually attacked was a nineteen-year-old who, the following day, showed Human Rights Watch the swelling in her mouth around a broken tooth, and bruises on her abdomen. She said she was groped by several men, who forced their hands into her pants: "I saw that those who were yelling at us started attacking a woman from our group. I tried to get to her, but I was pulled down to the ground and was then being hit, mostly in my stomach. I tried to get up, but I got hit in the face, and my tooth was broken. I fell back to the ground and was still being hit, and they restrained my hands. One of them unzipped my pants and tried to pull them off. I was kicking and trying to free myself. They called me a whore and yelled that they were going to make an example of me, so others wouldn't come to demonstrate. I felt that I was going to be raped, from what they were doing."

Another female protester told Human Rights Watch: "Not long after we arrived, many people surrounded us. Some men behind me were touching me all over, and put their hands under my clothes. I tried to stop someone who was doing this, and he grabbed my wrist and pulled my hands back. While they were holding me, they yelled that I was a whore and asked how much I charged to do sexual acts. I know the army could see us from where we were, because I made eye contact with them."

Militia Violence

In Basra, lawlessness and Iraqi militia activity escalated in September 2007 after British forces withdrew their troops from Basra Palace, one of Saddam Hussein's former residences, and moved them to the airport on the outskirts of the city. Until the Iraqi army's "Charge of the Knights" operation in Basra in March 2008, militias terrorized women in the city, according to women's rights activists and news reports. In 2007 alone, vigilantes reportedly killed 133 women, claiming religious or customary sanction. According to Basra security forces, extremists deemed 79 of the victims to be "violating Islamic teachings." Some 47 other women died in "honor killings," and 7 were targeted for their political affiliations.

In April 2010, I interviewed Major-General Abd al-Jalil Khalaf, who was sent to Basra in June 2007 as the city's chief of police. He told me that extremists were in complete control of the city and that none of them have been held accountable for the crimes they committed. His words were chilling:

"The ages of women who were murdered ranged anywhere from fourteen years to sixty. Before the women were killed, they were tortured and sometimes had their teeth or eyes extracted. The corpses had bruises all over their bodies. Some had their breasts cut off or arms amputated, and their hair was shaven off. Most of the victims had terrified looks frozen on their faces. And none of their families came to collect the bodies. Not only did the police not investigate these crimes, my officers were directly implicated in some of the killings since the militia had infiltrated the police force. . . . These men, who committed such atrocious acts, cannot be considered human."

Trafficking and Forced Prostitution

Since the 2003 invasion, widespread insecurity, displacement, financial hardship, social disintegration, and the dissolution of the rule of law and state authority have all contributed to an increase in trafficking and forced prostitution. There are no official statistics or estimates regarding the number of women who are trafficked within the country or internationally, but anecdotal evidence suggests that the major destination points are Syria, the United Arab Emirates, and other Gulf countries. According to some women activists, the number of victims is at least in the hundreds, if not thousands.

Traffickers transport their victims overseas by land, sea, or air mainly out of Baghdad and Basra by different mechanisms. In some cases, women are forced into prostitution through false promises of legitimate employment overseas. These women realize they are duped only after they arrive at their destination country and their traffickers confiscate their passports. Traffickers also transport women and girls internally and internationally through arranged and forced marriages. Families marry off their young women and girls to older men from outside their community who are either agents or brokers. Often the girl's family coerces her into marriage, hoping to escape desperate economic circumstances or to pay debts. Other times families are unaware of the fate that awaits their daughters. "These rich foreigners come, who seem normal and look respectable, and it turns out not to be the case but the families only find out later," said one women's rights activist in Basra. "Many of these poor girls who think they are escaping their hard life in Iraq end up in Syria dancing in nightclubs."

Typically, after the broker or agent takes his "wife" or "wives" to a destination point, he divorces the woman, sells her, and returns to Iraq to claim new victims. The younger the girl, the more lucrative the profits. The highest demand is for girls under sixteen. Traffickers reportedly sell girls as young as eleven and twelve, for as much as $30,000, while older "used" girls and women can be bought for as little as $2,000. The traffickers are aided by sophisticated criminal networks that are able to forge documents and pay corrupt officials to remove impediments.

Iraq's government has done little to combat trafficking in girls and women: there have been no successful prosecutions of criminals engaged in human trafficking, no comprehensive program to tackle the problem, and negligible support for victims.

Penalizing Victims

Instead of helping victims, women's rights groups say that trafficked women (and victims of sexual violence) often find themselves in jail. The government provides no assistance to victims repatriated from abroad, and Iraqi authorities prosecute and convict trafficking victims for unlawful acts committed as a result of being trafficked; for example, some victims who were trafficked abroad using false documents were arrested and prosecuted upon their return to Iraq.

Apart from document and passport fraud, victims are also jailed for prostitution, while authorities ignore their abusers.

In some cases, women and girls request to remain in detention centers even after a sentence is complete, fearful that their families will kill them. One fourteen-year-old girl originally from Rania, in Iraq's Kurdistan region, told Human Rights Watch in June 2010 that she ran away from home to Arbil, the region's capital, after her parents forced her to become engaged to a cousin. In Arbil, out of desperation, she accepted money and accommodation from a man in exchange for sex. An Arbil court convicted her of prostitution and gave her a six-month sentence. When authorities released her to a shelter because of her age, she insisted on staying in the prison. She said she considered the prison more secure. Seven months after her initial arrest, she says she does not know what to do: "My father says that he will kill me if he ever sees me."

Victims of sexual violence and trafficking have well grounded fears of reprisals, social ostracism, rejection, or physical violence from their families, and a lack of confidence that authorities have the will or capacity to provide the support or protection required. Police are generally reluctant to investigate cases of sexual violence, trafficking, and abductions. Policing in Iraq is almost exclusively a male profession, and officers give low priority to allegations of sexual violence and trafficking compared with other crimes, such as murder and theft. Women's groups complain that, too often, police blame the victim, doubt her credibility, show indifference, and conduct inadequate investigations. For these reasons, many women are reluctant to file a complaint.

Domestic Violence

Domestic violence has always been a problem in Iraq, but women's rights groups say that years of armed conflict and economic hardships have contributed to increased violence within families. The proliferation of weapons has also intensified domestic violence and increased the risks of serious injury or death for women and girls. This issue has not received the attention it deserves, women's groups say. "In conflict areas, women's issues are never a priority," one human rights defender in Baghdad told me in 2010. "Who wants to talk about domestic violence when violence is everywhere and people are dying on the streets?"

According to a female lawyer and women's advocate from Qurna, the economic situation is forcing women to stay in dysfunctional or abusive relationships out of necessity. "If they don't, who will provide for them or their children? So accepting domestic violence is preferable to being poor."

Social attitudes that stigmatize female divorcees also help keep women in abusive relationships. According to a 2008 World Health Organization survey on family health in Iraq, 83 percent of married Iraqi women interviewed said they were subjected to "controlling behavior" by their husbands, including insisting on knowing where they were at all times, and 21 percent reported physical violence. In a

2003 study in southern Iraq by Physicians for Human Rights, more than half of the surveyed women and men agreed that a husband has the right to beat a disobedient wife.

This level of violence within marriage is underpinned by Iraqi legislation. Iraq's penal code effectively condones domestic violence under Article 41(1). The "punishment of a wife by her husband" is considered a legal right on par with disciplining children, according to the text of the provision. While the penal code specifies that such punishment is permissible "within certain limits prescribed by law or by custom," there are no specified legal limits. According to a lawyer in Najaf who provides legal assistance to women's groups, it is "very difficult" to take any legal action against men who abuse their wives. If the woman does not show marks or scars from abuse, the case is automatically rejected.

Female-Headed Households and Widows

The International Committee for the Red Cross (ICRC) estimates there are between 1 million and 3 million female-headed households in Iraq as a result of decades of war and violence. Traditionally, a widow in Iraq would return to her family or in-laws after the death of her husband, but increasingly families are unable to provide any help. Without their husbands or support from their families, these widows become socially isolated and desperate for ways to support their children.

The Iraqi government has developed a social welfare program, which includes pensions for widows amounting to 50,000 to 120,000 dinars (US$43 to $102), according to the number of dependent children. Widows are also entitled to additional compensation of up to 2.5 million dinars (US$2,100) for a spouse killed because of "terrorism."

Aid experts have said the allowance is insufficient, especially for rural widows who typically have more children and fewer sources of income than urban widows. A 2010 survey by the International Organization for Migration found that 74 percent of 1,355 female-headed displaced families who have returned to their places of origin are struggling to secure adequate nutrition for their families.

Many widows do not receive an allowance because of corruption and government institutions' lack of capacity to reach rural areas. Others, lacking education and documents, do not even bother applying because the process is overly complex and requires excessive amounts of documentation. A 2008 survey conducted by the ICRC in cooperation with a local NGO in one district of Baghdad found that only 10 percent of eligible widows received a widow's pension. Another survey conducted by Oxfam and the Iraqi NGO Al-Amal in five governorates across the country showed that 76 percent of widows did not get any government pension.

Because of the extreme financial pressures on displaced and female-headed families, local human rights activists say they are seeing an increase in child marriages, forced prostitution, and trafficking in women. Activists have also said that the practice of *mut'ah*, or temporary marriage, has grown since 2003 because of poverty and a resurgence of religious parties and tribal customs. Permissible under Shi'a Islam, *mut'ah* is a fixed-term contractual marriage usually involving a payment by the man to the wife during the specified period, and can lead in some cases to permanent marriage. In modern times, it has been used for example by men who move to a city on a temporary basis. However, this practice can lead to abuses. Impoverished and jobless widows and girls, often from displaced families, are being pressured into these types of contracts as a way to lessen their families' poverty, according to women's rights activists. More troubling, women's rights groups in the south report that men working for local government, religious institutions, and charities use their positions to pressure widows to practice *mut'ah* in exchange for any charity or services. They are exploited for *mut'ah* (literally, "pleasure") marriages by the very institutions that are supposed to be helping them.

Hope for Change

As the tenth anniversary of the 2003 US-led invasion of Iraq approaches, the country's transition to a functioning and sustainable democracy built on rule of law is far from accomplished. Iraq's transition from a police state to a society based on respect for fundamental human rights depends in large part on whether Iraqi authorities will be able to adequately defend women's rights and end the violations against women and girls that have so far continued with impunity.

While the effects of the US troop pullout by the end of 2011 remains to be seen, women and girls find themselves vulnerable again in the face of further insecurity and diminished international attention to their plight. To bolster women's rights, the international community must continue providing financial and technical assistance to civil society organizations supporting women and girls who have suffered sexual violence, trafficking, or forced marriage, or who fear reprisals from their families in the form of honor killings. One of the few bright lights for women since 2003 that I have witnessed in different cities across Iraq has been the dramatic increase in women's rights groups and female activists ceaselessly working to advocate for legislative reform and provide services to marginalized women.

However, it will be impossible for these activists to embark on a program of reform unilaterally. There is hope but only if the Iraqi government acts decisively as a partner for change. Iraq's Kurdistan Regional Government has taken a series of positive steps in this respect. Most significantly, in June 2011, Kurdistan's parliament passed the Family Violence Bill, which criminalizes forced and child marriages; the verbal, physical, and psychological abuse of girls and women; and female genital mutilation.

On the national level, Iraq's central government must follow suit and adopt a two-pronged approach to legal reform. First, the government would provide a huge boost to women's rights by amending the penal code and all other legislation to remove any law that discriminates against women, or allows mitigation for violent crimes against women on grounds of "honor." The second necessary step is passing a law to combat human trafficking, in particular the trafficking of women and girls for the purposes of sexual exploitation. Under this law, victims would not be punished further, but referred to social welfare agencies for financial assistance as well as health and social services.

The Iraqi government could further serve the cause of women's rights by establishing or improving preventive and protection programs and facilities, including adequate shelters, for women at risk of violence or abuse. Facilitating widows' access to government services and aid by removing burdensome documentation requirements would be another step in the right direction.

Perhaps most important, a change of mindset from top to bottom in Iraq's government with regard to the role and value of women in society is essential, as is the need for justice to deter abusers. It should be unthinkable for a female victim to go to a police station in Iraq and hear the words spoken to Muna in Baghdad: "It is not up to us, we have nothing to do with your case."

CHAPTER 8

Saudi Women's Struggle

Christoph Wilcke

"My Gua....nows What's Best for Me" is a web campaign by conservative Saudi women who say they support the current male guardianship system that reduces women to the status of perpetual children, requiring them to obtain permission from a male legal guardian for just about anything grownups normally decide independently. They say they do not want to drive—preferring the convenience of having a foreign driver chauffeur them around. They do not want to travel alone, abroad or within the kingdom, and they probably wouldn't dream of working against the wishes of their male guardians, usually husbands, fathers, or brothers. After all, they say, those guardians know best, by virtue of being male.

It seemed odd at first in mid-2009 that a conservative group would launch such a campaign or that the campaign's website attracted over five thousand signatures within a few months. But, in a strange twist, the campaign is part of a renewed focus on women's rights in Saudi Arabia.

After decades of frozen progress, the continued denial of women's basic rights in Saudi Arabia is coming under sustained attack. The

Christoph Wilcke is a senior researcher for Human Rights Watch's Middle East and North Africa Division, covering Saudi Arabia, Jordan, and Yemen. He is the author of numerous reports including Looser Rein, Uncertain Gain: A Human Rights Assessment of Five Years of King Abdullah's Reforms in Saudi Arabia *(2010). Prior to joining Human Rights Watch in 2005, he worked with the International Crisis Group, the International Peace Institute, and Save the Children UK.*

upheavals in Arab countries in 2011 have given new impetus to calls for reform in Saudi Arabia, too, and calls for women's rights have been the most prominent among them.

No longer is it chiefly Western activists grabbing headlines about sexist discrimination. Courageous Saudi educated and middle-class women—even a few princesses—are now also taking up the cause. Online social media have allowed these activists to connect with one another and, crucially, with the many other women who were silent before but can now express their support for women's rights at the click of a mouse button. The nascent women's rights movement in Saudi Arabia may be on the cusp of becoming a broad-based wave, lobbying fathers, husbands, and brothers within their homes, and public opinion on the Internet. Those are their two means of exerting pressure, as there are no formal mechanisms for decision making in which Saudi women are allowed to participate.

Ironically, under the current system in Saudi Arabia, it will be men who institute changes for women, if at all. The leader of the movement for Saudi women's rights is King Abdullah himself. Giving women greater freedoms, especially in the public space, education, and the labor market, has been a declared priority for reform for the eighty-nine-year-old king since he ascended the throne in August 2005.

Abdullah surprised his fellow Saudis with an announcement on September 25, 2011, that Saudi women would be able to vote and stand as candidates in municipal elections in 2015 as well as be considered for appointment to the Shura Council. Both announcements are highly symbolic of the king's support for women's greater participation in public life, but are also likely to have next to no impact on their lives. Municipal councils are administratively toothless and politically meaningless, and female participation in the polls can be expected to be extremely low—if the low participation of men in the 2005 election is any indicator. The Shura Council is toothless but not politically insignificant, but women members will face an uphill struggle in getting their issues debated as long as they do not form a substantial number of its members.

Women activists regularly urge the king to support them. Manal al-Sharif, who courageously broke two taboos by driving a car and then publicizing the event online, wrote after being released from her prison cell: "I thank our guardians, first among whom is the custodian of the two holy mosques [King Abdullah], for ordering my release from detention, out of the compassion for his sons and daughters among the citizens of this blessed country for which he is known." Wajeha al-Huwaider, Saudi Arabia's most vocal and best-known women's rights activist, together with Fouzia al-'Uyuni, another veteran campaigner for women's rights, waylaid the king by raising placards on his visit to the Eastern Province, where they live, to bring cases of discrimination and violence against women to the monarch's attention.

The direct appeals by women activists to the king as the champion of their cause is both a strength and a weakness. On the positive side, this constellation allows relatively few activists to raise their issues directly to the highest level of decision making, where they believe they have a sympathetic ear. But the weaknesses of this setup also reveal the fragility of the movement and the lack of an institutional forum at which it can address women's rights abuses in Saudi Arabia. For all the new voices demanding women's rights, next to nothing has changed over the past five years. The government has not budged on guardianship rules or on the ban on women driving. In 2011, there are still no new laws to ban violence against women, and marriage and divorce rules as well as other issues of personal status remain discriminatory. Enforced sex segregation has eased in some public places, where women can walk around more freely, but even at most government institutions, women must still enter through the back door.

The Guardianship System

"Male guardianship" is a system of officially sanctioned practices that treat women as perpetual minors by denying them the right to make decisions about their own lives. The system affects almost all aspects of women's human rights, from their freedom of movement to their right to health. Failure to comply with the requirements of the system can be severe: in January 2010, a court in the city of Buraida sentenced Sawsan Salim to three hundred lashes and one-and-a-half years in prison for "appearing . . . without a male guardian" at government offices.[1]

Women require permission from their male relatives—often in writing—to travel, to undergo certain medical procedures, to work, to study, or even to open a bank account.

Saudi authorities require a woman to show her male guardian's consent to travel for each foreign journey or on yellow travel cards, valid for one year, in the case of domestic travel. In July 2010 Wajeha al-Huwaider traveled abroad and was astonished when her brother—her male guardian—received a government-issued text message on his mobile phone informing him of her trip. Nazia Quazi, a twenty-four-year-old dual Canadian-Indian national, traveled to Saudi Arabia to meet her father. Her Indian father works in Saudi Arabia and is her male guardian. He refused to give her permission to leave the kingdom because he disapproved of her fiancé. Nazia was trapped in Saudi Arabia for three years.

Hospitals, private and governmental, still require permission from male guardians for women to undergo certain surgical procedures. A Saudi woman, who preferred to remain anonymous, could not schedule surgery for herself in late 2010 because Saudi intelligence forces had detained her husband, an outspoken dissident, and kept him in solitary confinement. After repeated visits to the local Saudi domestic intelligence office, they finally granted her a visit with her husband so he could sign the guardian's consent form allowing her to undergo the operation. That was two months after her husband had been arrested, just days before her scheduled surgery.

The guardianship system can prevent women from escaping restrictive or abusive homes. One Saudi woman told Human Rights Watch in June 2010 that her brothers, who are her guardians, beat her and then married her off against her will three times for money to men who also beat her. Saudi Arabia's domestic Human Rights Commission, a government agency, said it was powerless to intervene against the will of the guardians.

In 2009, the Saudi government pledged to abolish the system at a review of its rights record at the United Nations Human Rights Council, but has taken no legislative steps to overturn male guardianship.

King Abdullah made only one small change to the system by decreeing, in January 2008, that women may stay in hotels without a male guardian. As crown prince in 2004, Abdullah had previously issued a decree permitting businesswomen to open businesses without guardian approval.

Fatwas Against Female Drivers

The most famous incident of women driving took place in central Riyadh in November 1990. Forty-seven women, inspired by female US soldiers driving military vehicles on Saudi streets, took to their cars in a symbolic drive around the block. The police arrested them, their employers fired or suspended them, and conservative Islamist clerics slandered them from pulpits as whores.

There is no law barring women from driving in Saudi Arabia, but senior government clerics have issued several fatwas, or religious rulings (that are not binding), saying women are prohibited from driving for fear of moral corruption if they mingle with unrelated men. These fatwas are based on the rationale of "warding off" situations that may lead to corruption, the same concept Saudi clerics invoked in the 1990s to forbid women from opening businesses, arguing that a woman's place is at home and there is no need for her to leave the home other than in times of emergency. The Interior Ministry in 1991 also issued a decree banning women from driving, though Saudi legal scholars say the 1992 Basic Law supersedes and annuls this decree, the text of which is not public. As these scholars have pointed out, the Basic Law's Article 26 guarantees human rights in accordance with Islamic Sharia law, and there is no Sharia legal provision against women driving.

Saudi women occasionally do drive, especially outside the cities in the desert, and several attempts have been made to ease the ban on women driving in the kingdom. Senior ruling Saudi princes, including King Abdullah, Crown Prince Sultan, and Foreign Minister Prince Sa'ud, have supported removing the ban in principle, and members of the advisory Shura Council discussed proposals to ease the ban between 2005 and 2007.

In practice, Saudi officials have barred women from driving and refused to issue them driver's licenses. In March 2008, Wajeha al-Huwaider posted on YouTube a video of herself driving in a rural Saudi area while narrating an appeal to Interior Minister Prince Nayef bin Abd al-'Aziz to allow women to drive. The video sparked some media interest but no driving revolution.

More than three years later, and more than twenty years since the landmark 1990 protest, another woman, Manal al-Sharif, also drove in protest of the ban and publicized her action by posting a video online. A computer security expert and divorced mother in her early thirties, she was fed up with being unable to get home after leaving the office. One day in May 2011, she had worked late but couldn't find a taxi, so she called her brother to pick her up, but he did not answer his phone. She had to order an expensive car service to get home, because, as a single divorcée, she is not allowed to hire a live-in foreign male driver, like other Saudi families.

Al-Sharif, who holds an international driver's license, decided to drive in protest, first on May 19, 2011, when she recorded herself on video, and again on May 21, when she took her children and brother along. Unlike her drive on May 19, which went undetected, traffic police stopped her on this second instance and called the religious police, a morality watchdog with arrest powers, to the scene. The officials briefly arrested al-Sharif and her brother, before letting them go. In the middle of the night on May 22, however, the criminal investigation police returned to arrest al-Sharif and took her to prison, accusing her not only of driving but also of "stirring up public opinion" and "harming Saudi Arabia's reputation abroad." The police had presumably found the video and noticed that a campaign for women drivers had scheduled a protest on June 17.

Al-Sharif's arrest and detention backfired. The officials who tried to smear her as immoral faced widely expressed sympathies for al-Sharif and for women driving. On June 17, more than fifty Saudi women took to their cars, often with supportive husbands or brothers accompanying them, largely without incident. Less than two weeks later, however, Saudi authorities began clamping down again, arresting at least seven women who continued to drive in Dammam and Jeddah. By September 2011, however, a senior traffic official leaked information that new guidance by the Interior Ministry directed traffic cops to no longer arrest women who drive. That same month, lawyer Abd al-Rahman al-Lahim was preparing a landmark case for discrimination against Manal al-Sharif concerning the refusal of the traffic department to issue her a driving license.

Sex Segregation

The Saudi government is unique among Muslim-majority countries in that it imposes almost complete sex segregation. While the policy is worded in as being gender neutral, in practice it prevents Saudi women from participating meaningfully in public life.

Sex segregation in the workplace has particularly adverse and discriminatory consequences for women by making them unattractive as employees. For employers, the need to establish separate facilities for women, and women's inability to interact with government agencies without a male representative, provide significant disincentives to hiring them. An additional disincentive is that employers must sometimes coordinate their female employees' transportation as a result of the driving ban.

The government's religious police, the Commission for the Promotion of Virtue and the Prevention of Vice, strictly monitors and enforces sex segregation in all workplaces with the exception of hospitals. When they discover unlawful mixing of the sexes, they are authorized to arrest the violators and bring them to the nearest police station, where they can be criminally charged.

Saudi jurists from the Permanent Council for Scientific Research and Legal Opinions have described the rationale behind this policy: "In an Islamic society, the call for women to join men in their workplace is a grave matter, and intermingling with men is among its greatest pitfalls. Loose interaction across gender lines is one of the major causes of fornication, which disintegrates society and destroys its moral values and all sense of propriety."[2]

The unease about women working and coming into contact with men is illustrated by the debate over lingerie stores. In March 2006, the Labor Ministry warned that under regulation 120 of 2,005 male workers in such shops, who are all non-Saudi, would be prohibited from selling lingerie to women and that female salesclerks would take over. Under fierce attack from conservative clerics opposed to women leaving the house to work, the ministry later announced it would not enforce the decree. The dispute over which was the greater evil—Saudi women working or coming into contact with foreign men—remained unsettled. The chief of the religious police, Ibrahim al-Ghaith, declared in December 2008 that he was not opposed to women working in lingerie stores, earning him a rebuke from the grand mufti, Abd al-'Aziz Al al-Shaikh, who opposed such work for women, saying, "We should not involve them in matters far from their nature." Finally, in June 2011, King Abdullah issued a decree replacing lingerie salesmen with saleswomen.

In education and sports, sex segregation has also resulted in unequal access to facilities. At the public King Saud University in Riyadh, female students are required to study in the older buildings with an inferior library, and the administration only allows them to use the main library in the men's colleges one day per week during limited daytime hours. No women are allowed in the King Fahd Public Library, also located in the kingdom's capital; women must call in advance for materials and send their drivers to pick these up.

Saudi girls and women may not practice sports with the same freedom as men. Saudi Arabia may be the only country in the world where girls, unlike boys, do not receive physical education in government schools, and that has no mechanisms for supporting competitive female athletes. Besides discrimination in schools and competitive sports, Saudi women also face greater obstacles in exercising for their health or playing team sports for fun. No women's sports clubs exist, and even exercise gyms have to masquerade as "health clubs," usually attached to hospitals, in order to receive a commercial license. The Olympic Charter prohibits discrimination against women and girls in sport, yet the International Olympic Committee has so far not taken the drastic steps necessary to bring Saudi practice in line international standards. In November 2011, Saudi Arabia conceded it would not oppose a Saudi woman athlete participating in the London 2012 Olympics, if invited by an international sports federation, appearing in Islamic dress, and accompanied by a male guardian. Human Rights Watch and other activists are now pushing the government to go much further by promoting female athletes to qualify for future Olympics, permitting girls to practice sports in school, and mandating government sports clubs open women's sections.

The risk sex segregation can present to the life and health of Saudi women and girls is sadly illustrated by reports of a tragedy in March 2002, when a fire at an elementary girls' school in Mecca resulted in the death of fifteen girls. According to journalists and eyewitnesses, the religious police did not allow the girls to exit the school without their headscarves, contributing to their deaths. The Ministry of Education denies this version of events.

Yet, over the past five years, there has been an increasingly vigorous and public domestic debate about what constitutes permissible interactions for men and women, such as at work meetings or large gatherings, referred to as "innocent mingling," or inappropriate seclusion for immoral purposes, such as a man and a woman alone together in a closed environment.

King Abdullah has encouraged women's education and entry into the workforce, and tolerated increased visibility of women in public, challenging the practices of strict sex segregation. The Nora bint Abdul Rahman University for Women, the largest women's university in the world with a capacity for forty thousand students, opened in Riyadh in May 2011. In 2009, the king opened King Abdullah University for Science and Technology (KAUST), the first mixed-gender university in the kingdom. To promote the normalcy of interaction between men and women, King Abdullah allowed *Okaz* and other newspapers to publish a front-page photograph of him surrounded by more than thirty-five partially veiled female participants in the 2010 National Dialogue in Najran. And, in an important symbolic message, King Abdullah fired a cleric who had criticized gender mixing at KAUST.

In the workplace, the Saudi Labor Law, which came into force in 2006, no longer includes an explicit provision requiring sex segregation, instead generally requiring that the law adhere to Sharia law. King

Abdullah has also encouraged women to enter the workplace by dropping certain licensing requirements. Royal Decree No. 187 of 2005 allows "private enterprises to open sections employing women without a license being required," and section 8 of labor regulation 120 of 2005 encouraged women to work in certain sectors. In 2004, Council of Ministers Resolution 120 allowed women to apply for business licenses.

However, women remain barred from certain professions. Although they may now study law, they may not actually practice as lawyers in court or work as prosecutors or judges.

Violence Against Women

One previously taboo issue that has attracted significant attention and public debate in the kingdom is domestic violence. Human rights activists including Dr. Maha Munif and Wajeha al-Huwaider, and groups such as the National Society for Human Rights (NSHR), have highlighted individual cases of domestic violence against women and children to generate public awareness and lift the veil of shame obscuring access to justice for its victims. In 2005, Munif helped establish the National Family Safety Program for victims of domestic violence after winning royal support. It now provides some services to victims of domestic violence, including operating shelters and setting up specialized domestic violence units within hospitals. In May 2010, al-Huwaider helped to produce a short film, *I Want to Feel Safe*, posted online, detailing how the guardianship system trapped women in their homes and exposed them to violence.

In 2007, the NSHR noted the "high rate of [domestic violence] cases" it received, and urged "issuing legislation that [criminalizes domestic] violence and imposes severe punishment for offenders." The 2009 NSHR report again observed a "noticeable increase" in domestic violence, and called for "activating a strategy that restricts [domestic] violence." Majed Garoub, the head of the Jeddah lawyers' committee, in a series of three articles published in *Al-Watan* in May and June 2010, urged the adoption of specific measures against domestic violence. To date, however, King Abdullah has not acted on the recommendations.

In late February 2010, Justice Minister Muhammad al-ʿIsa announced that a new law would soon accredit women lawyers to allow them to appear in court for the first time, but restrict their clients to women. They would only be permitted to litigate child custody, divorce, marriage, and other family-related cases. Despite these restrictions, activists hailed the announcement as a step toward increased access to justice for women as well as toward women's professional development. By July 2011 nothing had come of the law.

Many victims of domestic violence remain outside the system of help and redress. The story of Nathalie Morin exemplifies the impact on vulnerable women and children. A Canadian married to a Saudi man, she had been living in the kingdom with her children for years. Morin in 2010 first described to Human Rights Watch her husband's violence and neglect toward her and her children, including locking her up and denying them food. Human Rights Watch's appeals to the kingdom's Human Rights Commission produced no help. Then Morin contacted al-Huwaider and al-ʿUyuni in June 2011 to let them know she had found a key to the apartment and that her husband would be gone for five days. The women activists set out in an attempt to bring Morin out of her apartment for some shopping, but as soon as they arrived, police arrested them. Morin's husband was also there, and had set up their arrest after discovering that his wife had contacted the women. The husband told the police the women activists wanted to abduct his wife, and the police believed him without checking with Morin. Al-Huwaider and al-ʿUyuni were released after some time, but not before the governor of the Eastern Province intervened. Morin and her children remain captives of a man she describes as an abusive husband, unable to leave the apartment or the country or seek help. Saudi interpretation of Sharia law makes it extremely difficult for women to obtain a divorce, in which case the father would likely gain custody of the children.

Despite increased international attention, King Abdullah and his government have taken few concrete measures over the past five years to address the problems of domestic violence. The government has drafted, but has been unable or unwilling to pass, a law criminalizing domestic violence and offering protection, redress, and rehabilitation to its victims.

Forced and Forbidden Marriages

The Saudi government has not even begun to address many other matters affecting women's rights, such as forced marriages and divorce, equality in citizenship, and other personal status matters. Only after the marriage in 2008 of an eight-year-old girl to a man in his fifties, twice court approved but later dissolved with the consent of all parties, did the Human Rights Commission and the Justice Ministry indicate that they would draft a law addressing early marriage. To date, nothing has come of the effort, although in June 2010 the Justice Ministry amended the standard marriage contract to mention the bride's age but without setting an age limit.

Fathers and brothers force young daughters, or sisters, to marry against their will. An adult Saudi woman, whose brother is her guardian, told Human Rights Watch in August 2009 that her brother had raped her when she was a child, and later twice married her off to men against her will. She was now divorced, and lived in her brother's house with her infant daughter from the second marriage. He beat her, but she could not live elsewhere without his consent, as he was her sole guardian.

Some Saudi fathers also prevent their adult daughters from marrying, and the Saudi government recognizes filial "disobedience" as a crime, denying adult women the right to marry of their own free will or to live on their own. Lulwa Abd al-Rahman, a Saudi woman in her thirties, remains in the Protection Home in Jeddah for a third year, her fiancé told Human Rights Watch. She had fled her abusive father, who refused to allow them to marry four years ago because of the fiancé's allegedly inferior tribe. Her father also had her briefly committed to a mental hospital. An appeals court said Abd al-Rahman's behavior was unlawful "rebellion" against her father.

The experience of Samar Bawadi is another case in point. In July 2010, Jeddah's General Court ruled in her favor after she filed an *adhl* suit (overreach of guardian authority) against her father for refusing to let her marry. Badawi remained in prison pending trial, however, because her father had countersued her for "disobedience" after she fled his home for a shelter.

In 2008, Badawi and her nine-year-old son from a previous marriage escaped what she said (and Saudi officials confirmed) was her father's physical abuse. She found refuge at the Protection Home in Jeddah, a shelter for victims of domestic violence. Her father attempted to bring a "disobedience" charge against her, but the Saudi Public Prosecutions and Investigation Bureau decided not to prosecute her. Badawi's father again sued her in 2009 for "disobedience" for not returning to his home. Judge Abdullah al-'Uthaim, who presides over Jeddah's Summary Court, issued a warrant for her arrest after she had missed several trial dates. Al-'Uthaim said that "disobedience is among the serious cases requiring imprisonment," citing Interior Ministry Decree 1900 of 2007. In fact, this decree lists only one crime concerning parent-child relations among the serious crimes requiring detention pending trial: "assaulting a parent with beatings," which is clearly distinct from mere "disobedience."

Badawi left the shelter in July 2009 with the permission of Jeddah Governor Prince Mish'al bin Abd al-Majid to live with her brother, believing this would protect her from arrest and imprisonment in the outstanding disobedience case. When she found a man whom she wanted to marry, and her father refused, she filed the *adhl* suit against her father. In 2010, during the first court session in her *adhl* case, her father had her arrested based on the outstanding "disobedience" warrant. She was later released, won her case, and was able to marry.

Although several government-ordered investigations found the father to be abusive toward Badawi, no criminal prosecution against him ever got under way. Instead, Mecca Governor Prince Khalid bin Faisal in July 2010 recommended a committee look into reconciliation between father and daughter. The publicity Badawi generated about her case may have shamed the judges into releasing her from the clutches of her father, but the government banned her from foreign travel as a punishment.

Slow Dawn

Until now, there have been two constants for Saudi women that even the reign of the reform-minded King Abdullah has not changed: first, they face one of the most severe forms of discrimination against women in the world; and, second, the government is doing nothing substantial to correct this injustice.

But other things have changed: the battlefield of women's rights is now more clearly drawn, not only the line between conservative and progressive forces, but, more important, the issues and ideas for which each side is fighting. Five years ago, male guardianship was not yet recognized as the core systemic reason behind women's discrimination. Now, the government has acknowledged and pledged to abolish this archaic system, though it has done nothing.

Today, a rising number of brave Saudi women's rights activists repeatedly publicize cases of discrimination and rights violations. Some, like Badawi, have filed lawsuits against their abusers. She has followed up since her release and marriage with a lawsuit against women's disenfranchisement from the 2011 municipal elections.

Saudi courts steeped in patriarchal traditions are unlikely saviors of Saudi women. But they will increasingly be forced to provide written justifications for women's continued inequity. Meanwhile, courageous women like Samar Badawi will continue to challenge those justifications as not up to the times, not founded on solid legal grounds, and not fair or just. And with forty thousand new female students at Nora bint Abdul Rahman University for Women, there may soon be many followers.

PART 3
CONFLICT ZONES

CHAPTER 9

Devastating Remnants of War
The Impact of Armed Conflict on
Women and Girls

Jody Williams

At six years old, Song Kosal was a lovely little Cambodian girl. Her eyes sparkled, and her smile lit up her face so much that everyone who knew her was always trying to make her laugh. But one afternoon, in the blink of an eye, her life changed forever. And it wasn't just her life. What happened to Kosal transformed the lives of her family.

That afternoon in the summer of 1995, Kosal was working with her mother in a rice paddy in a quiet town on the Thai-Cambodia border where they lived. Much of that border was one of the most heavily mined areas in the world, belying the seeming serenity of that town. While helping her mother work, in the middle of that rice paddy, Song Kosal stepped on a landmine.

The immediate shock of the blast was overwhelming, but its aftermath was even more devastating. Kosal's right leg was severely injured. Ultimately, it was mutilated beyond repair and had to be amputated.

Antipersonnel landmines are particularly heinous weapons. They are designed, for the most part, to injure and maim and not to kill. Maiming requires an intense medical response, both immediate but

In 1997, Jody Williams became the tenth woman—and third American woman—to be awarded the Nobel Peace Prize. She was honored for her work as the founding coordinator of the International Campaign to Ban Landmines, which shared the prize with her that year. She is currently the chair of the Nobel Women's Initiative.

also more long-term: blood transfusions, surgeries, and rehabilitation, mental and physical. Suddenly a person who was healthy and strong is permanently maimed, and his or her life is altered irrevocably.

Damaged Families

If people ever do think about landmines, they tend to think about their impact on soldiers; however, soldiers are often the least affected, and when they are affected, they frequently have access to resources that civilians do not. They are supported by medical response teams and other systems. Most people don't think about the impact of landmines on civilians, especially on women and young girls. The majority of landmines have been used in poor countries that have minimal to nonexistent medical infrastructure. Sometimes it can literally take days to get a mine victim to even rudimentary medical care. Many who might have lived die simply because they cannot quickly get the help they need.

Imagine, then, how families like Kosal's, who are subsistence farmers, manage in such a situation. They barely get by, eking out a living because everyone in the family, even six-year-old girls who should be in school, is working. And now this young daughter can no longer contribute to the survival of the family. Not only can she no longer work, but she has suddenly become a drain on the family's finances.

Someone from the family, sometimes the mother and all of her children, depending on their ages, will have to accompany her to the hospital and stay there for the weeks it takes for surgery and recovery. The landmine survivor's physical and psychological needs will be great and will change over time. Had Kosal decided to use a prosthetic leg, it would have had to be changed as she grew and then less often for the rest of her life, as artificial limbs wear out and have to be replaced. Who will pay for this?

On a personal level, in a society in which marriage remains an important measure of a woman's worth, who will want to marry a young Cambodian woman, no matter how beautiful and how magical her smile, if she only has one leg? How could she help farm? How could she tend to children? Instead, will she be a burden on her family for the rest of her life? Not only in Cambodia but also in Angola, Bosnia, and Burma, or any of the other dozens of countries where landmines and other explosive weapons of war are found, young women face lives of unnecessary pain and difficulty.

It only takes a few minutes to explain the difference between weapons that go home with soldiers at the end of a conflict and those that remain a danger on now silent battlefields long after a war ends. Landmines, cluster bombs, grenades, and the other explosive detritus of battle sow a particular terror in communities around the world in which entire families try to survive on lands seeded with these indiscriminate weapons that can continue to kill and maim for generations after the end of a conflict.

Explosive remnants of war are a most tangible and blatant expression of both the immediate and the long-term effects of war on societies, especially on its most vulnerable members, women and girls. Landmines, cluster bombs, and other such weapons can serve as a prism through which people can begin to understand what conflict leaves in its wake.

The High Price Paid by Women and Girls

The impact of explosive weapons on women and girls is not the only curse of violent conflict. Just as most people tend to think of landmines in connection with soldiers and not civilians, too often visions of armed conflict include men fighting, while their families continue with their lives, waiting for their soldiers to come home. But that simply is not the case. In war and lower-level conflict situations that might not be called "war," such as the "war on drugs" that began tearing Mexico apart in 2006, women and girls too often bear the brunt of the immediate violence and endure repercussions long afterward.

Women and girls themselves are targets of violence, including sexual violence. At the same time, women are trying to hold families together, too often on their own. Often the percentage of women-headed households increases dramatically not only during the conflict but afterward, with many women widowed or abandoned. Resources decline and support networks begin to collapse; many families suffer increased poverty, and women-headed households are more likely than others to experience poverty and destitution.

If in periods of peace women's human rights are already violated or ignored, those violations are magnified in times of armed conflict. Whether they remain in the zones of conflict or flee inside their own countries or leave to live as refugees, there is little safe haven for women and girls. They can be abducted, raped, and tortured no matter where they are.

The Office of the United Nations High Commissioner for Refugees (UNHCR) estimates that in most refugee populations, approximately 50 percent are women and girls.[1] Many refugee women arrive in host countries as widows; frequently they have also lost children. Some have been raped or gang raped; many of their daughters have endured the same. Rape is used in epidemic proportions as a weapon of terror in armed conflict. Its multiple effects can include the shame and ostracization of raped women; abandonment by husbands who leave them to fend for themselves and their children on their own; and a dwindling chance of ever marrying again, or ever marrying at all in the case of young girls. If their families lived in poverty before, this indigence is only magnified for refugee women.

Women and girls are not necessarily safer in refugee camps, either. Often, they have come from small villages where the number of families can be counted on two hands or by the dozens. They can suddenly find themselves in inhospitable camps inhabited by thousands or tens of thousands of desperate people living in extremely close quarters. Many women and girls may experience gender-based violence, including domestic and sexual violence. Also, women and girls fleeing conflict or in the chaos of its aftermath may end up as victims of human trafficking. If not trafficked, they can also end up as child soldiers—a dire fate that can befall girls as well as boys.

Girls can often be an invisible element of the child soldier issue. While many attempts are made—often successfully—to reintegrate boy soldiers into society, that is not always the case for girls who have been forcibly recruited to serve male combatants, whether as "wives" or cooks or porters. Families and communities may not welcome them home with open arms at the end of conflict, especially when these girls try to return with children born of combatants. Reintegration programs for child soldiers in many cases do not tackle the specific needs of girls in this predicament. Often they do not address female child soldiers at all.

Women and girls also are at tremendous risk in situations of violent conflict that have not yet reached full-blown civil war, such as the war on drugs in Mexico, which has been engulfing the country. Since Mexico's president militarized the national response to the drug cartels there in 2006, the ongoing low-level conflict there has had a significant impact on ordinary citizens who are bearing the brunt of the cartels' brutal response. Mexican police and military are not innocents in the war on drugs, either. Impunity reigns. That and stresses caused by the conflict and militarization of the country are resulting in domestic violence, rape, and femicide spiraling out of control. In just one example, hundreds of unsolved cases of young women who were killed or disappeared in Ciudad Juarez earned this city the tragic name "City of the Lost Girls."

At the same time, women have courageously been at the forefront of efforts to end the violence and the impunity in Mexico, exposing them to further risks in an accelerating cycle of brutality. In response to their protests, Mexican women have been abused, threatened, or even murdered. In some cases, when other family members have taken up the protest after such an assassination, they too have been tortured, mutilated, or killed. In one of the more notorious cases at the end of 2010, a woman denouncing her daughter's murder was shot down on the steps of the main office of the municipal government where she was staging her most recent protest.

A Human Security Framework

Such examples are mere snapshots of what can and does happen to women and girls during full-blown armed conflict and in situations of systemic armed violence. Sometimes the distinctions between "systemic armed violence" and "armed conflict" can be hard to discern. For women and girls the distinctions are immaterial. No matter how the violent conflicts are parsed out and defined, women and girls are the most vulnerable and suffer the most. But while their situation is dismal, it does not have to remain that way.

Violence against women and girls in armed conflict is not new. But increasingly over the past few decades, a more sophisticated understanding of the multiple ways that conflict affects them differently from men and boys has evolved. With that awareness, a variety of efforts to tackle the many faces of the violence have been on the rise. The UN and various affiliated agencies, regional bodies, and individual governments have passed treaties, resolutions, and national legislation. Many NGOs have plans or programs dealing with the impact of armed conflict and violence on women and girls.

For example, in 1979, the United Nations adopted the Convention on the Elimination of All Forms of Discrimination Against Women (CEDAW). In October 2000, the UN Security Council adopted Resolution 1325 on women, peace, and security. In June 2008, the Security Council unanimously passed Resolution 1820, which deals with rape as a weapon of war and recognizes the impact of sexual violence in conflict on international peace and security. Most recently, in January 2011, the newly created agency UN Women was officially launched with the objective of ending grave abuses against women, including those occurring in conflict zones.

The list goes on, spanning at least three decades. But a key question that has yet to be answered is what, fundamentally, has changed for women and girls in conflict situations? Treaties and resolutions are important tools for change. The soaring words that often open these documents are inspired, sometimes almost poetic, and offer a passionate vision of a different world for women and girls. But words on paper can and must only be measured in terms of the impact they have had individually or collectively on the lives of women and girls in situations of armed conflict.

So far, such words have not done enough to stem the tide of violence against women and to address the impunity with which these crimes are carried out. While the UN Security Council's Resolution 1325 (on women, peace, and security) and to a lesser degree its Resolution 1820 (on the specific problem of sexual violence in armed conflict zones) are addressed in public fora and speeches, so far they have not had sufficient impact on the ground. Implementation of a treaty or resolution does not happen simply because a document exists. Without political will and a real commitment to achieving the goals of agreements, not much happens. This was the case, for example, with landmines until we created the International Campaign to Ban Landmines in 1992 to go to the root of the problem and get rid of these weapons entirely.

I didn't meet Song Kosal until a few years after she'd stepped on that landmine in the rice paddy. It was the summer of 1995, and the International Campaign to Ban Landmines was holding its first international conference on landmines in Cambodia, a country deeply afflicted by this problem. Kosal was still a very young girl and was quiet and shy. She was involved in a local program of Jesuit Refugee Services and was learning about how important it was for landmine survivors to become their own advocates for their rights as well as for a world free of landmines. The Cambodia conference was her first big meeting with campaigners from around the world. She's never stopped.

Grassroots Efforts to Achieve "Human Security"

I would argue—and I believe my now longtime landmine ban friend and colleague Song Kosal would agree—that it is essential to have a global grassroots campaign dedicated to stopping such violence. In tackling landmines, we quickly recognized that aiding landmine survivors alone, while critical, would not fundamentally alter the lives of people around the world living with landmines long after a conflict has ended. Similarly, aiding women and girls who have survived violence in conflict situations alone, while critical, will not fundamentally alter the global crisis of such violence. It will be necessary to also address the causes of the violence, including the subordinate status of women and girls all over the world, and make sure that perpetrators who commit these terrible acts are brought to justice, even if it takes as long as it will to clear all the landmines away.

One of the main reasons that the Mine Ban Treaty has seen such dramatic implementation and compliance is that the global ban advocates who make up the International Campaign to Ban Landmines have never lessened their pressure on governments to obey the laws that they themselves created concerning landmines. Relentless civil society pressure has kept their political will focused on the issue and on the ultimate objective, the complete eradication of landmines.

Finally, addressing the impact of armed conflict on women and girls requires a different vision of what might really bring sustained peace, security, and equality to the planet. Enough of "peace through strength." Enough of "if you want peace you must prepare for war." Enough of the worn-out, centuries-old framework of national security in this fundamentally changed and changing global world system.

A grassroots campaign to tackle the impact of violent conflict on women and girls would do well to ground itself in a human security framework. That framework rests on security of the individual, of human beings, and not solely on the security of the state. The twin pillars of human security in the globalized world are "freedom from fear" and "freedom from want." The success of the mine ban movement has already helped spur some governments to focus more on human security, and not just national security.

Song Kosal was a child victim of violence in war. But she did not remain a victim. She is a survivor of violence who chose to become a powerful advocate for a different world. Her empowerment is her own, but it also is supported in the vast global network of grassroots activists working to eliminate the violent terror of landmines. She is a powerful symbol of what a former victim can achieve, and an inspiration to all who seek to rid the world not only of crippling weapons, but of the equally debilitating violence that too many women and girls suffer today.

CHAPTER 10

Under Siege in Somalia

Dr. Hawa Abdi with Sarah J. Robbins

I ignored their call, so they came to my gate unannounced: six members of the Somali insurgent group Hizbul Islam, with a request to
speak with me in person. By this time, April 2010, their militia had
controlled our area for the past year—the latest in an endless line of
transitional leaders, warlords, and regimes I'd seen since the collapse
of Somalia's government. I was examining a severely malnourished
child, who hadn't eaten for at least four days, when a security guard
ran in with the news. I was not willing to abandon my patient for a
conversation with people whose only clear goals were to rob, to take
over, or to kill.

My medical practice began in 1983 as a one-room clinic on my family's farm, ten miles outside Mogadishu. As hard as it may be to
imagine, Somalia was peaceful when I moved here. But now, after
more than twenty years of civil war caused by interclan fighting, that
one room is a four-hundred-bed hospital; the land behind it, once fer-

*Dr. Hawa Abdi is a Somali obstetrician and gynecologist who in 1983 established a one-room
clinic near Somalia's capital, Mogadishu. Over time, this small operation evolved into one of
the largest camps and medical facilities for internally displaced people in the war-torn African
country; today, the camp houses approximately ninety thousand people, mostly women and
children. Dr. Abdi works alongside her two daughters, who are also doctors, under highly dangerous conditions, and was selected as one of* Glamour *magazine's "Women of the Year" in 2010.
This chapter, co-written with author Sarah J. Robbins, recounts a harrowing episode in 2010
when Islamist militants invaded her camp and held her hostage for several days. Grand Central
Publishing will release Dr. Abdi's memoir, co-written with Robbins, in 2013.*

tile, now utterly parched, offers refuge to more than ninety thousand internally displaced people—a fraction of the nearly half million who now live along that main road, which stretches northwest from our destroyed capital city. (About 1.5 million Somalis have been displaced by the violence.)[1] The need in our area is unimaginable, but my mission as a doctor is the same. I rise long before dawn with a singular focus: to meet my patients' needs.

As I spoke with the child's mother, one of my fellow doctors tried to reason with the Hizbul Islam soldiers—jittery, aggressive young men with henna-dyed beards, wearing red-and-white checkered scarves. He told them that in our area, we are known as a safe haven, a refuge; we treat all victims of the conflict equally, no matter what side they're on. The six men refused to leave, so I assembled my committee of elders and we sat down together to talk.

One of the militants began the conversation with an insult: "You are an old woman, and we are stronger than you," he said. "You have to hand over the authority of the hospital and the management of your camp to us."

"That's impossible," I said. "This is my property. I am the doctor here, and I have the knowledge for it. On what legal basis should I hand over a hospital to you?"

"You are a woman," said another with contempt. "You are not allowed to shoulder any responsibility and authority."

We continued this way, their argument an extreme interpretation of Sharia law to which I don't subscribe. According to their version of Islam, a woman is an object that is denied basic human rights. She is something to help them by staying in the home, cooking and cleaning for him. My Islam sees women as valued members of society—as equals.

"We will protect you here," they said.

"That's not your job," I said. The elders quietly reminded me that the men could shoot me at a moment's notice, but I refused to back down. When it became clear the conversation could not continue, the members of Hizbul Islam pushed back their chairs to leave.

"So they'll shoot me!" I told the elders. "At least I will die with dignity." I waited for word that the soldiers had left the property, and I returned to the sixty patients waiting in the outpatient clinic—and the additional hundred who had been admitted to the hospital that day.

As I walked back toward the clinic, I felt a mixture of anger and resoluteness. For more than twenty years, our country has suffered at the hands of so-called leaders who are motivated solely by owning and taking. I believe that a true leader must care for and develop her society, and in my place, the only way to do so is from the inside out.

Defying Death in a War-Torn Country

Today, when I recall this episode and how my work began four decades earlier, I remember a sad saying in our culture: "If you're waiting for a life, you should also wait for a death." My mother died of gynecological complications when I was thirteen years old. There was no pain medication in those days; I sat by her bedside, pressing down on her lower abdomen as she cried out in agony. As my younger sisters and I struggled without her, I resolved to become a doctor—to help other sick mothers, so their children would not suffer the same fate. In 1964 I received a scholarship to study medicine in the Soviet Union. I returned home seven years later to work in Mogadishu's biggest hospital as one of Somalia's first female gynecologists.

On my first day of work, I treated one woman with postpartum hemorrhage so severe that she would have died in five minutes without medical treatment. She was one of the lucky ones. By the time many laboring women reached us, they were already dying; many arrived by donkey carts dragged by their despairing families. "The pain began two days ago," they'd tell me, "but we have no roads, no transportation." Most women, lacking resources or the confidence in modern medicine, stayed at home, where the risks were even greater. I opened my practice in the rural area to help these women, and within a few months, I was seeing as many as one hundred patients per day. Though exhausted, I was proud: the Somali women coming to me recognized the power they had to save their own lives and their own families.

When the government collapsed, this critical work became a race against death. The clinic and my family's home next door transformed into a triage center and temporary housing for hundreds, then thousands—mostly women and children. With limited resources, I gave away what I had, but our farm's stores ran out by early 1992, when drought and famine set in. I sold my family gold to buy enough food to sustain the vulnerable children and give the gravediggers enough strength to work. Even in this darkest time, when we were burying fifty people per day, I was still able to provide free land, security, and medical treatment. We clung to one another and we survived, defending women from the rapists and bandits that threatened them from outside the camp, and the diseases and health complications that attacked them from within.

The fighting continued, and as our numbers grew to ten thousand, it became clear that security guards were not enough—we needed to ensure peace within our own borders. Over time we developed a system of government, dividing the land into seven sections according to water distribution, and appointing a committee to oversee each section. Today, each committee reflects the makeup of the area, including at least one woman, one elderly person, and one boy or girl under the age of eighteen. The women's sense of justice is often more acute than that of the men, who are more easily able to fend for themselves, to rectify a situation using force, or to simply leave, seeking a different life.

Our Rules

Our law and order on our property depends on two simple rules: First, there are no clan-based divisions within our society. Tribalism has destroyed our once unified country and has even shaken my own family. The law of the jungle still prevails outside our camp's borders, where one group wants more, gets angry, and attacks another, more vulnerable group. Inside the camp, we ensure that no one part is protected while another is left to perish. If one family cannot abide by this rule, our security guards force them to leave.

The other rule is that men cannot beat their wives. Before the government's collapse, Somali men were working, earning, and giving orders. But when society ceased to function, and when people began killing each other because of clan distinctions, we saw many men lash out against their families—perhaps they were trying to replace the control they used to have in their lives with a need to control things at home. During four months of nonstop fighting in 1992, we were approached by at least two abused women every day. Now our guards will follow the woman back to her hut and take her husband to a "jail" we've created in a storage room. Once the situation cools down, and the committee and the family determine the best way to handle the conflict, I will approve the man for release. So far, we've had no repeat offenders.

My own experience has taught me that women in armed conflict need determination above all else. While the men are off fighting, women and children suffer the majority of non-combat casualties;[2] when the endless gunfire and heavy shelling cease, women are the ones responsible for carrying on and supporting their families. While only some of our women can be committee leaders, a growing majority of them are breadwinners. In 2009, with the help of a Swiss foundation, we opened a Women's Education Center that now provides close to two hundred women with literacy education; job training; and lifesaving health, hygiene, and nutrition information. Education for mothers has never been more crucial, as children born today in Somalia face more than a 1 in 6 risk of dying before age five.[3] In our center we show women how to provide their children with clean drinking water and nutritious food, and we explain the complications of female genital mutilation, so that they can make an informed decision about their daughters.

My own two daughters were sixteen and eleven when the fighting began. Each studied medicine in Moscow and now work by my side, treating patients, meeting with our elders, and planning for the future. We live among the women we support, hoping to motivate them to seek a better life. And it's working: while twice as many Somali boys attend school as do girls,[4] the majority of our school's 850 students are female. We believe that by giving women the tools to survive and the confidence to succeed, we can establish enough stability to truly break the cycle of violence.

My Camp Under Siege

A week after my meeting with Hizbul Islam, on May 5, 2010, I heard gunfire in the distance. Ten minutes later, guards burst into my room to tell me that two men had been shot in the camp, and that one of our guards was severely wounded. As I was rushing to dress, the phone rang: Hizbul Islam had sent 750 men to surround us, and to take my camp by force.

Knowing we were outnumbered, I agreed to hand over my security personnel and arms on the condition that Hizbul Islam act peacefully. But when our thirty elders met the militia at the front gate, they were forced onto the ground and brutally beaten. Hizbul Islam's black flag hung inside our emergency ward while their mortar shells slammed into the cement walls and aluminum roofs of our hospital compound. A group of about two hundred—including the camp's elderly watchman—were led to the militia's detention center. Their crime? Working with women who were not of their clan.

I learned all this while pacing inside my room, listening to the explosions. I called my daughters, who were both out of the country at the time; they told me that they were praying for my safety and began alerting the media. When a BBC producer called me during some of the heaviest shelling, I told him what my guards had told me: Hizbul Islam's targets were the maternity ward, the surgical ward, and the pediatric malnutrition section. One woman recovering from a C-section I'd performed earlier that day had stood up to run, her wound opening as she disappeared toward Mogadishu. Terrified mothers had detached feeding tubes and IV lines from their dehydrated children's arms and noses to flee into the woods, away from the indiscriminate shooting. We knew those children would not survive. "Pray for us," were my last words before hanging up. "Pray for us."

Staff members and friends pushed into my room, wanting to help me flee; I insisted on staying. "Mama Hawa, then we are going to stay with you," said one boy who had grown up in the camp before my eyes. I swallowed my fear, and we huddled together and waited.

A round of bullets hit my front door, shaking the entire house; a group of their men stormed into my room and began beating our young men. "You've spoken to the radio, haven't you?" shouted one, as they dragged our boys away. As six nurses surrounded me, a soldier ordered us to hand over our mobile phones and demanded that I rise to put on the *hijab*. I managed a smile, saying, "My sons, I don't even know how to wear it." (Usually I wear a traditional Somali *gutiimo*—a fabric draped over one shoulder.) The frightened nurses covered my body with a large shawl, and together we walked silently down the stairs and outside, to a waiting bus. As we drove away to an unknown place, I was not as afraid for my own life as I was for the innocent, displaced, weak people whose hopes had been shattered once again.

We arrived at one of Hizbul Islam's offices, where the nurses and I sat together on a stack of mattresses in the middle of an empty room. We refused the food and drink we were offered, concerned it might be poisoned. After several hours like this, I suddenly heard my own terrified voice from the next room: the militia was listening to a rebroadcast of my BBC interview. One solider entered the room and handed me a mobile phone. "You have many supporters," he said, ordering me to tell them that I was alive and unharmed. I talked and talked, reaching out first to my daughters and then to the hospital's staff, assuring everyone that I was unharmed and urging them to speak out. Hizbul Islam, I said, didn't have an ounce of humanity. They'd done things far worse to others than what they'd done to me.

"No Hawa, No Water"

Ten hours after we'd arrived, the soldiers ordered us back into the bus and returned us to the camp, which was dark, silent, and ravaged. Without my daily order to start the generators, there was no electricity and no power for the water pumps. (I later learned that soldiers in the camp had taunted the residents by shouting, "No Hawa, no water!") Armed men led me into my ransacked house, guns slung over their shoulders. My eyes moved across my bookshelves, my desk, the walls: they'd destroyed every one of my family pictures, shredded my documents, shattered our CDs. My mattress was ripped open, my furniture slashed in a fruitless search for hidden money; though they went after my safe with a sledgehammer, they'd failed to open it. They'd even stomped on my daughters' framed college photos, saying that their association with their male classmates proved they were infidels.

My own room destroyed, I walked into my daughter's room trailed by forty people, who covered every inch of the floor to protect me. I ordered someone to start the generators and lay on my daughter's bed, but sleep was impossible with gunfire echoing around the camp. Without our guards, we didn't even have protection from a regular thief.

Dawn broke, and I looked out the window at a sea of thousands gathered around the house. When they saw me, they began shouting, "We want to see Dr. Hawa!" Hizbul Islam's guards had no choice but to ask me for advice; I told them that to maintain law and order, they had to let them in, about four hundred at a time. Which is how, during those terrible days of house arrest, I welcomed visitors between the hours of 6 a.m. and 1 p.m. I put on a brave face, though I could not stop thinking about my guard, who had died of his wounds, and the people suffering without medical care. I gave a local reporter a short interview, reiterating that Hizbul Islam had entered my private property, and that the needy women and children they'd attacked were my guests. The area's safety, I said, depended on the intruders' removing their black flag and leaving.

The next day, a group of soldiers entered my room, holding their guns. "Dr. Hawa, you are stubborn," said one. "You're not listening to what we're telling you. Do not give any interview to any person outside."

"I'm not going to stop," I said.

"You are an old woman," he said. "You need to sit."

"You are young and active," I said. "I do something for my people and my country. What have you done for your people and your country?"

The men looked at me, surprised, and I could see fear registering in the faces of the nurses and young people surrounding me. "You are men," I said calmly, as if it were a compliment. "You need to give something to these people in need."

Lifting of the Siege

The soldiers ended the conversation by telling me that they would bring me before their Islamic court. But they could not silence the outrage from the international community. After a seven-day siege, they had to respond to the outside pressure and to remove their troops from the camp. They left just five soldiers in my house as guards. While the immediate threat of violence had finally lifted, the hospital, the school, and the sanitation departments remained closed. We remained at a standstill, the camp's wreckage a reminder of Hizbul Islam's unimaginable cruelty.

So those five soldiers returned to my room with a different demand: "We told the media that the place is open," they said. "You need to open it."

In the midst of this very unbalanced situation, two thoughts ran through my mind: I needed to resume my work as soon as possible, but if I accepted their request to open my facilities today, they'd have the power to return tomorrow, to tell me to close them. I had to show Hizbul Islam the consequences of their actions, for their own survival. For as hard as it was for me to remember in the moment, these men who attacked me are also Somali: they are the husbands and the sons of the women I treat, the brothers of the other wounded men in the hospital.

"I'm not going to open it until you write me a letter of apology," I said.

The facilities remained closed for day after excruciating day, and I remained in my room, greeting my supporters and giving orders to staff in the ways that I could. Finally, one week after my request, their second-in-command came to me with a signed letter of apology, written in both Somali and in English. He was a tall man in his early fifties, eloquent and articulate; he'd urged the others to speak reasonably when we were sitting around the negotiating table together. He stood by me as I read the letter, which apologized first to me, Dr. Hawa, and then to the NGOs helping in the camp, the camp's staff, and the Somali people around the area who lost loved ones. When I looked up, he offered me his own heartfelt apology and assured me that nothing like this would ever happen again.

I shook my head, telling him he'd made a mistake. "I am Somali," I said. "I am a mother, I am a doctor, and I deserve to be respected. I care for so many people around you—this was a tragedy you could have prevented.

"Never do this again," I continued, but my voice caught on the words. I'd remained strong when Hizbul Islam took me from my place, when they destroyed all I had worked to build, when they challenged my ability to lead. I refused to succumb to emotion while for two weeks the people in my care had suffered because of something beyond my control. I'd known Hizbul Islam were wrong, but I'd no power to stop them—the only power I had was to return to work under my own conditions. Once I realized that, in spite of it all, I had achieved what I needed, I began to cry for the first time. Tears streamed down my face as he left the letter with me, closing the door behind him.

The Lesson of the Letter

That same emotion remains with me now, and so does my conviction, which has carried our society through. Thanks to the generosity of donors, we've rebuilt the hospital bit by bit, and we're expanding our maternal and child health services and our education programs. My daughters and I are back to work, restoring the confidence of the women and children in our midst.

We need their strength to help meet our growing challenges: soon after the attack, our NGO partners left the camp for security reasons. In December 2010, Hizbul Islam was defeated by al-Shabaab—the militant group that now controls our area in southern Somalia. They've blocked international aid from reaching us, and in April 2011 they stopped our hospital's attempts to fight a cholera outbreak, holding our volunteer doctors hostage and robbing dozens of dying people of the medical interventions necessary to save their lives. (They later released our staff, claiming it was a misunderstanding.)

Now we face our biggest challenge yet. The drought in our area in the summer of 2011 has led to the worst starvation I have ever seen—worse even than what we saw in 1992. Hundreds of people stand in line at our hospital, mostly desperate mothers holding children dying of severe malnutrition. We've taken the money we've raised to open a series of emergency feeding centers that will feed, for now, about twelve thousand people per day, but it is not enough. We need the investment of the international community to guarantee that we survive this difficult time and return to strength.

As all that I've built hangs in the balance, I think of that apology letter and the lesson it holds. It *is* possible for Somalia to achieve peace. Even when I've felt the world has forgotten us, my daughters and I have remained to demonstrate the potential within our borders.

The women who are my neighbors and my partners are the true leaders. Their sons are choosing to go to school or to our nurse training programs instead of picking up AK-4/s; their husbands are farming and fishing with us instead of leaving their families to an uncertain fate. For more than twenty years, Somalia's women have faced violence and displacement, poverty and hunger, disease and death, but they are still the backbone of our society.

I hope my story will inspire other women in conflict zones around the world to feel empowered enough to look death in the eye and pursue their rights with quiet determination. This will take time, since discrimination against women is a part of the culture in our country and many others.

Building, surviving the siege, and rebuilding our camp has strengthened my belief in the ultimate emergence of women's rights, in our war-ravaged area and beyond.

CHAPTER 11

Confronting Rape as a Weapon of War in the Democratic Republic of Congo

Anneke Van Woudenberg

"I was a sex slave kept naked in a hole in the ground and raped nearly every day for six months," fifteen-year-old Elise[1] told me as we sat under a tree in Minova, eastern Democratic Republic of Congo. "The [combatants] dragged me from my home when they attacked my village. They also took my best friend. They tore off our clothes and five of them raped me on the first day. Others raped my friend. Then they took us to their camp and threw us together in a dried-up well. We tried to crawl out to escape, but we couldn't manage. I was only taken out when they wanted to rape me."

She spoke with little emotion, but her toes were tightly curled and her hands clenched the ground as if she needed stability. "We were treated like animals," she said. "They would occasionally throw us scraps of food. My friend decided to resist when they came to rape her. [The combatants] punished her by hitting her repeatedly on the head.

Anneke Van Woudenberg is the senior researcher for the Democratic Republic of Congo in Human Rights Watch's Africa Division. She has authored and coauthored many reports, including "We Will Crush You": The Restriction of Political Space in the Democratic Republic of Congo (2008) and "You Will Be Punished": Attacks on Civilians in Eastern Congo (2009). Before joining Human Rights Watch in 2002, she worked as country director in the Democratic Republic of Congo for Oxfam Great Britain during the height of the war. She has provided regular briefings on the situation in this country to the United Nations Security Council, the United States Congress, and other international bodies, and is a frequent commentator in the media.

Then they threw her back in the hole with me. She died of her injuries. For days they left me with her corpse."

She paused for a moment, looked at me as if to make sure I was following her story, and then continued. "One day [government] soldiers attacked the camp and [my captors] ran away. Then there was silence. I screamed and screamed for help but no one came. I thought I too would die in that hole. I had no food and no water for days. But a woman who had also been kept as a sex slave by the combatants, and who had been rescued by the soldiers, told them she was sure there were more victims left behind at the camp. She convinced the soldiers to come back and then they found me."

She sighed and neither one of us spoke for a moment. Her story was almost too horrifying to take in. Yet her ordeal did not end there. "As I began to recover, I found out I was pregnant," she added quietly. "I don't even know who the father is, but I know it was one of those men who raped me." Her family rejected her when she returned home pregnant. They said she had brought them shame.

Alone with nowhere to go, Elise was taken in by a local woman who ran a makeshift rape counseling center, one of many unsung heroes in Congo.[2] She helped Elise through the pregnancy and the birth. As we spoke, Elise held her five-month-old baby boy in her lap. He looked healthy and was playfully pulling on his mother's scarf. "I named him Luck," she said, when I asked the baby's name. "I know it was luck that led the kind woman to send the soldiers back to find me, so I thought it was appropriate."

Elise's story is echoed across the Congo. During my twelve years of working in this war-torn country, my colleagues at Human Rights Watch and I have recorded thousands of stories of sexual violence and other brutal attacks on civilians. Scores of notebooks line the shelves of my office, their pages filled with one horrifying story after another.

Sexual violence has reached extraordinary levels in Congo. There are no exact statistics since collecting data in a war zone is exceedingly difficult, but the UN estimates that at least two hundred thousand women and girls have been raped since 1998, though most UN officials say they believe the number is much higher. In April 2010, the UN

Special Representative on Sexual Violence in Conflict labeled Congo "the rape capital of the world."

A study published in the *American Journal of Public Health* in May 2011 found that four hundred thousand women and girls ages fifteen to forty-nine were raped in a twelve-month period in 2006 and 2007. Its authors state that their findings only "represent a conservative estimate of the true prevalence of sexual violence" since it excludes younger and older victims, and many women are reluctant to report rape. If we suppose the number of rapes were the same for the previous and subsequent years (and it is possible they are much higher since levels of conflict were more intense in other years), the total number of women raped in Congo could be well over 2 million.

Conflict has been the single most important contributor to Congo's rape epidemic. While sexual violence certainly existed before the outbreak of war, two consecutive wars—the first from 1996 to 1997 followed by a second war from 1998 to 2003—significantly altered the scale of sexual violence in Congo. Since the official end of Congo's second war, conflict has continued in eastern parts of the country. The wars and the continued fighting drew in armies from neighboring countries and spawned dozens of Congolese armed groups. Nearly all fighting factions claimed they were defending local populations or working to install democracy and the rule of law. But in reality soldiers and combatants exploited Congo's immense mineral wealth and preyed on civilians. An estimated 5 million people have died since 1998, the vast majority due to the lack of food or access to medical services, making Congo's war the deadliest in the world since World War II.

Rape as a Weapon of War

Women and girls have been particularly vulnerable. Nearly all the fighting factions have used—and many continue to use—rape as a weapon of war. The battleground: women's bodies. Rape as a weapon of war is used to terrorize, to assert control, to force compliance, or to punish individuals and entire communities for perceived support to the enemy. It is often accompanied by extreme brutality.

Take for example the case of the Democratic Forces for the Liberation of Rwanda (FDLR), a Rwandan armed group based in the hills of eastern Congo. In 2009, following a shift in alliances, the Congolese national army launched a military campaign against the group. The FDLR responded by attacking Congolese civilians telling their victims they were being "punished" for their government's policy.

In the cases investigated by Human Rights Watch, most victims of sexual violence by FDLR combatants were gang raped, in some cases by as many as seven or eight combatants at a time. The FDLR sometimes tied their victims to trees before raping them, violently inserted objects into the victims' vaginas, such as sticks or the barrels of guns, cut them with machetes or knives, or brutally beat them during the rape. Some women and girls were killed after being raped, sometimes by being shot in the vagina. Others were killed if they resisted when the FDLR tried to rape them. Some victims were so violently raped that they later bled to death; others suffered debilitating and often chronic injuries. Scores of women were abducted and forced to serve as sex slaves in FDLR camps, where they were raped repeatedly for weeks or months at a time.

Elise was one of the FDLR's victims. There were many others. In one case on March 25, in the Ziralo area of eastern Congo, seven FDLR combatants attacked a sixty-year-old woman and her daughter. When her daughter resisted being raped, the attackers shot her in the vagina, killing her. Then they gang raped the mother. Before the FDLR departed they turned to the mother and said, "You voted for your President Kabila . . . now he is sending his soldiers to chase us out. Since your president sent soldiers to kill us, we will take it out on you and rape and kill you." The attack was a clear example of rape as "punishment."

The FDLR is not the only armed group to have used such tactics. Other armed groups have been equally responsible for the horrific acts of sexual violence.

Soldiers from the national army, tasked to protect Congolese women and girls, have been no better and have also targeted civilians. While Congolese army soldiers also raped to punish women and girls who they perceived as collaborators, in many other cases the sexual violence was linked to pillage and looting. The government's failure to pay its soldiers and provide them adequate food rations while on military operation has contributed to an environment where such violence flourishes.

In one case, in the village of Chambombo in eastern Congo, six government soldiers stopped a group of four women returning from the market. They asked the women for money. The women said they didn't have any since they used it all to buy the bags of beans they were carrying on their backs. The soldiers did not believe them and decided to search the women, especially in their vaginas, where they claimed the women must be hiding their money. The women were dragged into the nearby forest and each was gang raped. One of the women was six months pregnant. She bled severely following the rape and miscarried.

The use of rape as a weapon of war seems to have permeated Congolese society and increased attacks on women by other actors. Recent studies on the prevalence of rape have found mounting numbers of police and others in positions of authority, opportunistic common criminals, bandits, and sometimes predatory civilians are also responsible for sexual violence. It is not yet clear why such cases are on the increase. In part this could be explained by the large numbers of demobilized combatants who have returned to their communities with minimal rehabilitation efforts. But this is not an explanation that covers all such cases.

Many women's rights activists believe the increase is more profound and disturbing. Congolese women, they say, have always been seen as inferior to men, but the society has now been so extremely brutalized that social norms which used to protect women and girls have been completely eroded. In a letter to the UN Security Council in June 2008, seventy-one Congolese women's groups wrote, "The nuclear family, the base of our society, no longer exists. Today in Congo, the woman has become an object. We are not protected. We have no justice. There is a crisis of authority and a culture of impunity."

The culture of impunity for sexual violence and other serious crimes is at the heart of why rape continues. Few armed group leaders or officers in the Congolese army have been held to account for rape or other crimes that they or their troops have committed. To date, only a small fraction of the total number of acts of sexual violence committed by soldiers have been prosecuted, and the vast majority of those that have been taken to court are only junior ranking soldiers. Military commanders are powerful figures in Congo, perceived as being untouchable. Far too often, abusive commanders are promoted rather than arrested, sending a clear signal that serious abuses, such as sexual attacks on women and girls, will be tolerated. Prosecutions of sexual violence will have their greatest deterrent value when high-ranking commanders are held to account.

Rape as a weapon of war is not unique to Congo, nor is it new. It was used by combatants in former Yugoslavia, during the genocide in Rwanda, and by Russian soldiers in World War II to punish German women. What is new is that such extreme levels of sexual violence are now officially recognized as a war crime and a crime against humanity. The first-ever case in which this was made explicit was at the International Criminal Tribunal for the former Yugoslavia, whose judges ruled in 2001 that rape and sexual enslavement can be crimes against humanity. The ruling challenged the widespread acceptance of rape as an intrinsic part of war.

A Landmark Resolution

In June 2008 the UN Security Council adopted the landmark Resolution 1820, condemning the use of rape and other forms of sexual violence during wartime, and announced targeted measures against responsible parties to the conflict. For the first time, sexual violence against women and girls during conflict was seen as a threat to international peace and security. In February 2010, the UN secretary general created the new position of a UN special representative for sexual violence in conflict and appointed Margot Wallström to the post. Her first trip was to the Congo, which she subsequently described as the "rape capital of the world."[3]

Congolese women have played a vital role in pushing for sexual violence to be recognized nationally and internationally. They have not remained silent. Far from it. They have organized, protested, marched in the streets, and made their voices heard, often at great risk. Their protests, together with the efforts of human rights groups, humanitarian agencies, and Congolese women lawmakers, have helped bring about important action by the Congolese government and parliament.

In 2006, Congo's parliament adopted a new law on sexual violence to reflect the tactics being used against women and to increase the penalties for such a crime. For the first time, the law specifically criminalized acts such as the insertion of an object into a woman's vagina, sexual mutilation, and sexual slavery. Penalties for rape range from five to twenty years' imprisonment but are doubled under certain conditions, such as when committed by a public official, by several persons together, with a weapon, or in situations of captivity.

Congo's president, Joseph Kabila, publicly spoke about sexual violence in his country, largely as a result of the outcry by Congolese women. In November 2007, his wife, Olive Lemba Kabila, opened a countrywide campaign supported by UN agencies to raise awareness about sexual violence and push for an end to impunity. In 2009, President Kabila declared a policy of zero tolerance for human rights abuses and sexual violence by soldiers of the national army. The new policy emphasized that commanders would be held responsible for the behavior of their troops.

The implementation of the new laws and policies has lagged behind, but there have been some notable successes, which are beginning to eat away at impunity for sexual violence. In April 2006 a military court in the province of Equateur, in western Congo, tried and found guilty seven soldiers on crimes against humanity for the collective rape of at least 119 women and girls in the village of Songo Mboyo in 2003. It was the first time in Congo's history that rape was tried as a crime against humanity as defined in the Rome Statute of the International Criminal Court, and it set an important legal precedent. In April 2010, a general was arrested and charged with rape, the first time in Congo's history that such a high-ranking officer was arrested for the crime of sexual violence. In 2011, a lieutenant-colonel and three of his officers were found guilty for allowing their troops to rape forty-nine women and girls in the Fizi area of South Kivu on New Year's Eve. They each received a sentence of twenty years, and five soldiers who had participated in the rapes were sentenced to terms between fifteen and twenty years.[4]

The Congolese government has established a task force on sexual violence and appointed a minister to be in charge of working with the UN to implement a Comprehensive Strategy on Combating Sexual Violence. The strategy makes strong, detailed recommendations in four areas: combating impunity; protection and prevention; security sector reform; and multi-sectoral assistance for health, psychosocial support, and reintegration of victims.

All of this is a start, but it has not yet contributed to a decrease of sexual violence in Congo. Why not? In large part because the strong words of Congo's government, the UN and other international actors have not been followed by consistent and strong actions. Tackling sexual violence by armed actors and the Congolese army, who still account for the largest number of the rapes, means tackling vested interests and unseating those who are powerful and abusive.

"It will upset the peace process," I often hear from government and UN officials when I urge for a senior commander to be arrested for acts of sexual violence or other atrocities. Or they say an armed group leader must first be granted a high-ranking position and integrated into the army or government before an arrest can happen. "Not now," they say. "Such action should come later." The problem is that often the arrests do not follow the promotions and all such action does is to reward abusive commanders.

Touching the powerful "untouchables" is not easy and it can come with short-term political risks. Yet this is precisely what must be done if sexual violence and other atrocities in Congo are to come to an end in the medium to long term. Peace and the rule of law will not be established in Congo through turning a blind eye to the abusers or by promoting them.

Elise survived her ordeal. She has a future because she was taken in by an extraordinary Congolese woman who runs a rape counseling center and has helped thousands of victims like her in one small town in eastern Congo. There are centers and small help groups like this all over Congo run by courageous and resilient women (and sometimes men). They are organizing amongst themselves, speaking up and saying, "No."

Perhaps one of the most extraordinary things to come out of the curse of sexual violence in Congo is the birth of a women's movement, seen in the emergence of these small but empowering groups.

For Congolese women, like their sisters around the world, have learned that without a seat at the table, without women in leadership positions in local and national government, their actions will have minimal effect and their calls for ending impunity and making the tough short-term decisions to arrest those responsible for rape will not be heard. They are now organizing and working to get women into positions of power.

The international community should recognize that one way to end rape is to support women to gain political office, be part of their country's decision making, and to have a meaningful voice. Tough decisions must ultimately be made to punish perpetrators of sexual violence and hold leaders to account, and more women at the table will ensure that outcome is achieved faster and will be far more durable. In short, one of the best ways we can help end sexual violence in Congo is to support Congo's growing women's movement.

CHAPTER 12

"I Was Sold Twice"
Harmful Traditional Practices in Afghanistan

Georgette Gagnon

"I was sold twice," Samira told me one day in May 2010. A shy seventeen-year-old girl, she was "under protection" in a juvenile correction center in Kunduz province, in the northeast of Afghanistan. When Samira was two years old, her father engaged her to a boy whom she was forced to marry when she was thirteen. Her husband regularly beat her, blaming her for the huge debt caused by the high bride price he had to pay to her family. One day, her husband took her to a district in a neighboring province, where a friend of his was waiting in a car alongside the road. Her husband handed Samira to his friend. The man, living in a village that Samira was not familiar with, took her home and raped her, saying he bought her as a wife, allowing her first husband to pay off his debt. Only fifteen at the time, Samira had been sold a second time by a male family member.

A few months later, Samira ran away from home and took a bus to Kunduz city. As she was walking alone, a police officer arrested her, accusing her of "running away" with the intention to commit *zina*

Based in Kabul, Georgette Gagnon is the director of Human Rights at the United Nations Assistance Mission in Afghanistan (UNAMA), which seeks to support the Afghan people "in laying the foundations for sustainable peace and development." She previously served as director of Human Rights Watch's Africa Division—working on rights crises in numerous countries including the Democratic Republic of Congo and Sudan—and as director of Human Rights for the Organization for Security and Cooperation in Europe's Mission to Bosnia and Herzegovina.[1]

(sexual intercourse outside of marriage, a crime under Islamic law). The police did not look for her original husband or the man who bought her. The court convicted her of *zina* and put her in jail. After one and half years in prison, Samira was released and her first husband took her back to his house. Later, Samira ran away from home again to escape abuse at the hands of her husband and his family. She fled to a juvenile correction center, asking for protection as there was no safe house or protection center for women in northeastern Afghanistan. Samira was now "sheltered" in the juvenile correction center while local NGOs were looking for a solution other than returning her to her abusive husband or back to jail.

Harmful traditional practices[2] like child marriage, forced marriage, exchange marriage (mutual arrangements between families to exchange daughters, known as *baadal*), "giving away" girls as a means to resolve disputes (known as *baad*), selling girls, subjecting them to forced isolation in the home, and "honor" killings—cause suffering, humiliation, and marginalization, if not death, for millions of women and girls in Afghanistan. Such practices are grounded in discriminatory views and beliefs about the role and position of women in society, and have been reinforced in Afghanistan by widespread poverty and chronic insecurity for more than thirty years. Many Afghans, including some religious leaders, believe that practices that subordinate women to the will of men and sharply limit their realms of activity originate in the Holy Koran. In most cases, however, these practices are inconsistent with Sharia law as well as Afghan and international law, and violate the human rights of women.

The Far Reach of Harmful Practices

My team, the Human Rights Unit of the United Nations Assistance Mission in Afghanistan (UNAMA), carried out extensive research into harmful practices in 2010 in nearly all thirty-four provinces of Afghanistan. We interviewed almost two hundred Afghans, male and female government authorities, religious leaders, women's rights and civil society activists, and representatives of various community groups. We found that these practices are pervasive, occurring in varying degrees in all communities, urban and rural, and among all ethnic groups. We also found that such practices are further entrenched by the Afghan government's inability to fully protect the rights of women and girls. Our research concludes that most harmful practices are crimes under Afghan law and inconsistent with Sharia law.

Our countrywide discussions and analysis of cases, published in a report released by UNAMA in December 2010,[3] showed that many marriages in Afghanistan are "forced" because a woman's free and informed consent was missing. Many religious leaders and Islamic scholars informed us that under Islam, marriage is a mutual contractual agreement and consent is required by both the woman and the man for a marriage to be valid.

The marriage of girls before the age of sixteen, or under limited circumstances at fifteen, is prohibited under Afghan law. Yet the marriage of very young girls is common across all regions and among all ethnic groups. No official figures are available, but our studies show that half of all Afghan girls are married before the age of fifteen. Women in Balkh province quoted a popular saying: *"If you hit a girl with your hat and she doesn't fall over, it's time to marry her."*

Despite the prevalence of this practice, all Afghan men and women we interviewed identified child marriage as one of the most harmful practices in the country. The consequences of child marriage have been widely demonstrated to be lasting and damaging to the health, education and well-being of girls. According to a UN report published in September 2010, Afghanistan has one of the highest maternal mortality ratios in the world (1,400 maternal deaths per 100,000 live births in 2008).[4] Many deaths are of women who were married under the age of sixteen.

Although high bride price—the amount of money paid by the groom to the bride's family—is not specifically illegal under national, international, or Sharia law, a number of human rights consequences emanate from this practice. In the context of extreme poverty in Afghanistan, high bride price can lead to forced and underage marriages, the selling of girls, and a high level of domestic violence. Men who resent being in debt or having to work for years to repay loans sometimes take out their frustrations on their wives. This was the case of Samira's husband. She told me that she preferred staying in the juvenile correction center to going back home where she was abused by her husband, denied education, and risked being sold again.

Nowhere to Flee

Afghan girls who run away from home often have nowhere to go because their families and communities are reluctant to accept them. Few safe houses or women's shelters are available in Afghanistan, and even when girls manage to reach a safe house, they tend to be stigmatized as 'immoral' and are not accepted by their communities.

The police and judiciary in Afghanistan often fail to enforce laws that respect women's rights, and tend to take a selective rather than impartial approach to administering justice. They often pursue cases where women are perceived to have transgressed social norms and fail to act when women report violence or in cases of child marriage dismissing them as "private matters." This situation is demonstrated by the large number of women detained in Afghan prisons for "moral crimes" such as "running away." When social and cultural circumstances do not allow women and girls to oppose harmful practices, or to escape violence, they sometimes run away from home. Running away is not a crime under Afghan law. Yet law enforcement authorities often arrest, jail, and prosecute girls for running away and charge them with intention to commit *zina* (sexual intercourse outside of marriage), as in Samira's case. Several studies report that more than half of the country's female prison population (almost 450 women in mid-2011) is detained for "moral crimes."

An incident in Afghanistan's southern Uruzgan province was highlighted in the international press after the victim was pictured on the cover of *Time* magazine in July 2010. When Aisha was twelve years old, her father reportedly gave her and her younger sister away in marriage to settle a blood debt; her uncle had allegedly killed a relative of the man Aisha was sent to marry. At the husband's house, the in-laws housed the sisters with the livestock, used them like slaves, and beat them frequently for their uncle's crime. When Aisha was eighteen she fled, but her husband caught her and sliced off both her ears and her nose as punishment, leaving her bleeding and unconscious. (In Afghanistan, a man shamed by his wife is said to have lost his nose, so it seems that Aisha was punished in kind.) Aisha managed to survive the attack. Afghan women's organizations assisted her and eventually she traveled to the United States for reconstructive surgery, and was the subject of *Time*'s cover story. Her ten-year-old sister remains in Uruzgan with the abusive in-laws.

The practice known as *baad* (giving away a girl or a woman in marriage as blood price to settle a conflict over murder or a perceived affront to honor) is one of the most severe forms of violence against women in Afghanistan. *Baad* is practiced among communities throughout the country although it is illegal under Afghan law. Despite the occurrence of *baad*, many Afghan men and women we interviewed expressed strong opposition to the practice. Women in Faryab province told us that a girl married through *baad* "is never respected by her new family as they associate her with her male relative who committed the crime and accuse her equally of being a criminal. The girl is treated like a servant as a means of revenge. Sometimes she is forced to sleep with the animals in the barn."

Among the most tragic consequences of harmful practices is self-immolation— setting oneself on fire, a growing trend in some parts of Afghanistan. The doctor in charge of Afghanistan's only special burns unit told me that the main cause of self immolation is forced marriage and other such practices: "young women married to old men, sold, swapped for sheep or even opium," he explained. "Under pressure from abusive husbands and mothers-in-law, they sometimes go to mullahs and community councils to ask for help, but even there they face humiliation and abuse. So they try to kill themselves."

UNAMA Human Rights followed the case of a twenty-year-old pregnant woman who set herself on fire in Panjsher province in July 2009. Before she died, she explained to us that she had endured daily beatings from her husband and abuse from her sisters-in-law since her marriage in 2007. On the day she burned herself, her husband had accused her of not being a virgin on their wedding day. She poured kerosene over herself and set herself alight. She died of her injuries a few days later. Following pressure from women's groups, the husband was arrested and was sentenced to two years in prison for having caused his wife's suicide.

The Role of Religious Leaders

In Herat province, in May 2010, the *ulema* (religious scholars) council issued an edict banning women from traveling abroad without a *mahram* (a husband, father, brother, or other approved escort) even for the Hajj pilgrimage. It also condemned women working for foreign organizations and said their fathers and husbands have a religious duty to prevent such acts.

Conservative, traditional members of *ulema* councils who issue proclamations of this nature often do not explain their reasoning or clarify the religious sources on which they rely. Following extensive consultations with a wide range of Islamic scholars and experts, UNAMA Human Rights found that harmful practices are not consistent with the religious teachings of Islam, although certain interpretations of religious precepts are often used to justify some of these practices. Islam has a central place in Afghanistan's constitution and under Sharia law. Forced marriage, giving girls away to settle disputes, and many such practices are prohibited. My organization recommended to the Afghan government that it take the lead in promoting a comprehensive interpretation of Sharia law that shows how rights guaranteed in national and international law are consistent with, and complement, the fundamental teachings of Islam.

Some religious and community leaders perpetuate harmful practices, although such practices are inconsistent with the fundamental tenets of Islam. Many Afghan men and women we interviewed stated that the way to end harmful practices is to provide religious leaders with training and education. They said that the moral voice of religious leaders could be used to advise local communities that harmful practices discriminate against women are inconsistent with Islamic law.

Some religious leaders have spoken out in favor of women's rights. At a conference on International Women's Day 2010 in Jalalabad city, fifteen *ulema* members from Nangarhar province unanimously vowed to raise awareness against harmful practices in their teaching at mosques. We also found recent examples of religious figures condemning exchange marriages and high bride price.

An Encouraging Law

There have been some advances in the Afghan government's response to practices that harm women and girls. In August 2009, the government enacted the Law on Elimination of Violence against Women that criminalizes many harmful practices, and could eventually end them if it were fully implemented. The law seeks to eliminate "customs, traditions, and practices that cause violence against women contrary to the religion of Islam."

It makes illegal the selling and buying of women for marriage; forced marriage; marriage before the legal age; forced isolation; forcing a woman to commit self-immolation; and denying the right to education, work, and access to health services, among other harmful practices. The law prescribes preventive measures for seven government ministries to implement and establishes a national high commission for the prevention of violence against women.

The law's section that criminalizes a person's "prohibition" of an Afghan woman or girl's right to education is particularly important in view of the severe problems documented by two Human Rights Watch reports. The 2009 report *"We Have the Promises of the World": Women's Rights in Afghanistan*[5] described a range of factors impeding girls' access to secondary education, from security threats and cultural or traditional barriers such as early marriage, to the higher numbers of boys' schools and the shortage of qualified female teachers, especially in rural areas. The 2010 follow-up report *The "Ten-Dollar Talib" and Women's Rights: Afghan Women and the Risks of Reintegration and Reconciliation*[6] described the Taliban's attacks against girls' schools in some areas and quotes numerous threat-filled "night letters" sent to both students and teachers.

The Law on Elimination of Violence against Women is a major step forward in the legal protection of women's human rights. Yet it suffers from flaws, such as the failure to criminalize "honor" crimes, the lack of a clear definition of rape to distinguish it from consensual *zina*, and the requirement that a victim initiate or maintain judicial action. Despite these concerns, UNAMA together with most Afghan women's rights defenders believe that raising awareness about the current law and working for its full implementation is urgently needed to protect women and girls, while recognizing that revisions may be necessary to fully guarantee women's rights.

Our research for the United Nations found that law enforcement authorities often are unwilling or unable to apply laws that protect women's rights, in particular the Elimination of Violence against Women law, and that such inaction is one of the main factors that permit harmful practices. Although the provincial police and the judiciary are becoming aware of the law, they require much more guidance and support from Afghan national authorities on how to apply it. In many rural and remote provinces, communities and government officials do not even know about the law's existence and it remains unimplemented.

Implementation of the Law on Elimination of Violence against Women requires a huge investment in building the capacities of law enforcement personnel and in providing services to victims. Certainly convictions under the law could result in deterring perpetrators of violence against women, and more needs to be done to inform the Afghan public about the law's existence and the practices it criminalizes. Finally, there needs to be awareness raising about the negative social consequences of harmful practices across Afghan society. Religious leaders, communities, civil society, and international donors must support Afghan civil society in monitoring, education, and advocacy.

The bottom line is that little meaningful and sustainable progress for women's rights can be achieved in Afghanistan so long as women and girls are subject to practices that harm, degrade, humiliate, and deny them their basic human rights.

Ensuring rights for Afghan women, such as access to adequate health care, equal opportunities in education and employment, and participation in public life will require not only legal and constitutional safeguards on paper, but speedy, consistent, and committed enforcement. The Afghan government at all levels from the president down must take all possible measures to eliminate harmful practices, fully implement the Elimination of Violence Against Women law, and ensure women's rights are included in the current peace and reconciliation efforts.

CHAPTER 13

Letters in the Night
Closing Space for Women and Girls in Afghanistan

Rachel Reid

When Hossai, a twenty-two-year-old Afghan aid worker in the southern city of Kandahar, received threatening phone calls from a man who said he was with the Taliban, she didn't believe it. Or she chose to carry on regardless. The man had told her to stop working with foreigners. But Hossai didn't want to give up a good job with an American development company, Development Alternatives, Inc. (DAI). Within weeks Hossai was dead. On April 13, 2010, a gunman lay in wait for her. When she left the office, he shot her multiple times. She died the next day.

Days after Hossai's killing, another young woman working in Kandahar, Nadia N.[1] received a letter that appeared to be from Taliban members or sympathizers, which threatened her with death:

> We would warn you today on behalf of the Servants of Islam to stop working with infidels. We always know when you are working. If you continue, you will be considered an enemy of

Rachel Reid, the senior regional advisor on Afghanistan and Pakistan policy at the Open Society Foundations, previously worked as the Kabul-based Afghanistan analyst for Human Rights Watch (2008-2011), following a thirteen-year career at the BBC. She gathered the research for this chapter while working on the Human Rights Watch report, The "Ten-Dollar Talib" and Women's Rights, *published in July 2010.*

Islam and will be killed. In the same way that yesterday we have killed Hossai, whose name was on our list, your name and other women's names are also our list.

Nadia N. did believe the letter, and quit her job. Such "night letters," usually posted or pinned to doors at night, are a common form of Taliban intimidation. Often a letter is enough to scare women or men into compliance. Nadia N. reported the threat to the government, but expected nothing: "What can they do?"

The UN estimates that 462 Afghan civilians were assassinated in 2010, an increase of more than 100 percent over 2009. More than half of those killed were in the southern region where Nadia N. and her family lived. While the number of women among those killed represent only a fraction of the total number of assassinations, it is of high symbolic importance in a country where women represented only 36 percent of the labor force in 2010 as reported by the United States Agency for International Development (USAID)[2] and rarely occupy high-ranking positions. The threats and killings send a chilling message to those women who want to take an active role in their society.

Nadia N. had worked for an international NGO that supports children in need. The threatening letter she received referred to her working with "infidels," meaning nonbelievers, sometimes a pejorative term used for non-Muslim foreigners. But Nadia N.'s explanation of why she was targeted was simpler: "because I was working outside [the home]," an act some Taliban condemn for women. In talking to women about the threats and pressures in areas where the Taliban are strong, "working outside the home" is mentioned with depressing regularity. It is also a pressure felt in some conservative communities without a Taliban presence, but the Taliban are more likely to enforce their threats with brutal means. Nadia N. took the threat seriously, and gave up her job and stayed inside her home until the family could move away to another region relatively free from Taliban control. Nobody counts how many women receive these threats, and make this choice to retreat.

When the Taliban were in government in Afghanistan, between 1996 and 2001, their notorious restrictions were often about social control, placing great importance on gender segregation, and dress codes.

This included a series of edicts that restricted women's movement, requiring them to stay home or travel with a male chaperone (*mahram*). Such edicts resulted in significant restrictions on Afghan women's ability to work, at a time when they had started to make inroads into the work place. And perhaps most harmfully, Taliban rule led to a significant reduction in Afghan girls' access to education, particularly once they reached puberty. Enforcement was highly erratic and sometimes violent. The enforcers were the infamous "religious police," the Ministry for the Promotion of Virtue and the Prevention of Vice (*al-Amr bi al Ma'ruf wa al-Nahi 'an al-Munkar*).

"We Will Kill You in Such a Harsh Way . . ."

Today the Taliban target fewer women than men, not least because there are so few Afghan women active in public life in areas where these night letters and assassinations take place. Those who are singled out are condemned for their association with the government or foreigners, but also quite clearly for their presence, as women, in public life. This letter to Fatima K., received in February 2010 in a southern province, makes this chillingly clear:

> We Taliban warn you to stop working otherwise we will take your life away. We will kill you in such a harsh way that no woman has so far been killed in that manner. This will be a good lesson for those women like you who are working. The money you receive is *haram* [prohibited under Islam] and coming from the infidels. The choice is now with you.

Fatima K., like many recipients of such letters, was torn: at once terrified and desperate not to lose her income. "I am feeling very afraid now," she said. "But what to do? I can't leave my job because I need to work and do something for my family." She took extended leave and has not returned to her job.

When Rahela Z. received the following letter in 2009, she said she was "very afraid," and immediately resigned from her job, working as a civil servant in a southern province in Afghanistan:

[Name removed] You are working with . . . the government and organizations. You are warned by the Taliban to stop working with them otherwise the Taliban's court shall make a decision about you, which would have severe consequences for you and your family. You will lose your life.

Mahjabin Subhanzada ran an NGO, Mehboba Herawi, which works with widows, disabled women, and other women in economic need, to help them become economically self-sufficient. The NGO worked in many provinces, particularly in the conflict-hit south. Subhanzada was based in Helmand, one of the most dangerous provinces in the country. As one of the few women active in public life in the province, she was well known.

Subhanzada told a reporter in March 2010 that she had been receiving threats: "I have been warned to stop working, to stop encouraging other women to work."[3] She said she would reduce her movement to remote areas, spending more time in the provincial capital, Lashkar Gah. But on October 31, 2010, she and a colleague, Nazanin, were traveling just outside Lashkar Gah, when they were stopped by the Taliban. Both women were forced out of the car and shot by the side of the road.

Subhanzada was not the first high-profile woman to have been assassinated. In recent years a number of highly respected women have been killed, including provincial councilor and peace activist Sitara Achakzai, senior police commander Malalai Kakar, journalist and human rights defender Zakia Zaki, and women's affairs director Safia Amajan. None of their killers have been brought to justice. This is in part a wider failure to address rampant impunity in Afghanistan, which is connected to the decision by both the Afghan government and its international backers to prioritize building up Afghanistan's military capabilities at the expense of justice and rule of law. But many women activists feel that the government does not take seriously threats and killings of women in public life.

Threats and attacks against women have a domino effect, spreading fear to women who have not been directly targeted by night letters and other warnings. Freshta S. (a pseudonym) was teaching in a province in southeastern Afghanistan. She left her job because of the widespread threats against women. "The security situation deteriorated in the last three years," she explained in January 2010. "In my village the Taliban distributed 'night letters' and warned that women cannot go out and work. If they go to work then they will be killed. This scared me and my family, and since then I have spent all my days at home."

Afghan women who work for foreign organizations risk incurring the wrath of Taliban, particularly if they defy the Taliban's insistence on face-covering *burqas*. In March 2010, Selay M., who was working for an international NGO, received this night letter:

> [Name removed] You are working with a foreign organization, which is the enemy of religion and Islam. You receive a salary from them. You should be fearful of God. Every day, you shake hands with strangers without covering your face. We, herewith, inform you to stop doing this otherwise we will take such action against you that a Muslim has not yet done to another Muslim.

Sometimes threats are directed at wider female behavior in a community that is deemed to be un-Islamic. In late 2009 a large number of homes were sent the following threat letter in an attempt to stop women and girls communicating with popular music radio stations:

> To all those girls who live in Kohistan 1 district of Kapisa province and to those girls in particular who make telephone call to radio stations and introduce themselves and request songs. Hereafter, they are seriously warned that they should not call any local or international radios. If anyone does it again, particularly girls, they will face serious consequences: they will either be beheaded or acid will be thrown in their faces.
>
> From: The Islamic Brotherhood Group.

Attacks on Girls Seeking Education

The Taliban government severely restricted girls' access to education in the 1990s. Today in Afghanistan, female students and teachers are threatened and attacked, with disproportionately more girls' schools subject to attack. In February 2010, a girls' school in a northern province received the following night letter:

> You were already informed by us to close the school and not mislead the pure and innocent girls under this non-Muslim government; however you did not pay attention and you are continuing to keep the school open. We want to remind you that we are going to implement what we are saying, and we do not want to discuss this. This is the last warning to close the school immediately and put a lock on its door. We should not see you in the province too. If you remain in the province, remember that you along with your family will be eliminated. Just wait for your death. It will be a good thing to accept our order. It depends on you.

There is no uniform pattern of abuse with regards to attacks on girls' access to education. Some insurgent commanders impose strict conditions, such as *mahrams* for female teachers, and the most conservative Islamic dress burqas when any males are present). Other Taliban commanders have issued blanket bans on girls attending school past puberty. Some commanders appear to have a violent opposition to girls' education in general.

Asma A., who was a teacher at a girls' school in a southern province, was sent this night letter with a Taliban insignia in October 2009:

> You are teaching at the [name removed] School, which is a girls' school. You should be afraid of God. We warn you to leave your job as a teacher as soon as possible otherwise we will cut the heads off your children and shall set fire to your daughter. We can make you regret your actions.

Mullah Abdullah, who described himself as a "spiritual leader of the Taliban" in the southeastern province of Ghazni, gave one explanation of why girls' schools were subject to attack: "We are opposed to un-Islamic educations [sic] for women. We close those schools that teach adultery, nudity and un-Islamic behavior."

Afghan women who are professionally involved in the field of education are also at risk, as illustrated by the case of Madiha M., formerly a teacher in an eastern province. In early 2010, she was forced by both Taliban night letters and community pressure to give up her job: "I received a lot of threats," she told Human Rights Watch in February 2010. "I got night letters to my house. And the community where I was living, they also did not want me to work. They also threatened us saying I should not go out and should not teach. So finally I left my job."

Risks of Deal Making with the Taliban

At this writing in 2011, the Afghan government with growing support from its international partners is looking for ways to reach a peace deal with the Taliban. While women in Afghanistan are paying a heavy price in the current conflict, which shows no sign of a military resolution, many who fear the Taliban's violent misogyny view this prospect with trepidation. There are fears that a government dominated by warlords and corruption may be prepared to trade away too much, including women's rights to participate in political life, reserved seats in parliament, and access to education, particularly for girls who have passed puberty.

Those who remain close to the Taliban offer few assurances. Mullah Abdul Salam Zaeef was one of the founding members of the Taliban, and their ambassador to Pakistan while they were in government. After they fell, he spent some time detained by the United States at Guantanamo. He is now resident in Kabul, and retains some contact with Taliban leaders. He denies that women's freedoms would be eroded, but is clearly opposed to women's presence in work places (or parliament) without strict gender segregation, describing mixed work places as "corrupting."

"It is against Islam," Zaeef told me during an interview in May 2010.

"If you put a young adult man and woman in one room for some time, of course there will be some interactions, which is against Islam. This is like a virus here and it will spread."

Many individuals (including a few former Taliban) in the current Afghan government and parliament, in mid-2011, share much of the Taliban's conservative interpretation of Islam. Any deal reached with the Taliban that does not expressly protect basic rights and freedoms for women could give fundamentalist leaders more influence in government to roll back gains of the last decade.

There is a revisionist tendency among some of those promoting deals with the Taliban to describe them as primarily motivated by political or economic grievances. While there are many grievances that drive the insurgency, including outrage at civilian casualties and night raids, and the abuses and corruption of the Karzai government, the night letters serve as a reminder that whatever drives communities into the hands of the Taliban, the Taliban leadership itself, even at the provincial level, is clearly ideological. Writers of night letters intend to permanently close space for Afghan women and girls. This should not be forgotten as the government and its international backers move toward a peace deal.

The effort to whitewash Taliban crimes against women extends into the heart of government. In July 2010, I met with cabinet minister Farook Wardak, heavily involved in the government's peace initiative at the time. When I shared some of the night letters with him, he dismissed the possibility that they could be the work of Afghan Taliban, claiming to recognize the "handwriting of a Pakistani." He went on to tell me that Mullah Omar did not exist. Wardak is not the first Afghan politician to deny Afghan Taliban crimes because it is more convenient than confronting the complexity of a homegrown movement with some hardline conservatives at its core. These denials bode ill for the prospects of a rights-respecting peace process.

In Badghis province in February 2011, the shadow Taliban government "reintegrated" one of its judges, Mawlawi Isfandyar. Just six months earlier, a pregnant woman accused of adultery was lashed two hundred times and killed by gunshot, on the orders of Isfandyar. The man she was said to have had an affair with escaped. An online video of Sanubar's death caused revulsion around the country and the globe. Local people told human rights investigators that while Isfandyar was a judge in the Taliban government, he was known for ordering similar punishments of men and women. Despite this, the local intelligence services reportedly enticed him back to the government with the promise of getting his old job back.

The Afghan government has promised to introduce a process where communities can vet those who are being reintegrated. But the focus tends to be on excluding criminal elements, not just notorious human rights abusers. Even if a system to exclude abusive commanders or mullahs like Isfandyar is established, those who have been victim of the crimes of former Taliban commanders, particularly female victims, will likely be very fearful of retribution. A woman who has received a night letter threatening that her children's heads will be cut off is unlikely to want to stand up and point the finger at the man she suspects is the author.

There are vocal and courageous Afghan women activists articulating women's demands in the peace and reintegration process. These women courageously speak out against efforts to welcome abusive commanders back into positions of authority. The US and other international supporters have also stressed their commitment to a rights respecting process. But these voices are not sufficient. The Afghan government also needs to make clear that whatever the shape of a peace process in Afghanistan, it will not be one that compromises women's access to education, justice, and participation in political life.

President Karzai has referred to the Taliban as his "brothers." But he has not yet spared a word for the anxious sisters, mothers, and daughters who do not want to be forced behind closed doors in the name of peace.

PART 4

THE ECONOMIES OF RIGHTS
EDUCATION, WORK, AND PROPERTY

CHAPTER 14

Unequal in Africa
How Property Rights Can Empower Women

Janet Walsh

E mily O. was a farmer in western Kenya, able to feed her four children, keep them in school, and eke out a comfortable existence. This ended abruptly when her husband died. Like millions of other women in sub-Saharan Africa, Emily lost literally everything when she became a widow. Her in-laws and community felt that, as a woman, she had no right to own or inherit property.

Emily's in-laws invaded her simple home within days of her husband's death, stripped it bare, and even took her clothing. Even worse, they took her farm equipment and livestock. Emily hoped to at least stay in her home. But her in-laws insisted that to do so, she go through the clan's customary "cleansing" ritual—having sex with a social outcast—to rid her of her dead husband's spirit. They paid a herdsman the equivalent of US$6 to have sex with Emily, against her will and without a condom. She recalled, "I tried to refuse, but my in-laws said I must be cleansed or they'd beat me and chase me out of my home. They said they had bought me [with the dowry], and therefore I had no voice in that home." The in-laws eventually forced Emily out of her home anyway. She begged an elder and the village chief for help, but

Janet Walsh, deputy director of Human Rights Watch's Women's Rights Division, is the author of Double Standards, *a detailed report on the violations of Kenyan women's property rights published in 2003. In this chapter she describes the grave risks faced by African women whose rights to own land are curtailed by unjust laws, longstanding customs, and even their own families.*

they asked for bribes that she could not pay. Emily and her children were homeless until someone offered her a small, leaky shack. Her children dropped out of school. When Human Rights Watch interviewed Emily, her young sons were working as cowherds, and her daughters were doing domestic work in Nairobi, Kenya's bustling capital. Emily told us she had no hope of retrieving her land and property.

Emily's story illustrates a sad truth: African women's rights to own, inherit, manage, and dispose of property are under constant threat from customs, laws, and individuals¾including government officials¾who believe that women cannot be trusted with or do not deserve property. On much of the African continent, women constitute 70-90 percent of the agricultural labor force, yet according to the International Development Research Center, own only about 1 percent of land. The International Labor Organization estimates that African women receive just 7 percent of agricultural extension services and less than 10 percent of credit offered to small-scale farmers, in part because they seldom hold formal land titles.

Fragile Property Rights

Women's unequal property rights span geographic regions, ethnic groups, religions, and social classes. In sub-Saharan Africa, a woman's access to property usually hinges on her relationship with a man, be it her father, husband, brother, uncle, or cousin. When the relationship ends, the woman stands a good chance of losing her home, land, livestock, household goods, money, vehicles, and other property.

Although all women are vulnerable to these abuses, divorced women and widows suffer the most extreme violations. Widows are often evicted from their homes as in-laws rob them of their possessions and invade their homes and lands. These unlawful appropriations happen even more readily when the husband died of AIDS and families place the blame on the widow. In some places, widows like Emily are forced to undergo customary sexual practices such as "wife inheritance" or ritual "cleansing" in order to keep their property. "Wife inheritance" occurs when a male relative of the dead husband takes over the widow as a wife, often in a polygamous family, while "cleansing" usually involves sex with a social outcast. In both cases, sex is often coerced and seldom practiced safely. Divorced and separated women are often left with only the clothes on their backs while their husbands keep the home and other property.

Denying women equal property rights has devastating effects—including poverty, disease, violence, food insecurity, and homelessness—that harm women, their children, and Africa's overall development. Women who were left disinherited or propertyless after divorce in Kenya, Zambia, Uganda, Zimbabwe, and elsewhere in Africa have told Human Rights Watch that after losing their property, they ended up begging for water, scavenging in garbage dumps for food, seeing their children drop out of school, living in shacks in dangerous slums, and sleeping on cardboard boxes. They described being raped and beaten by in-laws who grabbed their properties, receiving death threats if they dared assert their property rights, and being unable to afford health care and housing after losing all their assets.

Violations of women's property rights are not only discriminatory; they may prove fatal in the context of HIV/AIDS. In sub-Saharan Africa, more women than men live with HIV, and women ages fifteen to twenty-four years are as much as eight times more likely to be HIV positive than men. Widows subjected to the customary practices of wife inheritance or ritual cleansing run a clear risk of contracting and spreading HIV. In one of Kenya's provinces where these practices are most common, the HIV prevalence is almost 14 percent of the population. A man who acts as a "cleanser" there told Human Rights Watch that he had "cleansed" about seventy-five women over several years. He said, "I don't use condoms with the women. It must be body to body. I must put sperm in her. . . . If no sperm comes out, she is not inherited. . . . I don't do anything to stop pregnancy. . . . I've heard about how you get AIDS. I'm getting scared. . . . There are inheritors who are infected with HIV. They don't use condoms."

Some officials claim that all women who are inherited or "cleansed" have consented to these practices, but this is clearly not the case. Jiwa S., a fifty-five-year-old widow from Kenya, told Human Rights Watch that her brother-in-law brought a cleanser to her home to have sex with her. She objected, saying, "I don't know this man's HIV status, and if I die my children will suffer." Her brother-in-law and four other men pushed the cleanser into Jiwa's hut and he raped her. The brother-in-law paid the cleanser with a cow, chickens, and clothing. Jiwa was forced out of her home and into a shoddy hut, and her brother-in-law took over her land and furniture. She reported this to the village elder, who did nothing. Jiwa developed a persistent cough and lost much weight. She feared she had contracted HIV from the cleanser.

HIV treatment is also jeopardized by women's property rights abuses. Many women in Zambia and Uganda told Human Rights Watch of struggling to stay on HIV medication because, having lost everything, they could not afford transport to clinics or the food they needed for treatment. In Zambia, Hilda M. told us, "All the property was taken by [my late husband's] relatives. They took a [minibus], TV, radio, DVD player, dining room set, and sitting room chairs. . . . My problem is that I do not have enough food now. These drugs are very strong. I need to have food to take them. If I had [my] minibus, I would use it for business and I would get money for food and transport. I have to catch a bus to the hospital to get my medication every month. My sister has to give me money for this, and when she can't, I have to walk. It is too far when I am feeling weak. I have missed some appointments when I do not have money for transport. Once I did not collect my medication for three days."

Divorced and separated African women fare no better. Take Mary A., a fifty-four-year-old Kenyan woman with eight children. When she and her violent husband separated, he kept all of the property, including vehicles, the land she cultivated, household goods, furniture, and bicycles. She received nothing. Her husband forced her out of their home, and she went to her parents. Mary stayed in her mother's hut, but was forced out when her mother died. She moved to a slum and learned that she was HIV positive, yet could no longer afford health care. Other women told us that their fear of losing their housing and the property they needed to survive and provide for their children kept them in violent marriages. The HIV risk is especially high for women in situations of domestic violence, which often involve coercive sex, diminish women's ability to negotiate safer sex and condom use, and impede women from seeking health information and treatment.

Underlying Factors

A complex mix of legal and social factors underlies women's property rights violations. First is the role of custom. Customary laws in many countries—largely unwritten but influential local norms that coexist with formal laws—often dictate that men inherit and have greater control over land and other property, and women should be "protected" but have inferior property rights. These customs reflect a tendency toward gender specialization in roles and responsibilities seen in all cultures. But customs should transform over time in response to societal shifts. The notion that giving women lesser property rights goes hand in hand with family and clan commitments to "protect" them is out of date in many places. Africa is rapidly urbanizing, people are migrating, and for many, life is no longer organized around communal clan structures. When a tradition is discriminatory and causes severe harms to individuals, families, and society, it should evolve or be superseded by legal rights that can provide better protection.

Formal laws and government institutions are also to blame for women's unequal property rights. Some countries' constitutions explicitly permit discrimination in personal and customary laws, which govern inheritance and divorce. Even in countries where succession laws establish equal rights to inheritance rights and family property upon divorce, enforcement is often weak. Local authorities are often unresponsive in the face of women's property rights abuses. When women try to report property violations to authorities, they are often asked for bribes, ignored, or told to go back to abusive husbands. Even judges sometimes resist enforcing women's rights to property. In Kenya, for example, women described attempting to pursue property claims in court, only to confront corruption, delays, and abusive treatment by judicial officials.

Most African countries have ratified international and regional human rights treaties requiring them to eliminate all forms of discrimination against women—including discrimination stemming from custom—and ensure that women have effective remedies if their rights are violated. Some governments have made strides in the right direction, such as enacting constitutional or statutory reforms recognizing women's equal property rights, reforming the processes and women's representation on bodies that oversee land transfers, and holding trainings on women's equal property rights for local officials and traditional authorities. In Kenya, for example, the constitution adopted in 2010 provides for the elimination of gender discrimination in law, customs, and practices related to land and property, and a landmark 2011 court ruling finding that married women have the right to inherit their parents' property. But the efforts to date across the region are utterly insufficient considering the scale of the problem. Nongovernmental and grassroots women's organizations are working tenaciously to provide services and information to women denied property rights in many countries. Their work is largely funded by international donors, not by the countries in which they work.

The United Nations (UN) and other international agencies working on poverty, development, agriculture, housing, food, health, and human rights have all condemned laws and practices that deny women equal property rights and promote reforms in this area. A joint 2009 publication by the World Bank, the Food and Agriculture Organization, and the International Fund for Agricultural Development presents findings from many studies on gender, land, and agriculture. It notes, for example, that if women and men in Zambia had the same degree of capital investment in agricultural inputs including land, agricultural output would increase by up to 15 percent.

The publication also explains that strengthening women's land rights would promote not just agricultural productivity, but also household human capital investments, such as nutrition and child schooling. Moreover, the UN report emphasizes that increasing women's land and property ownership contributes to the autonomy and social capital women need to participate effectively in community decision making and influencing public policy. On the down side, the World Bank notes that gender inequalities result in less food being grown, less income being earned through agricultural production, and higher levels of poverty and food insecurity.

Researchers have also found striking benefits from women's property ownership in deterring domestic violence and lessening the impacts of HIV/AIDS. The International Center for Research on

Women (ICRW) conducted a study in Kerala, India, to determine how women's property ownership related to the risk of domestic violence. Forty-nine percent of the women without property in the study reported that they had experienced domestic violence, compared to just 7 percent of women who owned land and a house. Another ICRW study on Uganda and South Africa showed that women's property ownership mitigated the impact of AIDS and enhanced women's ability to leave a violent situation.

Faced in many cases with extreme poverty and catastrophic HIV/AIDS rates, African governments can no longer afford to ignore women's property rights violations. They cannot hide behind the excuse that these abuses are private family matters, or customs they are powerless to change.

Human rights abuses committed by families or under the guise of custom are human rights abuses all the same, and governments have an obligation to prevent them and provide a remedy when they occur. Governments can take obvious steps, such as ensuring that constitutions guarantee women's full equality and that inheritance and divorce statutes treat men and women equally. They can hold accountable judges, police, land authorities, and other public officials if they fail to respect and enforce women's equal property rights. They can actively inform the public that women are entitled to property, and interfering with this right can result in jail or fines. And, most important of all, the government can play an active role in changing attitudes and promoting the transformation of customs that deny women their equal property rights. For this, they must support efforts of grassroots women and local groups that have legitimacy in their communities and the staying power needed to bring about change.

As for women, just level the playing field, and you can be sure they can take care of themselves. As Ruth O., a divorced Kenyan woman whose husband kept their eight modern houses while she wound up in a slum shack with no running water, put it, "What I want most is not to be helped but to be able to do something to help myself."

The African Union declared this the African Women's Decade, and African countries have pledged under the Millennium Development Goals to promote gender equality and empower women. With the extreme inequality in women's property rights, they have a long way to go before women like Ruth are in a position to help themselves. Eliminating women's property rights violations is not only a human rights obligation and a necessary measure for combating poverty; for many women, it is a matter of life and death.

CHAPTER 15

Cleaning House
The Growing Movement for Domestic Workers' Rights

Nisha Varia

I am the invisible woman
A ghost in your house
I go around the rooms without you noticing
Bringing order to your disorder
Cleanliness to your dirtiness
Care to your neglect
Love to your indifference
Company to what you abandon
Pity to your cruelty
Health to your sickness
I'm perfect and miraculous
Because you only miss me when I'm not here
You are only interested in what I say when I do not respond
In what I have done when I make a mistake

—from "Ode to the Invisible Woman"[1]

Nisha Varia is a senior researcher for Human Rights Watch's Women's Rights Division. She has conducted numerous research investigations on abuses against women migrant domestic workers in Asia and the Middle East and engaged in sustained campaigns for legal, policy, and programmatic reforms. She is the author of several reports including Slow Reform: Protection of Migrant Domestic Workers in Asia and the Middle East *(2010),* "As If I Am Not Human": Abuses Against Asian Domestic Workers in Saudi Arabia *(2008), and* Help Wanted: Abuses Against Female Migrant Domestic Workers in Indonesia and Malaysia *(2004). She previously volunteered and served as a board member for Andolan, a New York City–based community group organizing South Asian domestic workers.*

I magine not having the money to pay your children's school fees, rainproof your home, or ensure a loved one can get lifesaving medical treatment. Then imagine you live in a country wracked by unemployment with no jobs in sight. A community member offers you a job abroad with what seems like a dazzling foreign salary. You must leave your family behind for two years, and pay initial fees that leave you with large debts, but you hope the investment will pay off and transform your family's life.

Millions of women from South and Southeast Asia migrate for domestic work for these reasons. I have spent the past decade documenting the array of abuses that often confront them when migrating to destinations in Asia and the Middle East. They are a segment of the estimated 50-100 million people—mostly women and girls—who work as nannies, housekeepers, and caregivers worldwide, some in their own countries and some by migrating abroad.

I first got involved in activism around migrant domestic workers' rights as a volunteer for Andolan, a small community-based group organizing primarily Bangladeshi domestic workers in Queens, New York City. We held our meetings sitting on the living-room floor of the lead organizer, a former domestic worker named Nahar Alam. In response to cases of immigrant women being paid as little as $200 per month for working around the clock or having their passports taken, we organized street protests against diplomats who abused their domestic workers with impunity, linked survivors of abuse with pro bono legal assistance, and conducted outreach to raise awareness about migrant workers' rights.

As a researcher for Human Rights Watch, I learned that these problems were much more widespread than I could have ever dreamed. While employing a full-time, live-in domestic worker is a luxury for most households in the United States, it is fairly common in parts of Asia and the Middle East.

Households across Malaysia, Singapore, Hong Kong, and the Middle East including Saudi Arabia, Kuwait, and Lebanon depend heavily on live-in domestic workers to clean their homes or care for children, the sick, or the elderly. Kuwait's 1.3 million citizens and some foreign residents employ more than 660,000 domestic workers. Outside of the

Gulf, the ratios are typically not as high but still often amount to one migrant domestic worker for every three or four households.

While their earnings are often only a fraction of the prevailing minimum wage in any given country, migrant domestic workers help to prop up entire economies. The sheer scale of this massive movement of women and girls across borders results in billions of dollars of remittances sent to their home countries. Most of the migrant domestic workers employed in the Middle East and Asia come from Indonesia, Sri Lanka, India, Ethiopia, and the Philippines, and increasingly from Bangladesh, Cambodia, and Nepal.

For many of us, an incredibly precious and important part of our lives is the well-being of our children, the comfort of our elderly parents, and a safe, clean home where we can count on tasty meals. Yet society gives little recognition to the daily labors required to nurture a family and a home. Despite the invaluable services migrant domestic workers provide to both the families and countries where they work and those they have left behind, they have been left highly exposed to abuse.

While there are some who are "lucky" and successfully earn money abroad, migration for domestic work remains a dangerous gamble. Local recruiters often deceive prospective migrants about their working conditions abroad, and only after they have started working do women—and in some cases, girls—learn they will be working around the clock for salaries much lower than promised. Saddled with debts and subject to strict immigration laws that punish migrant domestic workers who "run away" from their employers, many get trapped in forced labor or jobs where they encounter chronic exploitation and abuse.

For example, when I visited Saudi Arabia in 2006, Sandra C., a Filipina domestic worker, told me about her experience working there:

> A recruiter came to my village and said I [would have to give up] six months pay for recruitment fees. In the Philippines I signed a contract for two years for a monthly salary of 750 riyals. . . . My problem when I came here is that my employers didn't give me 750 riyal salary, they gave only 600. After six

months, they still didn't give my salary. I only got five months' salary out of three years.

There were ten rooms in that house. I would get up at 6 a.m. in the morning. I would work until 7 p.m., and get one hour of rest. Then I would work until 2 a.m. We did not have any rest, not even a minute. There was no day off. My employer said, "If you want a day off, go to the Philippines." I could not leave the house. I [only] left the house three times in one year.

I could call my family in the Philippines three times a year. They would deduct the cost from my salary. . . . It has been three years and I want to go home. My husband died because of kidney problems. There was no communication and I didn't know. My employers didn't want to let me go. My employer told me, "You don't deserve to go to the Philippines because you have not finished your contract." I said my contract is two years, they said it was three years. They kept my documents.

My employers were always shouting at me, for little things. My employers were always angry. I would say, "Sorry, madam." She would say, "What, sorry? Do your work. We will take you to the police." They said they would put me in jail when I asked for my ticket. "You are like my slippers, you are a dog!" She would say all bad things. "You are worth nothing, you are not educated!" Why did she treat me like this?[2]

The large number of women and girls affected, and the intransigence and failure to protect by governments, has been daunting. Embassies of labor-sending countries in places such as Malaysia, Saudi Arabia, and Lebanon have been so flooded with complaints of abuse that they shelter hundreds of domestic workers on any given day.

Indispensable but Invisible

Despite the key economic role they play both at home and abroad, migrant domestic workers largely remain invisible to the public eye, hidden and isolated in private homes. The devaluation of work traditionally performed by women in the home, such as cleaning, cooking, and caring for children, has led to the widespread discounting of these workers as "helpers" or second-class "members of the family." Many labor laws codify these attitudes by excluding domestic workers from the basic protections guaranteed to other categories of workers, such as a weekly day off or limits to hours of work.

In Asia and the Middle East, immigration policies link migrant domestic workers' visas to their employers, contributing to a profoundly unequal power relationship that enables abuse. Employers can have domestic workers repatriated at will, withhold consent from a worker who wishes to transfer to another employer, and in some cases impede their ability to leave the country. Employers often pay thousands of dollars to hire a migrant domestic worker, and may use this to justify taking her passport, restricting her communication, and prohibiting her from leaving the home unaccompanied to prevent her from running away or "becoming pregnant."

In the worst cases, the level of control that employers exercise over domestic workers leads to forced labor and slavery-like conditions. An Indonesian domestic worker I interviewed in Jeddah, Saudi Arabia, Siti Mujiati W. told me, "My employer didn't allow me to go back to Indonesia for six years and eight months. . . . I never got any salary, not even one riyal! My employer never got angry with me; she never hit me. But she forbade me from returning to Indonesia."[3] Some of the most heartbreaking moments I remember are when women I interviewed told me, their voices cracking with tears or filled with anger, that their employers prevented them from returning home even when their parents were on their deathbed, or that they had not heard their children's voices in years.

While there are countless migrant domestic workers who do have positive experiences, decent working conditions are a matter of luck and not a guarantee. I have interviewed hundreds of domestic workers who have endured hellishly long working hours without rest; been forced to work months or years without pay; were starved, beaten, or burned with hot irons; or suffered routine humiliation and were locked up in the homes where they worked. My colleagues and I have collected statistics about tens of thousands of complaints of abuse made to authorities but have every reason to believe that even more are left unreported.

Domestic workers may not be aware of their rights in foreign countries, speak the local language, or simply have access to a phone. Others are repatriated before they have a chance to make a complaint. Police may ignore their requests for help or fail to conduct proper investigations. Domestic workers are often subject to counteraccusations of theft. In the Gulf, they may be subject to allegations of adultery, and in Saudi Arabia, to witchcraft. For the few prosecutions of abusive employers that do move forward, the trials are lengthy, and domestic workers are often confined to crowded shelters and unable to work while they wait for the conclusion. The most common problems—cases of unpaid wages—are typically resolved through negotiations in which the worker too often receives less than she is due.

One of the most haunting experiences I had was visiting an orthopedic hospital in Kuwait in 2009 that had two entire wards devoted to domestic workers with spinal cord injuries from falling from tall residential buildings. These women were either climbing out of windows in desperate escape attempts or attempting suicide out of depression and despair. Kuwait is hardly alone. We documented similar deaths in Singapore and Saudi Arabia, and in 2008, calculated that on average at least one migrant domestic worker was dying of unnatural causes each week in Lebanon.

Slow but Steady Path of Reform

Despite seeing the number of migrant domestic workers climb each year and learning about new cases of abuse almost every day, I feel hopeful about change. Over time I have been witness to an inspiring, growing movement to recognize domestic workers' rights that has won important, albeit incremental, victories.

When I began this work several years ago, many journalists, local activists, and labor ministry officials—the very sectors of society that should have been championing women workers' rights—were often employers of domestic workers themselves and among those who argued against providing them with a weekly day of rest or allowing them to keep their passports. Local media coverage would often be confined to short blurbs about maids who had fallen to their deaths or who were accused of stealing valuables.

In the last decade, once fledgling migrant workers' organizations have grown in strength, number, and sophistication. They have innovated to influence public opinion and provide desperately needed services. Examples include help desks at airports, SMS hotlines, pocket-sized "know your rights" booklets in migrants' native languages, legal aid, and shelters. Activists in Lebanon participated in a marathon wearing T-shirts emblazoned with "Don't run away from their rights" on the front and "Support a day off for domestic workers" on the back, while a group in Singapore organized an essay competition for school children to write about the migrant women who raised them. The most inspiring have been the current and former migrant domestic workers organizing their colleagues, usually under daunting constraints.

Once an invisible issue, there is now frequent and nuanced coverage of the working conditions of domestic workers in regional and international media, the blogosphere, and even several Facebook groups. The same newspapers that refused to cover our press conferences now write independent features critiquing their governments and demanding greater accountability.

And legal reforms are inching forward. Jordan amended its labor law to include domestic workers, and countries such as Singapore, the United Arab Emirates and Lebanon have established standard employment contracts. The contracts provide weaker protections than those in most labor codes and are difficult to enforce, but they represent a step toward formalizing work conditions, and now pressure to overhaul inadequate labor laws and restrictive immigration policies is mounting. Some governments are improving mechanisms to recover domestic workers' unpaid wages, and while many perpetrators of physical and sexual violence go free, others have been prosecuted and convicted. The change has been uneven and slow, but it is change in the right direction.

Demanding greater protection of domestic workers' rights has also met with setbacks. In 2009, Indonesia took a stand on abuse against its workers in Malaysia and banned further migration until greater protections were in place. Since the vast majority of domestic workers in Malaysia are Indonesian, the ban should have given the government strong bargaining power. Instead, Malaysian recruiters and employers turned to Cambodian domestic workers who tend to be younger, have less information about their rights, and have fewer avenues to seek help. After two years of negotiations, Indonesia was able to conclude a Memorandum of Understanding with Malaysia in June 2011 that allows domestic workers to keep their passports instead of having to surrender them to their employers, and guarantees them a weekly day off. But Indonesia was not able to secure the minimum wage it had tried hard to negotiate. The recruitment fee structure that allows employers to deduct several months of a domestic worker's salary remains intact.

Similarly, when the Philippines became increasingly vocal and concerned about abuse of its citizens in Saudi Arabia in 2011, Saudi government officials suspended new hires of Filipina domestic workers and instead created a new agreement to recruit from Bangladesh, which has been less demanding of labor rights protections. Labor-sending countries have yet to cooperate effectively to advocate strongly for a floor of minimum standards.

A Historic New Convention

Despite these setbacks, even international cooperation is on the rise. In June 2011, years of labor activism paved the way for a new treaty establishing global labor standards on domestic work by members of the International Labor Organization (ILO). The first of its kind, ILO Convention 189 on Decent Work Concerning Domestic Workers addresses the rights and circumstances of domestic workers, ensuring that domestic workers receive the same legal protections as other workers, including a minimum wage, limits to hours of work, a weekly day off, maternity benefits, and social security. This treaty will help reverse decades of exclusion from labor laws, provides guidance on sensitive issues such as labor inspections of private homes, and has specific provisions to protect against harassment, violence, and child labor.

After years of struggling to attract attention to an issue that most consider marginal, it was enthralling to sit in a room with hundreds of representatives from around the world—senior labor officials, national trade union leaders, representatives of powerful business groups, and domestic workers themselves—deeply engaged in negotiations on such nuanced issues as what proportion of compensation could be payment-in-kind instead of cash (e.g., room and board), or how to regulate the standby hours in which domestic workers may not be working but have to be on call.

After activists initially lobbied to open discussion on such a convention, the ILO conducted a global survey that amply demonstrated how discrimination and exploitation have been able to flourish when domestic work has been excluded from many national and even some international labor protections. Despite indifference and hesitation by many governments at the beginning of the process, only a handful failed to vote in favor of the final convention. The case for reversing the historical neglect of domestic workers had been successfully made, and many governments spoke compellingly on the urgent need to make exploitation and discrimination against domestic workers a thing of the past.

The ILO has a unique tripartite structure in which workers' groups, employers' groups, and governments all participate in the discussions and have a vote. Interestingly, the trade unions that typically represent workers' interests in these negotiations had traditionally focused on the formal sector and had limited experience with domestic work as a labor issue. The three-year process of consultations and developing labor-friendly positions has resulted in a tremendous sensitization of the global trade union movement about the labor rights violations faced by domestic workers and greatly strengthened alliances between trade unions and domestic workers' organizations.

National and regional domestic workers' organizations also used the negotiations around the convention as a central organizing point for a nascent global domestic workers' movement, notably the International Domestic Workers Network. Many labor activists and scholars additionally see the domestic work movement and convention as an exciting vanguard for innovative approaches to extend formal and comprehensive protections to workers in the informal sector.

Key elements of the convention require governments to provide domestic workers with labor protections equivalent to those of other workers, including for working hours, minimum wage coverage, overtime compensation, daily and weekly rest periods, social security, and maternity leave. The new standards address the protection and education of children—who comprise an estimated 30 percent of domestic workers—oblige governments to protect domestic workers from violence and abuse, and to ensure effective monitoring and enforcement.

The new convention also makes clear governments' responsibility to regulate private employment agencies, investigate complaints, and prohibit the practice of deducting domestic workers' salaries to pay recruitment fees. These provisions are particularly important for migrants, as are stipulations that migrant domestic workers must receive a written contract that is enforceable in the country of employment and that governments should strengthen international cooperation to protect their rights.

The convention received overwhelming backing with only some employers' representatives and nine governments refusing to vote in favor. Members of the Gulf Cooperation Council (Bahrain, Kuwait, Oman, Qatar, Saudi Arabia, and the United Arab Emirates), along with Bangladesh, Indonesia, and India, reversed early opposition to a legally binding convention and expressed support in the final vote. While some may be understandably cynical about these votes, the public support of the principles underlying this convention is a huge shift from the arguments these governments previously made to defend separate and unequal treatment, such as claiming these workers should be treated as "members of the family" and not "workers." The recognition of domestic workers' rights opens up space for change, and gives workers a chance to hold governments to their word.

Now begins a lengthy process for countries to sign on to this convention and reform their national laws to be in compliance. Widespread ratification and implementation is critical, but the existence of these standards is already having an impact. Governments currently in the process of drafting new legislation on domestic work, such as Kuwait, the United Arab Emirates, Indonesia, the Philippines, and Lebanon, will consult these standards as they finalize their laws. Singapore, one of the few countries that did not support the convention, is feeling the pressure to introduce reforms anyway in order to remain an attractive destination for domestic workers who can choose from other countries that may offer better wages and conditions. For activists, the convention provides a powerful tool for our advocacy. The domestic workers' rights movement has grown and diversified, with more resources and momentum to fight for these standards to become realities on the ground.

There is a tough road ahead. Discrimination and exploitative practices against domestic workers are deeply entrenched in many parts of the world and will not fade away quickly. But there is at last a snowballing momentum for change, a growing number of successes to point to as models, and a shift in attitudes that demands a greater valuing of women's labor and rights.

> *Let it be extinguished, so that not a single girl leaves school to scrub floors*
> *Let it be extinguished, so that not a single young woman has to wash clothes for others*
> *Let it be extinguished, so that not a single mother has to neglect her children to raise those of another*
> *Let it be extinguished, so there not a single older woman looks back after 40 years and sees her life lost in the lives of others.*

—from "Ode to the Invisible Woman"[4]

CHAPTER 16

Ending Trafficking of Women and Girls

Mark P. Lagon

I vividly remember the day in 2009 when I sat among a group of survivors of human trafficking gathered in Washington by Polaris Project, the NGO I then headed. They were all women sharing with one another the progress and setbacks they had had in the course of the previous year. An animated woman from Malawi, victimized as a domestic servant, pointedly interjected how curious it was that Americans seemed so interested in protecting the rights of animals, when people like her were treated worse than animals.

She captured the essence of the crime of trafficking: it dehumanizes. This affects women in forced labor as well as the sex trade. And it exists surreptitiously in the United States and in other developed countries, not just far away in the developing world.

Enlarging the dignity and progress of humanity depends on asking both why fighting human trafficking is essential to the state of women's rights globally, and what vital role gender equality plays in solving the problem of human trafficking.

First, human trafficking is not about migration. Much as "trafficking" sounds like a description of illicit movement across borders, and

Ambassador Mark P. Lagon, Ph.D., is chair of International Relations and Security at the Master of Foreign Service Program, Georgetown University. He is also adjunct senior fellow for Human Rights at the Council on Foreign Relations. He served as US ambassador-at-large directing the Department of State Office to Monitor and Combat Trafficking in Persons, and executive director and CEO of Polaris Project.

often does involve migration, conceptually and legally someone who has never left their country of birth, never crossed a border, can be a human trafficking victim. A woman of the disadvantaged *Dalit* caste (formerly known as "Untouchables"), spending every day of her life in India, trapped in unpaid bonded labor in a rice mill, with no meaningful choice or ability to leave the situation, is a human trafficking victim. So too is a runaway teenager in the US from a broken family prostituted in an American city. Human trafficking is, in short, the exploitative robbery of someone's autonomy.

Second, trafficking of women is not confined to sexual exploitation. The early campaign movement against human trafficking in the late 1990s focused on commercial sex, seized with the need to address the huge flow of victims from the former Warsaw Pact countries and Soviet republics. But many women are trafficked for labor, and not solely sexual exploitation. In 2007, I met a group of young women in a shelter outside Bangkok who had left Burma for Thailand in search of a better economic and political life, when wooed in a group of eight hundred young workers by labor recruiters in Burma. Once in a Thai seafood processing labor camp, remote in the forest on the outskirts of Bangkok, they were imprisoned by barbed wire fences with sharp edges facing inward and coerced to work inhumane hours. When a handful escaped the compound, they were caught by guards and were beaten in front of the camp's workers. One young woman told me of how her head was shaven to intimidate her peers.

Brutal Effects of Supply and Demand

On the supply side, a combination of criminal networks, corruption, poverty, and misinformation about employment opportunities and the nature of work promised, make people vulnerable to the lures of trafficking. This pattern is true of both sex trafficking and slave labor. Significant efforts are being made to address these "push" factors, but they alone are not the cause. As for sex trafficking, any effort to successfully combat it must confront not only the supply of vulnerable women and children, but also the demand that perpetuates it.

There are now international norms against trafficking. In 2005, the

UN Commission on the Status of Women adopted the US resolution entitled Eliminating Demand for Trafficked Women and Girls for All Forms of Exploitation. This was the first resolution of a UN body to focus on the demand side of human trafficking, with the goal of protecting women and girls by drying up the "market" for victims, particularly for commercial sexual exploitation. Professor Donna Hughes, a pioneer in the human trafficking abolitionist movement in the US, reports having interviewed pimps and police from organized crime units and finding that when the pimps need new women and girls, they simply contact someone who can deliver them, setting in motion the chain of events that perpetuates sex trafficking. Hughes writes, "Where prostitution is flourishing, pimps can not recruit enough local women to fill up the brothels, so they have to bring in victims from other places."[1]

The Hungarian sociologist Karl Polanyi in 1944 dubbed the industrial revolution's redefinition of the roles of land, money and labor as "the commodity fiction." While his Marxist notion is overdrawn, human trafficking is indeed about people being coarsely turned into commodities. Moreover, when those "commodities" are girls or women who are sold for their bodies' sexual consumption, left, right and center can agree this is an acute violation, and that those girls and women should not be stigmatized. Leading feminist scholar Catharine MacKinnon is surely right in observing that sex trafficking is always a form of violence against women.[2]

At its heart, human trafficking involves groups of people being consigned to less-than-human or non-person status. The recruiter, the exploiter, the "customer" creating demand, law enforcement and immigration officials, and society at large all consign such groups to that status. The groups can be minors, minorities, and migrants (irregular and regular). Most often that group is comprised of women and girls. The question in the title of MacKinnon's essay and edited volume, "Are Women Human?" is the nub of the problem: why are women treated as less than human by trafficking, and what is the solution?

Visiting Jordan as anti-trafficking envoy of the US Department of State, an official of the UN Development Fund for Women (UNIFEM) told me that the country was somewhat less repressive than others in the Middle East. Yet she emphasized that even in Jordan to be a foreign worker, and importantly a woman, makes someone highly vulnerable. Domestic workers, for example, are vulnerable to human trafficking because legal guest workers and women are not accorded equal rights or legal recourse as compared with citizens and men. The new International Labor Organization convention on domestic workers negotiated in 2011 should help.

In area after area, addressing women's rights generally is an essential part of shrinking and ultimately abolishing human trafficking. If girls have access to education and meaningful job opportunities, this will reduce vulnerability to recruitment into sexual or labor exploitation. If women can own or inherit property and wealth, they will be less vulnerable. If there are safe migration alternatives, women will be less likely prey for traffickers. If women in the sex industry are no longer seen as "dirty" and to be blamed for their existence, sex trafficking victims among them will be more likely to be identified by law enforcement and less likely to be treated by them as criminals.

What Needs to Be Done?

The priorities to end trafficking lie in news ways of thinking about the problem, an uncorrupted rule of law, and survivor empowerment.

First, an "idealist" rather than a "materialist" approach is most viable. It is true that the root cause of trafficking is poverty, which creates the desperation that leaves women and girls vulnerable to recruitment into trafficking situations. This materialist premise leads to the conclusion that fighting poverty broadly and creating economic opportunities is the solution. The international community must indeed fight poverty and create means of growth and prosperity for the half of the world that is female. Authors such as Nicholas Kristof and Sheryl WuDunn, NGOs such as Vital Voices, private sector actors like Goldman Sachs (with its 10,000 Women campaign), and microcredit lenders like Mohammed Yunus's Grameen Bank are right to call for creating economic opportunity for women as a means of addressing trafficking.

But we cannot just wait for the end of poverty. We need to act now and address the ideas that reduce women to second-class citizens, seen as unworthy of education or property rights, and that make their purchase for commercial sex or forced labor seem normal and inevitable. Of course, changing perspectives and cultures is enormously hard. Yet changing mindsets about women in society—especially the mindset among governing authorities and law enforcement agencies—must be priority number one in a campaign to end trafficking in women.

The second priority is that women should have access to justice when their rights are violated, including by trafficking. More than half of the countries around the world have adopted anti-trafficking laws since the 2000 UN Palermo Protocol and US Trafficking Victims Protection Act were put in place. So too have most of the fifty US states. Still, implementation often is lacking.

Women are denied justice when they are deported or not provided adequate witness protection, or are relegated to shelters ostensibly to protect them but where their rights are denied or unrealized. Countries of destination still fail to provide adequate protection, or are only willing to help those who testify against traffickers at great personal risk to themselves and their families. Further, justice that the women could use, in other words financial compensation, is not enforced as it should be.

The State Department *Trafficking in Persons Report* documented 7,992 prosecutions globally in 2003, which went down to 6,017 in 2010. Of those 6,017, only 607 were for labor-related rather than sex trafficking.[3] In Brazil in 2010, 2,617 victims of forced labor were identified and assisted by government authorities, but only eight perpetrators were convicted, seven with fines only and one with a 3.5-year sentence commuted to community service.[4] The US has only eighty beds for victims of child sex trafficking; in 2008-2009, three times that number of child sex-trafficking victims were incarcerated rather than protected and assisted. The number of victims who are arrested continues to go up, according to the US government's own statistics. Implementation clearly lags behind the intent of law.

A crucial part of law becoming justice in practice is ending the apathy and corruption of officials. As anti-trafficking envoy, I visited Chiapas in Mexico and witnessed police stand idly as minors were prostituted on their street.

Corruption can come in petty forms: the policeman or judge "on the take," the immigration official complicit in irregular migration, or fraud trapping guest workers in stark exploitation. It also takes place at higher levels. For instance, Moldova was one of the eight countries given large anti-trafficking aid packages pursuant to a Bush Administration presidential initiative announced at the UN General Assembly. Subsequently, the State Department assigned Moldova the lowest rating level in the 2008 *Trafficking in Persons Report*[5] when the head of the US-funded agency in the country was himself found complicit in trafficking.

The third priority is survivor empowerment. In human trafficking, we refer often to the ubiquitous "3 Ps," drawn from the Palermo Protocol and US Trafficking Victims Protection Act: prosecution of traffickers, prevention of the crime, and protection of victims. Prosecution ensures accountability, but is often overemphasized in international and domestic law relative to the other two Ps. Prevention usually takes the form of awareness campaigns, posters, and billboards on the one hand, and long-term, more diffuse efforts to create economic opportunity on the other.

Experience has taught us that protection is the primary P. For instance, the migrant communities affected by traffickers are often those with the best information about traffickers and how they operate. Yet people in these communities fear to come forward for fear of retaliation, as they are not protected but rather very likely to be retaliated against. Overall, protection must center on the real and genuine empowerment of survivors. This implies more than physical shelter, to include psychological and health services, and the protection of human rights. In Bucharest I met two women, Anca and Silvia. They were diverted into coercive prostitution in the United Kingdom as migrants from Romania. British authorities ended up arranging their return to their home country, Romania, but the two women did not receive any healthcare in the United Kingdom for serious untreated diseases they may have acquired during their time in coerced prostitution.

Survivor empowerment also requires training survivors in occupational skills to give them better alternatives in life. In Tamil Nadu, India, I met one of the ten thousand citizens receiving restitution for bonded labor since a 1976 law on that crime was enacted in India. Sitting with her in a one-room home provided by the state, I was moved by her pride in ownership and in autonomy to steer a course of freedom with her husband and children. Broad efforts to offer economic opportunities to potential victims should not crowd out helping survivors as a practical targeted focus.

One woman who ties together all these strands of changing ideas about trafficking, ending corruption, and survivor empowerment is Mexican journalist Lydia Cacho, a feminist calling for women to take charge of their fate. She is the author of an exposé of senior officials who were complicit in organized crime including human trafficking. When corrupt police intimidated her, she pursued litigation up to Mexico's Supreme Court to call that intimidation to account. Although she lost in court, she was undeterred and highlights trafficking in her newest book, *Esclavas del poder: Un viaje al corazón de la trata sexual de mujeres y niñas en el mundo* (*Slaves of Power: A Journey to the Heart of World Sex Trafficking of Women and Girls*).[6] Moreover, Cacho's NGO, Centro Integrale de Atención a la Mujer (CIAM) runs a shelter for battered women in a disguised location in Cancún. Victims of sex trafficking, often with children to provide for, are offered a holistic, explicitly feminist approach to taking economic control of their lives.

Key Players

Who are the key players to turn these priorities into reality? Lydia Cacho has shown extraordinary pluck and bravery, but an overreliance on social entrepreneurs might make more conclusive, systemic change more difficult. A remarkable alliance of feminists, Christians and other humanitarians, labor activists, and legislators has galvanized concern about the scale and severity of trafficking. Building civil society is extremely important, but it will take more than innovative social entrepreneurs and charismatic figures.

First, human trafficking needs to become a high priority for mainstream human rights and women's rights groups as well as groups more focused on ending violence against women. NGOs in all three communities need to place trafficking of women centrally in their agenda and resource priorities.

Second, for impact beyond social entrepreneurs, the human trafficking movement should emulate the violence against women movement. The coalition of nonprofits opposing violence against women in the US, for instance, exhibit an institutional maturation and a common voice on policy and government appropriations issues that the anti-trafficking community must develop.

Third, beyond governments and grant makers, others such as the business community, major philanthropic foundations and multilateral institutions should back this work with logistics and funding support.

These are answers to the "what" and the "who" of a strategy to stop women and girls from being turned into mere commodities. They all rest on a simple symmetry: fighting the calamity of human trafficking is central to the struggle for women's equality globally, and the problem will be truly solved only as women achieve full equality.

CHAPTER 17

Do No Harm
"Post-Trafficking" Abuses

Elaine Pearson

Over the last decade, I have interviewed scores of trafficking victims: people enslaved and forced to work under horrific conditions in sweatshops, brothels, and even other people's homes. The images of the men, women, and children I interviewed still haunt my thoughts.

Champa A.,[1] a Nepali girl I interviewed in Kathmandu, told me, "I went there when I was fifteen. All of us trafficked girls, thirty to forty of us, were kept in one room. We were only given two meals per day.... We were locked in, and we weren't allowed to leave. A few girls ran away. But they were caught, when they were brought back they were beaten up, and had hot water poured over them. When we got ill, it was only when I was completely bedridden that I got taken to the doctor. We were treated like animals.... I stayed there for two years in total. My family didn't know I was there."

Champa's experience is horrifying. Yet she was not telling me here

Elaine Pearson is deputy director of the Asia Division at Human Rights Watch. She has lived and worked in Asia, including in Bangkok, Hong Kong, and Kathmandu. She previously worked for the International Labor Organization as well as the UN Development Fund for Women, and led the first trafficking program at Anti-Slavery International in London. She has advised governments on anti-trafficking policies and programs, and has led trainings and developed curricula for government officials, police, and nongovernmental organizations on human rights and trafficking issues.

about the terrible treatment she experienced when forced to work in a brothel in India, which she had earlier told me about. She was describing the treatment she received in a private shelter in Nepal, after she was "rescued" by police and sent for "rehabilitation."

While there can be no equating the scope and immense suffering imposed by traffickers and the abuses that can accompany anti-trafficking responses, mistreatment of women and girls following rescue from trafficking is also a serious concern. The latter includes not only coercive and at times abusive confinement of trafficking victims after their rescue, as experienced by Champa, but also abuses by corrupt officials and approaches to rescue that can end up feeding a vicious circle of trafficking, the same women and girls cycling in and out of trafficking situations. While there is fortunately growing awareness of the importance of tackling such "post-trafficking" abuses, there is still a long way to go to fully incorporate concern with victim's rights at all stages of the response to trafficking.

The Imperative of Anti-Trafficking

Under international law, trafficking is the movement of people, through deceptive and coercive means, into a situation of slavery, forced labor, or severe exploitation.[2] For children, no deceptive or coercive means are required; the evidence of severe exploitation is enough to prove trafficking. Champa was trafficked into a brothel when a recruiter approached her and offered her a job in a carpet factory in India. Instead, she was forced into a brothel to sell sex at age fourteen.

Others are trafficked into marriage, factory work, domestic work, and other areas. Mende Nazer from Sudan was trafficked into domestic work at age twelve or thirteen when armed men attacked her village, abducted her, and sold her to a family in Khartoum who enslaved her as a domestic worker. She subsequently wrote a book about her experience.[3] Twenty-seven-year-old Noi K. had been working as a sex worker in Thailand, when a man offered her the opportunity to work in a brothel in Australia where, according to him, she could make more money. Upon arrival, her passport was taken away, she was indebted to the tune of US$45,000, forced to work in the brothel six days per week, and had no freedom to refuse clients.

There are myriad causes of human trafficking. Many of the factors that put women and girls at risk are similar to the push factors for migration. These include poverty and inequality, as well as the lack of employment opportunities, education, adequate labor migration opportunities, and sufficient labor protections, particularly for informal or unrecognized sectors of work. Women and girls are especially at risk due to gender inequality, the denial of property rights, limited access to education, low economic status, and obstacles to participation in the political process.[4]

While the illicit nature of trafficking makes it difficult to gather accurate statistics about how many people are trafficked annually. However, the International Labor Organization (ILO) estimated in 2005 that at least 12.3 million people are in forced labor, debt bondage, and slavery, of whom 20 percent are trafficked.[5]

In 2000, the United Nations adopted a new treaty for signature, the Protocol to Prevent, Suppress, and Punish Trafficking in Persons, Especially Women and Children, also known as the Trafficking Protocol. This was the first international instrument dealing with trafficking in all its forms, whether people are enslaved in sex work, farm work, deep-sea fishing, domestic work, marriage, or even trafficked for their organs. The protocol has helped focus attention on the problem of trafficking and many governments have begun to take steps to prevent it and protect victims. New laws criminalizing trafficking have been widely adopted and training programs have been established for law enforcement officers on identifying and responding to trafficking cases.

Many of these interventions have helped large numbers of people out of slavery and to rebuild their lives. Yet human trafficking persists, and unfortunately, for many around the world, like Champa, the nightmare is not always over when they leave a trafficking situation.

Measures Fall Short

For all of its contributions, the Trafficking Protocol focuses too little on the human rights of trafficking victims. Because it is attached to the Transnational Organized Crime Convention, the Protocol reflects governments' primary focus on stopping trafficking as transnational criminal activity and as a form of irregular migration, rather than assisting rescued victims. Under the Protocol, measures for aiding trafficking victims are encouraged but not mandatory.

The same year the protocol was adopted, the US government passed the Trafficking Victim Protection Act, which increased penalties for trafficking-related offences and established the State Department's annual Trafficking in Persons report, which evaluates and ranks countries according to their anti-trafficking efforts. Initially, the report focused overwhelmingly on prosecution of traffickers. Countries that continually score poorly in the rankings can be subject to sanctions. The adoption of the protocol and the US law led to a flurry of anti-trafficking activity including new anti-trafficking laws and training programs for law enforcement officers. However, these activities generally did not pay adequate attention to safeguarding victims' rights. Initially, protections such as residency permits or access to support services were only granted to victims willing to cooperate in criminal investigations and prosecutions against their traffickers, sometimes at great personal risk to them and their families.

Governments and NGOs have also worked on trafficking prevention, particularly through awareness-raising campaigns targeting potential victims and increased border surveillance efforts. Many of these efforts have reduced trafficking and alerted potential victims to the risks involved and what legal rights they have.[6] However, some had a negative impact by increasing discrimination or abuses against victims. For example, many women traveling alone from trafficking hot spots such as Eastern Europe and Southeast Asia were subject to more profiling and paperwork in order to obtain visas. Authorities have sometimes conflated trafficking and sex work, detaining and harassing sex workers in countries such as Australia, Thailand, Cambodia, and Nepal on the pretext that they are trafficked.

These approaches reflected the main concern of governments to address organized crime, prostitution, and irregular migration under the rubric of "trafficking." A consequence of this emphasis has been to neglect and sometimes directly undermine the needs of victims.

Serious concerns about the lack of human rights safeguards prompted former United Nations High Commissioner for Human Rights Mary Robinson to establish principles and guidelines on human rights and human trafficking in 2002. These guidelines state that anti-trafficking measures "shall not adversely affect the human rights and dignity of persons, in particular the rights of those who have been trafficked."[7] How did it become necessary to state the obvious—that efforts to end the abuses of trafficking should not harm those who have been trafficked?

Abuse in Shelters

Shelters have too often been the location of post-trafficking abuses. It seems obvious that trafficked persons, as victims of crime and victims of human rights violations, should not be immediately deported or locked up in immigration detention centers. It seems equally obvious that victims should have access, if they choose, to shelters that provide support and assistance and help them to recover. However, neither of these positions is universally accepted. Victims are still routinely detained as illegal immigrants and deported. In some countries that have signed the Trafficking Protocol, victims are forced to remain in government or private shelters against their will.

Even shelters often lauded by governments as models of good practice detain people. For instance, the government of Thailand has been widely applauded for its home for women and girls, Baan Kredtrakarn, which accommodates Thai and non-Thai victims of trafficking and exploitation. Yet the home is essentially an island prison which non-Thai women and girls are not permitted to leave. The US Trafficking in Persons report noted that in Thailand, "Foreign adult victims of trafficking identified by authorities continued to be detained in government shelters . . . foreign trafficking victims . . . fled shelters, likely due to slow legal and repatriation processes, the inability to earn income during trial proceedings, language barriers, and distrust of government officials."[8]

The proponents of shelter detention argue for it on various grounds.[9] First, the safety of trafficking victims is at risk, particularly if they are participating in criminal proceedings against traffickers. Second, for non-nationals, the legal status of residents is precarious—victims would be subject to arrest and deportation if allowed out. And third, as various shelter managers have sometimes told me, "Victims consent to it, so it's not actually detention." However, victims may not be provided with information about the conditions of staying in the shelter or fully understand their rights and the options open to them, including the length of their detention; regardless, consent cannot be construed as absolute. Their circumstances may also change during their stay, and they may be too afraid to question authorities or those offering them shelter.

Women and girls trafficked into the sex industry are often detained because many governments evidently believe that shelter detention is "for their own good," and that they will flee if the doors are not locked. Shelter staff in countries such as Cambodia, Nepal, and Bangladesh told me that these victims are in fact "bad girls" who will simply get into trouble if allowed to roam free.

Other, underlying reasons for detaining trafficked women and girls may be even more straightforward. It is cheaper, easier, and far more convenient to confine them. It also ensures that victims are available when police need to interview them or bring them to court. And closed shelters have a ready population available on call to easily show donors the fruits of their anti-trafficking efforts. The continuing stream of high profile visitors to Thailand's Baan Kredtrakarn is evidence of the public relations value of this aspect of Thailand's response to trafficking.

But by routinely detaining victims of trafficking, shelter managers run the risk of inflicting further trauma and harm to victims by essentially using similar methods to those of the traffickers themselves: holding them captive and violating their right to make decisions for themselves.

In Thailand, UN Special Rapporteur on Trafficking Joy Ezeilo voiced concern about "long stays at shelters," turning the shelters into "detention centers and a vehicle for violations of human rights, especially the right to freedom of movement and to earn an income and live a decent life."[10]

Besides detention and abuse in shelters, trafficking victims face further violations after they have escaped from traffickers. As Human Rights Watch has documented in Malaysia, Cambodia, and Thailand, corrupt officials complicit in trafficking hand victims back to traffickers, and beat, rape, or rob victims. Poorly planned and orchestrated rescue operations often end up with frightened victims who are so unwilling to trust officers that they end up being released, arrested, or deported with no end to the trafficking cycle.

Putting the Rights of Trafficking Victims First

As a result of advocacy by various human rights and anti-trafficking organizations, governments have begun to improve their efforts to protect the rights of victims. For instance, the European Trafficking Convention obliges states to provide basic assistance to all victims of trafficking, and not only those who agree to act as witnesses or assist in criminal investigations. Those identified by authorities as possible victims are entitled to a "reflection and recovery period," during which they can receive support and make an informed decision about whether and how to cooperate in the prosecution of their exploiters. Over the past few years there has been a welcome trend to de-link victim support from cooperation with law enforcement.

In recent years, some organizations and government bodies have focused on evidence-based and accountable anti-trafficking efforts.[11] This means not only sharing and replicating good practices, but also learning from bad practices by collecting evidence from victims and other migrants with firsthand experience of the counterproductive effects of anti-trafficking measures.[12]

The US State Department Trafficking in Persons report is a potentially important tool to strengthen accountability. The report has improved over the years and now includes information about the negative human rights consequences of counter-trafficking interventions, as it did with a critique of Thailand's shelter detention policy in 2011. During her Thailand mission, UN Envoy Ezeilo also investigated human rights violations in anti-trafficking responses, and raised concerns about "the frequent misidentification of trafficked persons as irregular migrants subject to arrest, detention and deportation."

Governments and NGOs, particularly in Southeast Asia and Europe, have started to focus more on promotion of safe migration, recognizing that many people are so desperate for work that they will accept even the risk of trafficking if there are no alternatives. But the tension between safe migration and approaches that prioritize crime fighting have by no means been resolved. Governments still often prioritize border control as a means of trafficking prevention at the expense of freedom of movement.[13]

Many shelters around the world provide safe haven for trafficking victims without locking them up. For instance, the Cambodian Women's Crisis Center does not detain victims but maintains security cameras, has enough staff to accompany women on trips outside the shelter, and maintains good relations with local police in case they need greater protection. Some NGOs, such as the Italian organization Associazione on the Road, provide various types of shelters depending on the victims' specific needs.[14]

NGOs run by formerly trafficked women have pioneered innovative approaches to address the needs of victims of trafficking. In Nepal, I first met Champa sitting on the floor of a one-room office of a grassroots NGO called Shakti Samuha ("Women of Power") conducts educational activities, provides individualized vocational training, coordinates legal aid, and has a small shelter, where victims are not detained. Shakti Samuha's staff understand and address the stigma and harassment their clients can face when identified as former sex workers. Their individualized vocational training programs have also seen at least one client qualify to work and travel abroad legally—a far cry from other institutions that frighten former victims and pressure them to return to their home village. Groups like Shakti Samuha understand from firsthand experience the need for individual-based approaches rather than the institutionalized model that is still favored across much of Asia.

NGO and government officials have also learned that the best way of identifying and assisting victims of trafficking may not always be a raid on premises to rescue them. For instance, in the United States, the Florida-based Coalition of Immokalee Workers has had great success in identifying victims of trafficking in agriculture through persuading migrant farm workers to reach out to enslaved workers and explain their rights and options.

Another positive development, particularly in Europe, North America, and Southeast Asia, is the growing acceptance that trafficking can take place for a range of exploitative purposes and into many different sectors, not just the sex sector. The increasing focus on trafficking for forced labor has resulted in more victims being identified and helped.

On a trip to Thailand in 2009, I met Bu from Laos, who was trafficked to work in a fish-processing factory. When officials raided the factory, Bu told me how the officials asked her if she was trafficked, "I said no, because I didn't want to go to the Home. I've heard the stories that it's like prison and I have heard you can get stuck there for many months. At least if I go to the IDC [Immigration Detention Center] then they will send me back to the border after a few weeks. I need to earn money—that's why I left. I didn't like being locked up in the factory, why would I like being locked up again?"

When victims deny they are victims of trafficking in order to avoid so-called support and assistance measures that are supposed to help them, it's clear these provisions are not working.

More than a decade after the Trafficking Protocol was enacted, counter-trafficking interventions must be assessed and evaluated. Governments and donors must listen and learn from the experiences of victims. They should devote attention and resources to identifying and combating human rights violations arising from anti-trafficking efforts. Only then will the values underpinning the broadening global commitment to protect and assist trafficking victims be fully realized.

PART 5

VIOLENCE AGAINST WOMEN

CHAPTER 18

A Needed Revolution
Testing Rape Kits and US Justice

Sarah Tofte

In 1996, when she was seventeen, Helena was abducted by a stranger from a car wash, driven around barren areas of Los Angeles County, and repeatedly raped. Immediately afterward, Helena reported the crime to the police. She made this courageous decision despite the parting threat from her assailant that he would come to her home and kill her and her family if she told anyone about the rape. Before he abandoned her to shiver in her car in a vacant industrial lot, he took Helena's driver's license with her home address on it, so she knew he had the information he needed to follow up on the threat. Still, as she told me fourteen years later with a tinge of sadness, "I believed in the criminal justice system, and it never occurred to me not to ask the police for help. Of course, at the time, I had a very different idea about how they would handle my case than how things actually worked out."

When Helena reported the rape to the police, she—like many in the United States who inform a hospital, the police, or a rape treatment center of a sexual assault within a week of the crime—was asked to

Sarah Tofte is the director of advocacy and strategic partnerships at the Joyful Heart Foundation, an organization dedicated to helping victims of sexual assault. Formerly a senior researcher with the US program at Human Rights Watch, she is the author of groundbreaking reports on the problem of untested rape kits in the United States, notably in California and Illinois. In this chapter, she discusses the origin of this crisis, and what it means for rape victims and public safety.

have a sexual assault forensic evidence kit collected at a hospital. The examination is a lengthy, invasive four-to-six-hour process in which a medical professional swabs, plucks, and brushes into envelopes any DNA left in or on a rape victim's body. The envelopes are sealed and then placed in a cardboard box. The cardboard box is referred to as a "rape kit."

After Helena reported her rape, it would be more than a decade before she heard again from the police. For thirteen years, Helena phoned the police department handling her case, and for thirteen years, her calls went unreturned. Then one day, in early 2010, she read a newspaper article about the rape kit backlog in Los Angeles, which quoted me and my report on this subject. Helena found my contact information, and a few days later called me at my office at Human Rights Watch. "I think my rape kit is in the backlog in Los Angeles," she told me by way of introduction during our first phone call, "and I would like to know if I can get it tested."

A Powerful Tool . . . If Used

Today's rape kit is the result of some thirty years of improvements made by medical and forensic professionals, police, prosecutors, and victim's advocates. The kits—and the way they are collected—have evolved in response to advancements in DNA technology, increased knowledge of what type of forensic evidence is most likely to have value in a rape case, data from crime laboratories regarding which forensic collection practices are most likely to ensure the integrity of the evidence, and studies regarding victims' needs during forensic examinations.

With an understanding of the power of DNA evidence in a rape case, criminal justice professionals have spent decades honing the forensic collection process. Their work has facilitated a victim's access to the rape kit and prohibited law enforcement from charging a victim for the cost of collecting it. They have developed protocols to ensure that the process of collecting a rape kit is handled in the least psychologically and physically harmful way for the victim, while using techniques most likely to preserve valuable evidence. In this regard, the United States has perhaps the highest standard of care in the world. Unfortunately, this high standard is not sustained in the way rape kit evidence is handled once it is collected.

Helena—like many other victims who reached out to me about the rape kit backlog—assumed her rape kit had been tested in the early days of the investigation of her case. The last time she saw her kit, it was in the hands of a police officer. She had guessed that she never heard from the detective about a result because, despite her sense that the rapist's DNA had been over her body in the form of his semen and saliva, the crime lab found no useful information in her kit. But when Helena read in her newspaper that Human Rights Watch had found 12,500 untested rape kits in police and crime lab storage facilities Los Angeles, she began to have doubts that her kit had been tested, and this prompted her to contact me. When I called, the Los Angeles Sheriff's Department confirmed that Helena's kit had been in a backlog.

Helena's assumption that her rape kit was tested was understandable. As DNA has played an increasingly important role in our criminal justice system, even laypersons grasp how vital DNA evidence is in resolving rape cases. Rape kit testing can identify an unknown assailant, confirm the presence of a known suspect, corroborate a victim's version of events, discredit a suspect's story, identify serial rapists by connecting individual crime scenes, and exonerate innocent suspects. Rape kit testing sends a crucial message to victims that their cases matter, and puts assailants on notice that the criminal justice system takes their crimes seriously.

Lost Opportunities for Stemming Violence Against Women and for Justice

Untested rape kits often represent lost opportunities for justice—if a kit is still unopened, it is usually a sign that the rape case did not move very far through the criminal justice system. Yet experts estimate that there are hundreds of thousands of untested rape kits in police and crime lab storage facilities across the United States.

There are two kinds of rape kit backlogs—untested rape kits in crime labs, and untested rape kits in police storage facilities. Those kits sitting in crime lab facilities are ones that law enforcement have requested for testing, but are held up in a long line because a lab does not have adequate staff and money to test each kit in a timely manner. Those kits sitting in police storage facilities have never been requested for testing, and often are connected to rape cases that were closed without an arrest, or remain open and unsolved. The vast majority of untested rape kits in the United States reside in police storage facilities.

The exact number of kits stacked in either police or crime lab storage is unknown, because the federal government does not track rape kit data, and only one state, Illinois, requires law enforcement to account for their rape kit evidence. But over the past decade, police departments have reported staggering backlogs in their storage facilities: 4,000 untested kits in Illinois; 12,500 in Dallas; 11,000 in San Antonio; 10,000 in Detroit; 4,000 in Houston; and 1,200 in Albuquerque.

Given the value of rape kit testing, "Why," as one victim, Stephanie, said to me, "did I go through the rape kit exam if they were not even going to open it?" The answers say a lot about how poorly the United States responds to violence against women, and how far the US has to go to realize its commitment to advance women's rights.

Scarce Funds and Feeble Intentions

Some experts attribute America's failure to get things right when it comes to rape kit testing to funding constraints. Indeed rape kit testing is more expensive than other kinds of DNA tests, in part because a DNA technician will, by the very nature of the crime, need to extract and separate at least two individuals' DNA from a swab—that of the victim and that of the assailant(s). Each kit can cost an average of $1,200-1,500 to test. The rapid expansion of DNA evidence in the criminal justice system has put an incredible stress on crime laboratories, but the sharp rise in the number of DNA test requests has not been accompanied by an increase in personnel and resources needed to test rape kit evidence in a comprehensive and timely manner.

This lack of resources is one reason why rape kits that are sent by the police to a crime lab for testing wait for weeks, months, and in some cases even years to be tested. This backlog at crime laboratories across the country is one reason that Congress created the Debbie Smith DNA Backlog Reduction Grant Program in 2004. Named after a rape victim whose case took seven years to solve because of a backlog, the goal of the program was to provide the resources states needed to eliminate their rape kit backlogs. But the program expanded to allow states to test backlogged DNA evidence from any crime, not just sexual assault. Yet, even when money is available, rape kit testing is not a priority for crime lab officials dealing with other kinds of DNA backlogs.

Scarce resources alone are not to blame for untested rape kits in crime labs, and cannot explain the rape kits stuck in police storage facilities that were deemed unworthy of testing by detectives. A 2009 National Institute of Justice survey of law enforcement officers found that evidence in sexual assault cases was the least likely among all violent crimes to be given testing priority. The cases most likely to have DNA evidence tested were property crimes. To understand why rape kits are such a low priority for police, it is important to place the rape kit backlog in the context of the criminal justice system's historically anemic response to sexual violence.

Progress on Some Fronts

The United States has struggled to make progress in the way the criminal justice system addresses violence against women and girls. Only in the last forty years have laws and systems been put in place to record the prevalence of sexual violence; provide advocates who guide victims through the system; educate and raise awareness about the causes and consequences of sexual violence; prohibit a victim's prior sexual activity from being entered into evidence; eliminate the requirement that there be a corroborating witness to the rape in addition to the victim; and create procedures to collect physical evidence from victims. Police and prosecutors have been extensively trained in how to move cases forward, and special sexual assault investigative and prosecutorial units are now common in most major cities.

Despite all these reforms, the number of reported rapes that lead to an arrest, much less a conviction, remains intractably small. In 2010, the arrest rate for rape was 24 percent, which was exactly what it was in the late 1970s when the FBI first began tracking such data. Too many rape cases in this country don't just remain unresolved—they remain uninvestigated. As the executive director of the Illinois State Coalition of Sexual Assault, Polly Poskin told me, "The other day, I learned that the oldest kit in Illinois's rape kit backlog was from a rape that occurred in 1979. When I think about what that reporting victim went through in 1979 to report her rape and what she would go through in 2011, the progress of our response is remarkable, amazing, and encouraging. Yet when I remember that her rape kit is in a backlog with untested kits from 2008, 2009, I realize how very far we still have to go in getting rape cases investigated using all the evidence we have available."

Most reported rapes are perpetrated by someone the victim knows, and law enforcement operate on the misguided assumption that these so-called acquaintance rape cases are too hard to prove or are false reports by victims motivated to harm the accused. Consequently, these "non-stranger" rape cases often languish after they are reported, and, even when they do move forward, law enforcement see no need to test a rape kit in the case, since they already know who the suspect is.

This approach to non-stranger rape cases ignores the reality of sexual violence and rape kit testing: government studies show that very few reporting victims give false reports of rape, research has found that non-stranger assailants are the most likely to be repeat offenders, and rape kit testing can provide investigative information in all kinds of rape cases, including non-stranger cases.

New York City adopted a policy of testing every rape kit booked into evidence, after discovering a backlog of sixteen thousand kits in 1999. The tested kits have resulted in at least two thousand cold hits (when the DNA profile from the rape kit matched a DNA profile from a separate crime scene or offender in a local, state, or national DNA data bank) and two hundred active investigations, arrests, or prosecutions. Testing the rape kit backlog also exonerated a wrongfully convicted defendant. While the DNA test results identified assailants in stranger rape cases, they also created leads in cases that police and prosecutors were not expecting. For example, prosecutors told me of tying the same assailant to multiple acquaintance rape cases that might otherwise have been difficult to move through the criminal justice system: "We had an assailant who raped drug addicts coming to him to buy drugs. These are women who may be particularly vulnerable to rape because of their addictions or their socioeconomic status, but whose cases are hard to get a jury to believe. But when we could connect the same guy to a number of rapes, we could get a conviction." Since the rape kit testing was completed in 2003, the NYPD has seen its arrest rate for rape increase dramatically, from 40 to 70 percent of reported cases, and there are increased numbers of prosecutions and convictions for rape.

Rape kit testing will not solve all rape cases, but it has the ability to move more of them forward. National studies have shown that cases in which a rape kit was collected, tested, and contained DNA evidence of the offender's contact with a victim were significantly more likely to move forward in the criminal justice system than cases in which there was no rape kit collected

Unclogging the Backlog

In order to clear the rape kit backlog in the United States, and ensure that it never recurs, state and federal rape kit policies need to change. States should require that every rape kit now booked into police evidence that was never sent to the crime lab for testing be counted, inventoried, and then sent on to the crime lab for testing, regardless of how old the case is, whether it was identified by other means, or whether the perpetrator was known to the victim or a stranger.

Once the kits that have been sitting in police storage facilities are shipped to the crime lab, police departments must adopt policies that eliminate detective discretion from the process of rape kit testing by making it mandatory that once a rape kit is booked into police custody and a victim has given permission, the kit is automatically sent to the crime lab. This will ensure that a new backlog doesn't develop once the old one is cleared out.

Crime laboratories will need more personnel and funding if they are to keep up with an increase in rape kits coming to them for testing, and state and federal governments should find money in their coffers to give labs the support they need to do their job.

Above all, states should empower survivors of sexual assault by giving them regular access to information about their kit, and their cases. California has a victim notification statute that requires law enforcement provide information about the status of their rape kit to the victim. While the statute could be stronger, it points in a hopeful direction. Providing victims with information about their rape kits will hold the government accountable to each individual victim.

While progress on rape kit reform has been slow, it is happening. Cities and states are going into their storage facilities and counting their rape kits to assess whether they have a backlog. In 2011, jurisdictions including Dallas, Detroit, Cleveland, and San Antonio publicly acknowledged that they have backlogs—the first step toward fixing the problem. Jurisdictions with backlogs are finding the resources to test their rape kits, and changing their policies to prevent future backlogs. Los Angeles announced this month that their backlog of 12,500 untested kits is nearly eliminated and policies are in place that require that every rape kit submitted to the sheriff's office or the police department be tested. San Francisco passed a citywide law that requires efficient, comprehensive rape kit testing. Cleveland changed its policy to ensure that every rape kit in police storage is sent to the crime lab for testing, and Detroit has established a task force to assess the nature of its backlog and identify sustainable solutions.

The federal government is offering leadership, resources, and research to fix the problem. Congress has introduced several rape kit reform bills that would require stronger funding for and tracking of rape kit evidence. The White House announced a new rape kit backlog pilot project overseen by the National Institute of Justice, which will award three to five applicant jurisdictions grants to come up with a plan to eliminate their rape kit backlog, implement the plan, and research best practices. And a broad coalition of sexual assault, human rights, and criminal justice groups have joined forces to advocate for systemic change.

This amazing change comes too late for the victims like Helena, whose rape kits were collected under policies which kept them hidden and unopened in cold storage facilities long enough for justice to run out. In February 2010, Helena learned that her rape kit had been tested and the DNA profile entered into the DNA data bank (which contains profiles from individual offenders as well as individual crime scenes). Thirteen years after the rape, Helena found out the DNA in her rape kit matched the DNA of a convicted offender in Ohio.

The rapist, Charles Courtney, had been a long-haul truck driver. Less than six weeks after he raped Helena, he raped his wife at knife-point while they were in Indiana. After he was convicted for that crime, he served a short jail sentence and his DNA was entered into the DNA data bank. If Helena's kit had been tested when it was collected in 1996, it would have matched Courtney's offender profile at this point, and he might have been apprehended and held accountable for raping Helena. But her kit wasn't in the system. In 1998, after he was released from prison, he abducted and raped a teenager in Ohio, under circumstances very similar to Helena's case. It took authorities three years to test the Ohio teenager's rape kit but, once they did, it matched Courtney's profile in the database.

When Helena learned about her rape kit test, and the identity of the rapist, she told me, "'That night was the first night I slept through the entire night since the rape. It was the first time that I didn't have a nightmare that the person who raped me wasn't going to find me at home and kill me." Courtney was extradited from his Ohio prison cell to a courtroom in Los Angeles. He is facing kidnapping charges in Helena's case. The statute of limitations for rape in California is ten years, and ran out before he was identified as the man who raped Helena.

I wish the story ended with Courtney facing justice, but it turns out there was one more piece of information about Helena's case that compounds the ways in which our criminal justice system failed her. In early 2011, as Courtney's trial for abducting Helena neared, prosecutors informed Helena that her rape kit was actually tested in 2003, when the Los Angeles Sheriff's Department was doing a small rape kit backlog clean-up project. Helena's kit was selected for testing. The results were entered into the DNA data bank and identified Courtney as her assailant. For reasons no law enforcement official has yet explained to

Helena, it took police and prosecutors seven years to act on this DNA hit in her case. Over the course of those seven years, the statute of limitations for rape ran out.

For seven unnecessary years, Helena lived not knowing whether the rapist was free or not to rape her again.

As a leading rape treatment provider in Los Angeles told me after hearing about Helena's case, and all the missteps along the way, "What other crime would be disregarded in this way?"

CHAPTER 19

Violence Against Immigrant Women in the United States

Meghan Rhoad

"**H**e moves things around in the diaper bag," Elsa M. says, and her eyes anxiously shift from the child on her lap to the bag by the door. "Even this scares me. I get scared about little things like that because I don't know what his intentions are, after everything he has done to us." She is referring to the man who is her husband, the father of her children, and the violent abuser who has filled years of her life with terror. They have recently separated but share child custody, and each time he takes the kids, she is petrified, to the extent that she questions his motives even when he merely shifts the contents of their youngest child's diaper bag. She describes a recent trip to Wal-Mart where she had the feeling of being watched while walking the aisles. She is almost certain a pick-up truck followed her car out of the parking lot.

In many respects, Elsa's experience mirrors that of millions of American women caught in abusive relationships. The subtle manipulations and outright threats of her abuser echo words recounted by

Meghan Road is a researcher in the Women's Rights Division at Human Rights Watch, specializing in violence against women and the US immigration system. She is the author of the reports Detained and at Risk *(2010) and* Detained and Dismissed *(2009), on sexual abuse and insufficient health care in US immigration detention centers. Before joining Human Rights Watch, she served as a women's law and public policy fellow at the National Women's Law Center in Washington DC, and prior to that worked on international advocacy projects on issues such as reproductive health and gender discrimination in inheritance law.*

women of varied backgrounds in any number of domestic violence shelters. But Elsa's abuser had an additional tool for trapping her in a cycle of violence. He held the ultimate trump card: he was a US citizen and Elsa, born in Mexico, lacked authorization to live in the US.

Globally, more than 100 million women live outside the country of their birth, more than double the number in 1960.[1] Migrant women face additional barriers to accessing justice for violence committed against them, whether it happens in their workplaces, on the street, or in their homes. These barriers can include lack of awareness about local laws and procedures, language and cultural differences making it difficult to report violence, geographic isolation from authorities and services (for example with migrant farmworkers), fear of retaliation against family members in their home countries, and discrimination on the part of law enforcement authorities. For those migrant women who lack authorization to live and work in their country of residence, the possibility of deportation can be manipulated by abusers to trap them in violent relationships and ensure their silence.

"Little by little I came to be in a relationship where he had the biggest control over me because of my being illegal. He had total control over me," Elsa says. "He knew I had this fear and he took advantage of that. If I would talk to him and say the relationship was bad and wasn't getting any better, he would remind me of that incident [when I was picked up by immigration authorities before], almost like a threat."

With her immigration status as leverage, Elsa's husband was able to abuse her with impunity for years. When the abuse hit a new high during her last pregnancy and she finally called the police, he received a citation and spent one night in jail. Returning irate and bent on revenge, he made good on his longstanding threat to turn her into immigration authorities if she ever reported the domestic violence. Sitting in her sister's apartment in Nogales, Arizona, in the spring of 2008, Elsa and I were no more than a mile from the border with Mexico where she expected to soon face deportation and separation from her four US-born children.

American immigration policy was not crafted with the intention for it to become an enabler of violence against women like Elsa, but there is little doubt that it now serves that function. The government estimates that 11 million people currently live in the US without authorization and about 43 percent, or 4.6 million, are women. Whether their immigration status is referred to as undocumented, illegal, or unauthorized, these women possess the same human rights as anyone else—in particular the right to freedom from violence, and equality before the law. However, under current US immigration law and policy, undocumented migrant women face escalated threats to those fundamental rights because of their status.

Some migrant women, like Elsa, are caught between two bad choices: reporting abuse and exposing their precarious immigration status, or avoiding deportation while living in communities around the country and risking further ill treatment. Some experience violence along the Mexican border, where the journey into the US has become increasingly perilous. Others encounter violence while in the custody of immigration authorities. As discussed here, these are three distinct problems, but the different policies, practices, and programs linked to each reflect a common prioritization of immigration law enforcement over the protection of women's safety. Too often they fail at both.

Justice Within Reach?

For a decade and a half, women's rights advocates have pushed policymakers to ensure that women are not forced to make the impossible choice between reporting crimes and avoiding deportation. Fortunately, Congress has taken some steps to address this. In the landmark Violence Against Women Act of 1994, Congress created a process by which battered spouses of US citizens and legal permanent residents could apply for permanent residency without the approval of their abusive spouses. Then in 2000, Congress established two visas that provide a path to permanent residency for migrants who assist in the investigation or prosecution of criminal activity: the T-visa for trafficking victims and the U-visa for victims of crime, including domestic violence and sexual assault.

These avenues for immigration have the potential to put justice within reach of many women who would otherwise suffer in silence. But these solutions are neither perfect nor sufficient. Not every woman who has experienced abuse meets the eligibility criteria. U-visas, which only became available in 2008 after years of delays in developing the regulations to implement the 2000 law, are capped at ten thousand per year despite the fact that they cover a wide range of crime victims. To be eligible, a victim must have a certification from law enforcement indicating her cooperation with the investigation or prosecution. This helps law enforcement acquire important information that they need to bring criminals to justice and ensure general public safety. It also acts as a barrier to false claims. However, real victims may face difficulties because police departments and prosecutors vary widely in their approach to providing certification, which is completely at their discretion. Further, limited awareness of the mechanism among both victims and law enforcement officers is a problem that, while slowly being addressed, severely undermines the visa's impact.

Apart from the visas' technical issues, immigrant women face a much larger obstacle to accessing justice. In the United States, immigration is a matter handled by the federal government. However, there is a growing trend of involving local law enforcement agencies in federal immigration law matters. This trend has taken a number of forms, from programs by which the federal government effectively deputizes local police officers to carry out federal immigration functions to state legislative initiatives, like Arizona's Senate Bill 1070, which assert a state right to assume those functions when dissatisfied with the federal government's handling of them. The result has been to remove the distinction between the authorities that would protect undocumented immigrant women from violence with the authorities that would deport them.

One such development is the rapidly expanding Secure Communities Program (SComm) operated by federal immigration authorities in over thirteen hundred local law enforcement jurisdictions around the country. The program, which is to be implemented nationwide by 2013, purports to target dangerous criminal offenders for deportation by running the fingerprints of anyone arrested by local police against a federal immigration database. However, records of the program's operation show that 79 percent of people deported through the program were nonviolent and low-level offenders. Moreover, observers have raised concerns about whether the program in practice contributes to racial profiling, leads to pretextual arrests for minor violations in order to check immigration status, and alienates immigrant communities from police departments, thereby undermining public safety as a whole. These types of concerns motivated the states of Illinois, New York, and Massachusetts to announce that they would not participate in the program—an option the federal government says they do not have.

The debate over SComm has brought to the surface the issue at stake for women in many of the federal and state initiatives to blend immigration functions with community policing. In a report on her January 2011 visit to the United States, the United Nations Special Rapporteur on Violence Against Women, Rashida Manjoo, specifically addressed SComm, concluding that "such initiatives make immigrant women more vulnerable to abuse, as attempts to stand up for their rights are countered by threats to report them to immigration."[2] Michael Hennessy, head of the police in San Francisco for more than thirty years and a vocal opponent of the program, has seen this happen in his jurisdiction. In a May 2011 op-ed in the *San Francisco Chronicle* he wrote, "In a recent case in San Francisco, a woman called 911 to report domestic violence, but the police arrested both her and her partner. Although no charges were ever filed against the woman, she is now fighting deportation. There should be no penalty for a victim of a crime to call the police."[3]

On the Border

Nowhere in the US is the subordination of migrants' safety—particularly migrant women's safety—in immigration enforcement policies more stark than on the border with Mexico. Just outside of where I sat talking to Elsa M. in Nogales, the borderline dividing Arizona from the Mexican state Sonora sees the largest flow of undocumented migration along the border. Those who make the crossing face a multitude of perils, including injuries from crossing rough terrain;

heatstroke, disorientation, and even death from days of walking under the desert sun. They also face robbery, kidnapping, and beatings by their smugglers or the bandits who roam the border areas, and harassment and abuse by Border Patrol or anti-immigrant vigilante groups. For women and girl migrants in particular—although not exclusively—the crossing also carries the risk of sexual assault.

The visibility of sexual violence has grown with an increasingly militarized environment on the border over the last decade and a half. The number of agents patrolling the border doubled between 2002 and 2009, the border wall has expanded to cover large portions of the almost two-thousand-mile southwestern border, and ever more sophisticated technology is used to detect unauthorized crossings. In directing resources, the government targeted the easier passage points with the expectation that the terrain and dangers in the remaining areas—many in Arizona—would be deterrent enough. Doris Meissner, a federal immigration official during the Clinton administration, told the *Arizona Republic* in 2000, "We did believe that geography would be an ally to us. . . . It was our sense that the number of people crossing the border through Arizona would go down to a trickle, once people realized what it's like."[4]

That expectation has not borne out. Even when the risks of crossing could not be higher, they are often eclipsed by the incentives that make migrants willing to brave various dangers in successive attempts to cross the border. The draw varies for each person, but for many it is primarily the chance to find a job that can feed a struggling family back home. Sometimes it is to escape a violent relationship. More and more frequently, as the US increases the number of deportations of longtime residents, it is the drive to reunite with children left behind in the US.

However, redirecting the flow of cross-border migration into areas that entail the assistance of smugglers, longer treks through difficult terrain, and sometimes routes dominated by drug-runners, has had a largely negative—even fatal—impact. Between 1995 and 2005, the number of border-crossing deaths doubled. One study of crossing-related deaths found that women were 2.7 times more likely to die during the journey than men.[5]

In remote parts of the desert, hikers find so-called rape trees where women's underwear has been strewn across branches, reportedly by perpetrators marking the site of sexual assaults. A woman interviewed by Human Rights Watch in April 2011 described the dangers she and her companions faced during their crossing:

> The smugglers have us locked in for three to four days inside a house, on the floor, like animals, then they take us to another house with no light, nor food, nothing, then they tell us that we are going to walk for one night. We buy a little food and then, once inside the desert, they tell us that we still have to walk for four nights. Women start to faint and fall, and guides do not say anything. They use drugs during the crossing, they are very rude, they tell those who fall to "fuck their mothers," they leave them there, they don't get them up. . . . We continued, and at night, the "coyotes" [smugglers] wanted to rape [two] young women, thirteen and eighteen years, but we didn't leave their side and they did not do it in the end.[6]

Statistics are lacking on how often women migrants are raped during the crossing, but organizations working with migrants report that it is not uncommon, and when it happens, it is most often attributed to the smugglers taking the women across, including some who were high on drugs at the time, or to bandits that prey on migrants. In a few reported cases, US Border Patrol agents have been accused of assault.

While international law grants governments wide latitude in controlling their borders, human rights obligations, including the duty to respond to violence against women, exist in parallel. In a May 2011 address, United Nations High Commissioner for Human Rights Navi Pillay urged countries to "look at the real need for migrant labor emanating from their economies and societies, and ensure that they put in place adequate, safe, and legal means for migrants to enter and work in their countries. This could reduce the necessity of risky irregular movement, particularly those facilitated by smugglers and traffickers."[7]

Addressing the accessibility of legal immigration options is of tremendous importance for alleviating the human suffering that is rife along the border. Even short of a comprehensive overhaul of the immigration system, there is much that can be done to address women's safety. Border Patrol and other agencies operating in these areas should be better trained and equipped to identify victims of sexual violence and provide them with access to medical care, legal services, and information about U-visas when victims are willing to cooperate with law enforcement in the investigation of the crime. The agencies should analyze their practices, including the timing and manner of deportations, to ensure they do not increase the risks to migrants' safety. They should also implement adequate oversight measures to prevent abuse of migrants by their own officers.

Abuse in Custody

In May 2010, reports surfaced in the Associated Press that the federal Immigration and Customs Enforcement agency was investigating allegations that a guard at the T. Don Hutto Residential Center, an immigration detention center in Texas, had sexually assaulted several female detainees.[8] The guard allegedly groped women while transporting them to an airport and a bus station where they were being released. While largely covered in the media as an isolated incident, this is only the latest in a series of assaults, abuses, and episodes of harassment that have quietly emerged in scattered media reports, court filings, and nongovernmental studies across the rapidly expanding national immigration detention system.

Because of a shortage of publicly available data and the closed nature of the detention system, the extent to which immigration detainees are subject to sexual abuse nationwide is unclear, but the known incidents and allegations are too serious and too numerous to ignore. In California, a transgender detainee accused a guard of forcing her to perform oral sex on him while she was detained in 2003.[9] In Florida in 2007, a woman reported that an officer charged with transporting a woman took her to his house and raped her.[10] He was ultimately sentenced to serve seven years in prison for sexual abuse.[11] At another facility in Texas, five women were assaulted in 2008 when a guard entered each of their rooms in the detention center infirmary, where they were patients, told them that he was operating under physician instructions, ordered them to undress, and touched intimate parts of their bodies. In April 2010, he was sentenced to three years in prison to be followed by community supervision for the assaults.[12]

The issue of abuse in custody has gained urgency as immigration detention has become the fastest growing form of incarceration in the United States. Federal immigration authorities detained more than 350,000 immigrants during their deportation proceedings in 2010, and women make up roughly 9 percent of the average daily detention population. They include asylum seekers, victims of trafficking, survivors of sexual assault and domestic violence, pregnant women, and nursing mothers. In addition to reports of sexual assault, the detention system has been plagued by reports of life-threatening failures to provide medical treatment. Yet time after time, the government has chosen to expand detention operations when alternatives to detention—for example, releasing immigrants from custody but requiring that they check in regularly while their cases proceed—have proven effective and cost-efficient.

While detention has ballooned, the federal government has persistently avoided instituting effective accountability mechanisms for human rights abuses committed in detention. This failure has been particularly striking in the area of sexual abuse and harassment. The US Congress enacted the Prison Rape Elimination Act in 2003 to require the government to develop rules to prevent rape of people in custody. While the rules will eventually cover prisons and jails nationwide, the government has maintained that the rules should not apply to immigration detention, despite expert recommendations to the contrary and evidence that Congress intended the law to cover immigration detention centers. Consequently, immigrant women held for administrative immigration proceedings could be left out of protections against sexual assault that will apply to prisoners convicted of criminal offenses.

Months before we spoke at her home in Nogales, Elsa was being held in an immigration detention facility in central Arizona when her husband came to visit her. She had to wear a prison uniform, including an uncomfortable bra that aggravated the intense pain she felt from being made to abruptly stop nursing. Her husband, on the other hand, whom she had reported to the police for domestic violence, was apparently savoring his success in getting her detained and on the path toward deportation. He had promised she would pay for the night he spent in jail and now she was paying. It had taken two attempts. The first time, when she was due to give birth in ten days, US Immigration and Customs Enforcement (ICE) declined to detain her. But three months later, he got his way. Now, sitting across from her at the detention center, new baby in tow, he told her that he was watching her every move. He said he had friends among the guards at the detention center who passed him surveillance tapes so he could watch her. Although almost certainly a lie, it seemed plausible enough at the time to Elsa, from a husband who had friends in law enforcement and who had already shown he could get ICE officers to do his bidding by arresting her. Message delivered, he left Elsa to ruminate behind bars, while he headed out to go on about his day.

Elsa's abusive and vindictive husband could not have scripted this scene better. And he could not have done it without US immigration policy. The good news is that this was not the final outcome. Ultimately, US immigration policy came through for Elsa. She was granted permission to stay in the US pursuant to the Violence Against Women Act, but only after years of suffering abuse, then detention, then painful uncertainty when her complex immigration case was being litigated. Her experience stands for the proposition that the US can and should do better.

Women's safety need not be a casualty of immigration law enforcement. What is needed is for policymakers in the US and other migrant-receiving countries to take a hard look at the impact their current immigration policy is having on violence against migrant women.

Indeed, lessons learned in the US could be applied in Europe and on other continents struggling with similar issues. In 2009, the Parliamentary Assembly of the Council of Europe called for member states to "do everything in their power to ensure that all women, including migrant women, living within their territories have access in law and in practice to the relevant victim protection and rehabilitation facilities." The Assembly added that no "cultural relativism" may be invoked to justify practices that infringe the rights of migrant women.[13] The International Organization for Migration has highlighted the issue of violence against migrant women in countries like South Africa, where Congolese women and others who sought to flee brutal conditions in their own countries often find themselves "vulnerable to robbery, rape and abuse."[14]

Common sense measures can be taken to protect women's safety that will not defeat immigration law enforcement efforts. Limiting the involvement of local law enforcement in immigration matters can encourage women to report crimes to their local police. Assessing the dangers to migrants posed by border security programs can lead to more strategic enforcement efforts that minimize human suffering. Making sure that immigration authorities are properly monitored will go far toward preventing and detecting a range of abuses.

These steps begin with one central premise: that a government's responsibility for managing immigration coexists with, rather than trumps, the responsibility to address violence against women.

CHAPTER 20

Behind Closed Doors
Domestic Violence in Europe

Gauri van Gulik

Born in southeastern Turkey, Selvi was twenty-two years old and pregnant with her fifth child when I met her in June 2010, while conducting research for a report on domestic violence. Her husband started his attacks when she was pregnant with their first child. "That first time, he hit me, he kicked the baby in my belly, and he threw me off the roof," she said. "The baby survived but I think [the child] has a mental illness." The violence increased in frequency and severity, and by the time I met Selvi, even included their children.

Selvi's husband controlled every aspect of her life and was extremely jealous. She told me: "He rapes me all the time, and he checks my fluids 'down there' to check I didn't have sex [with another man]." In 2008 Selvi finally built up the courage to go to the police, after her husband had "broken her skull and arm." The police brought her husband to the station, gave the couple some food, and sent them home, telling her, "There's no problem, we spoke to him, you're back together." This happened three more times, the violence worsening after every attempt to escape.

Gauri van Gulik is a researcher and advocate for the Women's Rights Division at Human Rights Watch, covering Europe and Central Asia. Her fields of expertise include reproductive health and issues affecting women migrants. She is the author of the 2010 Human Rights Watch report Fast-Tracked Unfairness, on the obstacles faced by many abused women seeking asylum in the United Kingdom, and the 2011 report "He Loves You, He Beats You" on domestic violence in Turkey.

The abuse was continuing when I spoke to Selvi in June 2010, during a heart-wrenching interview in a small community center. Her husband gambles, rarely works, and frequently abuses her and the children. She was too afraid to send the children to a government dormitory. Indeed, she had simply given up on escaping the life-threatening violence. "I just cannot go to the police anymore," she said.

Selvi's story represents everything that can go horribly wrong when domestic violence is not taken seriously.

Widespread Violence in Europe

Selvi is not the only woman suffering this abuse, and Turkey is not the only country battling it. Domestic violence is a worldwide epidemic, and the European continent is no exception. This violence affects people of both genders, but the vast majority of domestic violence is still endured by women. Children also suffer horrible violence and the effects of children having to witness violence between parents or other trusted grownups are long lasting.

Women throughout Europe are slapped, kicked, beaten, locked up, sexually and psychologically abused, genitally mutilated, raped, forced to work, and killed by men in their immediate social environment. According to the limited statistics available, at least one woman in every five in Europe has been subjected to physical violence at least once in her lifetime, and it is safe to assume this is merely the tip of the iceberg.

Across the continent of Europe, such violations of fundamental human rights affect millions of women. The inescapable conclusion is that violence within the family or household is the most widespread and serious human rights abuse women face in the region. And these women usually suffer in silence, as the majority of women never speak about their experiences.

What sets countries apart is not the occurrence of violence, but what the government does—or does not do—to protect women against it.

It is exceedingly difficult for women to reach out for help when their husbands or partners beat them. Obstacles range from the internal psychological battles of guilt and fear to external roadblocks along the way to protection. It starts with the family, and the pressure to keep things as they are. This may be explicit, to keep the family's honor intact, as I saw in some places in Turkey. But it is often more subtle with a similar effect. Pressure takes the form of statements like "It's better for the children," or "He takes care of you," or "We all went through it; you have to be humble."

There can also be economic pressure. In The Netherlands, a woman explained how hard it is to leave an abusive spouse, especially when you have children. Bianca told me, "Even though we might be able to get support from the state eventually, I didn't make enough money to get a house for us. . . . Things had to get very bad before I dared to uproot the family." In the Turkish capital Ankara, Deniz told me, "There was no way I could support myself and the baby. When I told my family that [my husband] was crazy, that he beat me and had even used a stun gun on me, they refused to support me and said, 'You have a baby, just bury it [the suffering], he's your husband.' I had no place to go and no way to get work. I was trapped."

Passive Authorities

When a woman does decide to escape, she often runs into disbelief, a lack of protection by the police, a lack of shelter, and a lack of access to justice. Even though eliminating domestic violence has been an international legal obligation for decades, government authorities still do not take this problem seriously in many countries.

What happens when a woman goes to the police to ask for help? Does she have anywhere to live if she leaves her abusive spouse? Will a prosecutor open a case against her abuser, if so she will have access to justice? Incredibly, after decades of incremental progress, the answer to those questions is still no in many countries. The refusal to deal with domestic violence cases seriously, or in other words, without due diligence, is a human rights violation. The person who commits violence against a woman has committed a crime. A government that does not adopt, fund and implement all necessary laws and actions to prevent and to punish this violence violates international human rights law.

In Turkey, a prosecutor stressed to me the importance of the family unit: "It's better not to get involved. We might save a woman, but destroy a family." In Belgium, social workers told us of reluctant police officers who cannot arrest perpetrators of domestic violence who still form a real threat, because "the prisons are full." When a colleague and I spoke with Aisha, a woman living in Belgium, she spoke of her fear and desperation because of this lack of action by the police. She suffered twenty-six long years of daily abuse and violence resulting in broken bones, burns, and awful panic attacks. When her husband almost killed their daughter after beating her and running after her with a knife, she decided she had to take action. She went to the police three times in total. Even though the police did take her complaint seriously, the husband was not removed from the house (there are no emergency protection orders in Belgium) and the police did not arrest him because of "lack of prison cells." "I don't know who to trust anymore," Aisha told us. "Maybe my nightmares will go away, but I am still frightened of him. Aren't twenty-six years enough?"

The attitude of officials is sometimes even worse if a woman fleeing domestic violence escapes not only from her house, but from her country as well, or has moved to another country to live with her husband.

I met Masha in Istanbul when she was still visibly suffering the physical consequences of her husband's beatings. Masha was born in the Ukraine, and she had a visa because she married a Turkish husband. He threatened to divorce her if she complained to officials, as divorce would mean she would have to leave the country. Masha is an educated nurse and she was brave enough to go to the police in a hospital despite the risks. She was met with hostility and a cold "Please bother the police in Ukraine with this, we have nothing to do with you."

One woman, Fatma, who moved to Belgium to join her husband, was beaten and forced to beg by him, a dangerous drug addict. She told us: "Every day, he beat, kicked, and threatened me. I was scared to go to the police. . . . When I finally went the police just said they contacted him but couldn't reach him. Now I don't know where he is and I am terrified." On top of that, Fatma might be removed from the country because her residence permit is linked to her husband and she no longer lives with him.

Besides the obvious fear of police that many women without official documentation have, other services available to citizens or official residents of a country may be out of reach for non-citizens. My colleagues and I saw shelters in countries throughout the region, including in The Netherlands, Belgium, and Turkey, turn battered women away because they did not have a residence permit. So at their most vulnerable moment, non-citizen women are refused, even by some nongovernmental shelters, if they do not have documentation.

New Tools to Fight Violence and Injustice

At least at the regional level, there have been some important developments and countries have come to the realization that the epidemic of domestic violence can and should be stopped, and that countries can learn from each other's best practices. Both the European Court of Human Rights and the Council of Europe, the forty-seven-country regional human rights body of which it is part, have given informed, detailed, and practical guidance to governments on what their duties are and how they could fulfill these.

In 2009, the European Court of Human Rights gave judgment in a landmark case, *Opuz v. Turkey*, which directly addressed the failure of the Turkish state to take reasonable measures to prevent domestic violence perpetrated against the applicant, Nahide Opuz, and the murder of her mother.

Much like many of the cases we would later document in Turkey, Nahide Opuz had suffered years of brutal domestic violence at the hands of her husband, including stabbings, beatings, and death threats. For four years from 1995 onward, Nahide and her mother requested protection from the police and a prosecutor, claiming their lives were at risk. After one complaint, authorities questioned and then released the husband. Despite numerous complaints, the police and prosecuting authorities did not adequately protect the women: Nahide's husband murdered her mother in 2002.

The European Court of Human Rights held that Turkey had failed to fulfill its obligations to protect the right to life of Nahide's mother and that it was in breach of the right not to be subject to torture or cruel, inhuman, or degrading treatment for its failure to protect the applicant against ill treatment perpetrated by her former husband. It also held that Turkey was in violation of the right to nondiscrimination, confirming that domestic violence is a form of discrimination against women.

This judgment constitutes the first time the court has elaborated the exact nature of state obligations under the European Convention on Human Rights with respect to violence in the family and the first time it has explicitly confirmed that gender-based violence is a form of discrimination under the Convention. Relying heavily on international and comparative law, the court emphasized what activists have long known: that domestic violence is not a private or family matter, but an issue of public interest that demands effective state action.

Two years later, in May 2011, the Council of Europe adopted the Convention on Preventing and Combating Violence against Women and Domestic Violence. This historic convention has the potential to improve the lives of women and other victims in forty-seven member states and other countries, with a total of some 800 million citizens. The convention defines and criminalizes various forms of violence against women, including forced marriage, female genital mutilation, and stalking, as well as physical, sexual and psychological violence. The Convention obliges states to create innovative mechanisms, particularly a range of protective measures including evicting violent spouses, lifting professional secrecy under certain conditions, establishing free twenty-four-hour telephone hotlines, and taking gender into account in the examination of asylum requests. It truly raises the bar.

Negotiations for this landmark treaty were not easy. Countries resisted several parts of the text, especially in the field of asylum and immigration. But after years of negotiating, the text of the convention is now open for ratification. Women's rights groups, lawyers and other human rights defenders from Albania to the United Kingdom have already started using it to push their governments to improve legislation and, more important, the practical protection of women against violence. Countries are signing up not just to a piece of text, but to a set of clear measures they will have to take and be held to account for.

What we have learned is that it all comes down to implementation. In recent years Turkey for example has taken important legislative steps toward addressing violence against women. But despite these impressive legal advances including penal code reforms and a protection order system, remaining gaps in the law and failures of implementation make the protection system unpredictable at best, and at times downright dangerous. The legislative process is undermined by the government's failure to better prevent abuse in the first place, change discriminatory attitudes, and effectively address the barriers that deter women and girls from reporting abuse and accessing protection. Countries should learn this lesson before it costs even more lives.

It is time for a swift advance toward better safeguards in Europe, and other continents, for women seeking to flee domestic violence.

A sense of urgency throughout the system, from top to bottom, in every country would mean budgets expressly dedicated to combating domestic violence, making an effective response part of the official police curriculum, and improving women's empowerment and participation in the workforce. Above all, it means accountability for failing to protect women. It is what we owe to Selvi, Deniz, Bianca, Aisha, and the countless abused women whose names we may never even know.

PART 6
WOMEN AND HEALTH

CHAPTER 21

Maternal Mortality
Ending Needless Deaths in Childbirth

Aruna Kashyap

I will never forget the grief etched on Suraj's face. It was in February 2009, and I was interviewing the middle-aged laborer in the Indian state of Uttar Pradesh, doing research for No Tally of the Anguish, a Human Rights Watch report on maternal deaths in India. In a quiet voice, Suraj recounted the death of his daughter Kavita, soon after she gave birth:

> We took her to the community health center and they said, "We cannot look at this here." So we took her to [the hospital in] Hydergad. From Hydergad to Balrampur, and from there to Lucknow—all government hospitals. From Wednesday to Sunday—for five days—we took her from one hospital to another. No one wanted to admit her. In Lucknow they admitted her and started treatment. They treated her for about an hour, and then she died.

Sadly, the pain I saw on Suraj's face is far too common in India, and

Aruna Kashyap, a Mumbai-based researcher for the Women's Rights Division at Human Rights Watch, is the author of the 2009 report No Tally of the Anguish: Accountability in Maternal Health Care in India. *She previously provided legal aid with the India Centre for Human Rights Law, where her work included assisting victims of sexual violence or abuse, and juveniles in conflict with the law.*

Kavita's case is not isolated one—neither in India, nor in many other parts of the world.

Childbirth should evoke images of joy and celebration, not death or disability. Yet, every year, more than 350,000 women and girls die because of pregnancy, childbirth, and unsafe abortions. A majority—as many as three-fourths of such deaths—are preventable. Many more women are disabled or injured from childbirth. Between 50,000 and 100,000 new incidents of obstetric fistula (tissue damage between the vagina and the bladder or rectum leading to incontinence) are detected annually. Other long-term consequences include uterine prolapse (weakened muscles after childbirth leading to displacement of the uterus), infertility, and depression; short-term complications include hemorrhage, convulsions, cervical tears, shock, and fever.

These preventable deaths and disabilities are a disheartening reminder of the disparities in access to quality health care. Nearly 99 percent of all preventable maternal deaths and disabilities occur in sub-Saharan Africa and South Asia. According to the latest global estimates for 2008, Afghanistan, Bangladesh, India, Indonesia, Pakistan, the Democratic Republic of Congo, Ethiopia, Kenya, Nigeria, Sudan, and Tanzania together accounted for 65 percent of the world's maternal deaths.[1]

Much research has already been done into the causes of maternal deaths and injuries. Globally, approximately 80 percent of all maternal deaths are thought to be caused by hemorrhage, sepsis (severe infection spreading through the bloodstream), eclampsia (pregnancy complication characterized by seizures or coma), unsafe abortions, and prolonged or obstructed labor. Other indirect causes include malaria, tuberculosis, and HIV/AIDS. In countries with high rates of HIV, malaria, or tuberculosis, the proportion of deaths due to such causes may be higher.

A Tragic End to a Complex Story

But understanding the medical causes is only a part of the story. Typically, a maternal death marks the tragic end to a complex story with a variety of medical, socioeconomic, and cultural elements. Contributing factors include early marriage, women's inability to get access to and use contraceptives of their choice, and husbands or mothers-in-law dictating how women may seek care. Other contributing factors include poor nutrition, poverty, lack of health education and awareness and domestic violence. The risk of maternal mortality is also compounded by health system-related issues such as poor access to affordable quality health care, including basic and comprehensive emergency obstetric services, lack of emergency transportation, and effective referral services.

The truth is that the world has known for a long time how to prevent deaths and disabilities resulting from childbirth. Maternal mortality and morbidity could have been eliminated with genuine political will, adequate resources, and strong monitoring to rectify shortcomings in health care systems. Instead, governments often choose to engage in politics around numbers, disputing the minutiae of how many women die or are injured, rather than tackling the real barriers that pregnant women face when they seek care. Governments spend a lot of time debating whether the estimated maternal mortality ratio (the number of maternal deaths in every hundred thousand live births) is accurate or whether the countries' own estimates are better suited methodologically than global estimates jointly provided by WHO, UNICEF, UNFPA, and the World Bank.

While estimates and statistics are important, they do not expose the obstacle courses that women like Kavita must navigate on their way to seeking medical care. Take India as an example: information collected by the government seems to show that the maternal mortality ratio has been on a steady decline. Debates rage about whether India is "on track" to meeting the UN Millennium Development Goals (MDG) on eliminating preventable maternal mortality, which mandates a 75 percent reduction in its maternal death rates between 1990 and 2015. The 2010 WHO report says India is not "on track," but the Indian government disputes these claims.

Much energy has been spent on these arguments. But these declines, whether or not they are accurate, fail to tell us how pregnant women like Kavita have to beg desperately for access at the hospital gate or how many women die at home, unable even to make the trip to a hospital. In their anxiety to report fewer deaths, many officials do not record maternal deaths at all. As I traveled around in Uttar Pradesh state, I heard numerous horrific accounts of such incidents, only to find that the district health records reported "zero deaths."

And yet India also has some of the strongest examples of how maternal deaths can be tackled effectively. While Kavita's death showed how hospitals in Uttar Pradesh are ill equipped and transfer patients from one place to another uselessly, Tamil Nadu state has resolved the same problem with an innovative solution. Tamil Nadu state has been investigating maternal deaths at the district level since 1996, analyzing patterns that emerge from a series of maternal death investigations and brainstorming to arrive at workable, practical solutions that can be implemented.

Auditing Deaths in Childbirth

Like their colleagues in Uttar Pradesh, officials in Tamil Nadu state too found that women were being shunted around from one hospital to another. They also found that pregnant women and their families often got scared that they wouldn't be able to afford the cost when they were referred to another hospital.

Through a series of maternal death investigations, Tamil Nadu district health officials discovered that families that were asked to take a pregnant woman to a larger hospital equipped to handle her case did a simple, heartbreaking calculation: Was it more expensive to transport a dead body back to their village for cremation or to take her home and seek affordable care there? Could they haggle effectively with nurses and staff at the larger hospital to get admission or was it simpler to turn around and return to their village? To make families feel less anxious and to ensure that women who were referred were immediately admitted and provided emergency care if needed, the district health officials instituted the system of "accompanied transfer." A nurse from the referring hospital would accompany the pregnant woman and her family to the next hospital and ensure that she was admitted and received medical care.

Similarly, district health officials in Tamil Nadu found that there was a lack of communication and organization between hospitals to provide emergency care. So district health officers started advertising their mobile numbers to all families, nurses and doctors to provide emergency support. That effort was then expanded into a control-room service, which coordinated services among anesthetists, surgeons, blood banks, and so on.

When district health officials learned that they had a severe shortage of blood for transfusions when pregnant women were hemorrhaging as well as a shortage of trained staff, they started blood donation camps and trained all nurses and doctors to provide blood transfusions—with the result that every hospital had a minimum of five bottles of blood in all blood groups at any given time, and also trained staff available around the clock.

These measures sound simple. But such decisions need strong political will. At the time Tamil Nadu health officials decided to conduct maternal death audits (as it is known in medical parlance), the health administration decided to challenge notions of "higher success" by reporting "fewer deaths." They braved criticism to protect staff nurses and doctors, encouraging them to report maternal deaths instead of hiding the causes. They refused the practice of appeasing public sentiment by suspending or transferring frontline health staff, and instead thoroughly investigated staff access to training and support. They accepted "command responsibility" where policy or programmatic decisions needed to be changed.

Maternal death audit reports did not sit on the shelves gathering dust in Tamil Nadu. Officers actually read them, discussed them in platforms where families were invited, decide to change what was going wrong and implemented those decisions. They demanded explanations from private hospitals that contributed to a maternal death. They conducted awareness drives in villages, dispelling the myth that a maternal death was "fate." The entire health system was galvanized to root out maternal deaths and today Tamil Nadu state has one of the lowest maternal death rates in the country. The Tamil Nadu experience shows that maternal death investigations, if conducted properly, can be a powerful tool to analyze and correct health system failures and gaps to avert maternal deaths.

Solving Women's Grievances

Talking to families of pregnant women or mothers who have died is critical, but health authorities need not wait until women die to understand the struggles women endure. Many pregnant women or mothers who have delivered in health facilities have useful information to share with health authorities that will help them change systems to address their needs. Some women I interviewed were horrified by their childbirth experiences in public health facilities. Many had very little information in advance about what to expect.

A woman named Hina told me about her treatment at the primary care center where she went to give birth. It was during the biting cold of a December winter in Uttar Pradesh. The center has only two beds, so most women were laid out on the floor. But the women had not been warned that they had to provide their own sheets or covers. Hina and several other women ended up giving birth on the cold hard floor of the labor room. A nurse gave Hina a brick to support her back during childbirth. Her past two deliveries had been in the comfort and warmth of her home. Her experience in the public health facility convinced her and her neighbors never to visit a public health facility for childbirth again.

Others also complained about illegal user fees charged in health facilities for services that are supposed to be free. One man with limited financial resources was forced to sell ten kilos of wheat to pay bribes to health workers for his wife's childbirth. There were different rates for boy and girl babies, given the high preference for sons in these areas.

These are not insurmountable problems. But what is lacking is a system equipped to pay attention to such problems and resolve them. One way of tapping into such information is with appropriate and accessible grievance redress mechanisms for women to share their experiences and to use the information to seek remedies. Contrary to popular belief, most health workers are not opposed to such grievance redress mechanisms, and many actually support these systems. They recognize that in many instances, the absence of such mechanisms contributes to the pressures they face.

Distraught families often express their anger at the lack of proper care for pregnant women in health centers or hospitals by organizing protests. Sometimes, in the event of a death, those protests can be hostile. What is needed is an urgent effort to reform and provide redress. But the state usually chooses aggression instead, responding with hostility even to peaceful protests.

For example, in December 2010 when tribal women organized a peaceful protest against a spate of maternal deaths in a government hospital in a predominantly tribal region of Madhya Pradesh state in central India, many were arrested, leading to further discontent in the community. Health workers are often the visible targets in such incidents, accused of neglect when they may not have had the resources to do what was needed. Many health workers I interviewed felt that there needed to be a system where pregnant women and their families could share their problems and find sustainable and effective remedies. Yet nothing meaningful is done to set up proper grievance redress mechanisms.

Token measures like complaint boxes in health centers and hospitals are seldom used, and when women have used them the help of local activists, the complaints sat unanswered. Formal institutions such as courts and human rights commissions are inaccessible and their procedures lengthy, fraught with procedural difficulties, and seldom provide avenues that resolve pregnant women's problems. Time and again, civil society groups as well as the UN Special Rapporteur on the right to health has stated that special ombudsman systems should be set up to deal effectively with grievances that pregnant women report.

Through the Millennium Declaration, 189 countries pledged to achieve eight development goals by 2015, including a 75 percent reduction in maternal mortality. In 2009, in a special session of the UN Human Rights Council, governments committed to adopting a human rights approach to preventable maternal mortality and morbidity. In September 2010, the UN secretary-general announced a separate Global Strategy for Women's and Children's Health as well as a global mechanism to monitor countries' progress under the strategy.

"Monitoring progress" has become a mantra for eliminating unnecessary maternal deaths. But monitoring should not be reduced to statistical calculations without empowering women, families and communities to tell of their experiences and grievances, and how to learn from them. The key to combating death in childbirth is investing in a way that amplifies the voices of women and girls—through thorough investigations of preventable deaths—and effective and accessible grievance redress mechanisms.

THE
UNFINISHED
REVOLUTION

IN IMAGES

EGYPT'S ARAB SPRING

Photographs by Platon for Human Rights Watch

In April 2011, Human Rights Watch commissioned the international portrait photographer Platon to shoot portraits of the Egyptian human rights campaigners, social media activists, women's rights organizers, torture victims, and heroes of the Tahrir Square movement that brought an end to Hosni Mubarak's thirty years of repressive rule—and helped inspire similar movements for human rights across the Middle East and beyond. Among the subjects of Platon's portraits are the brave women's rights activists shown here.

As Minky Worden writes in her introduction, the Arab Spring is a reminder that the movement for women's rights that has changed lives in some parts of the world has not yet become a truly global revolution. In the Middle East and elsewhere, political revolutions alone are not enough to secure fundamental rights for women and girls.

Veteran Women's Rights Advocates From left to right:

Azza Soliman, 45
Director of the Center for Egyptian Women's Legal Assistance. She has taken a leading role in advocacy aimed at amending pernicious laws in Egypt and other Arab countries that discriminate against women.

Amal Abdel Hadi, 63
Author of several books and an Egyptian physician who has worked extensively on issues related to sexual violence, particularly female genital mutilation in Egypt. She is a board member of the New Woman Foundation, one of the few NGOs in Egypt to break the silence on issues of violence against women.

Nawla Darwiche, 62
A women's rights leader and founding member of the New Woman Foundation.

Above:
Sarrah Abdel Rahman, 23, is a social media activist whose popular "sarrahsworld" YouTube commentaries report from Tahrir Square. She aspires to be a television producer/journalist.

Left:
Dr. Nawal El Saadawi, 80, is an Egyptian writer, veteran women's rights advocate, psychiatrist, and author of more than forty fiction and nonfiction books, many of which address the persecution of Arab women. In 1981 she was imprisoned after being charged with "political offenses." In 1982, she founded the Arab Women's Solidarity Association. One of the earliest to report on the taboo topic of female genital mutilation, Dr. El Saadawi's decades-long struggle for women's rights and against FGM helped pave the way for the adoption of a historic 2008 law that banned the practice in Egypt.

FEMALE GENITAL MUTILATION
IN IRAQI KURDISTAN

Photographs by Samer Muscati/Human Rights Watch

One day when Dashty (right) was 12, her mother told her to expect company. Anticipating friends, Dashty was shocked when she saw the midwife enter the house. After Dashty resisted, her mother beat her as other women held her down. She said she spent twenty days recovering in bed from the traumatic operation. "Since that day, my personality has changed and I'm depressed," says Dashty, now in her thirties, who lives close to her sister Sara (left), in their village of Meer Ghasem. "I've lost my love for this world because of what happened at the hands of people I trusted." © 2009 Samer Muscati/Human Rights Watch

A significant number of girls and women in Iraqi Kurdistan suffer female genital mutilation (FGM) and its destructive aftereffects, as described by Nadya Khalife in her chapter. This harmful traditional practice is still prevalent in many other countries, primarily in the Middle East and in Africa. The World Health Organization estimates that between 100 million and 140 million girls and women around the world have undergone some form of the procedure, which is often rooted in local culture. In 2010, Nadya Khalife authored a detailed Human Rights Watch report that resulted in a fatwa affirming that FGM is not an Islamic practice, and in the Kurdistan parliament's adoption of a 2011 family violence bill to curb the practice.

Top right:
A traditional midwife in Iraqi Kurdistan holds ashes that are sifted and applied to the wound after a girl has undergone female genital mutilation.

Bottom right:
Iraqi Kurdish girls play soccer before attending a seminar on female genital mutilation held by the Association for Crisis Assistance and Development Cooperation (WADI), a German-Iraqi human rights organization.

A 40-year-old man and an 11-year-old girl sit in her home prior to their wedding in the rural Damarda Village, Ghor province, Afghanistan, on Sept. 11, 2005. When asked how she felt that day, the girl responded, "I do not know this man. What am I supposed to feel?"

CHILD MARRIAGE

Photographs by Stephanie Sinclair/VII

In most societies, marriage is a celebrated institution signifying a union between two adults and the beginning of their future together. But as Graça Michel and Mary Robinson describe in their chapter, the experience of marriage is vastly different for the millions of girls worldwide every year who are wed while still children—many not yet even teenagers. Child marriage robs girls of the ordinary life experiences other young people take for granted. It denies their right to education, often restricts friendships with peers, and perpetuates the cycle of poverty in their communities. Young married girls have little power in relation to their husbands and in-laws in many of these cultures.

They are therefore extremely vulnerable to domestic violence. This violence may include physical, sexual, or psychological abuse. The experience of pregnancy can also be traumatizing for a girl who is still a child herself, and can result in a health crisis such as fistula (fistula's terrible effects are described by Agnes Odhiambo in chapter 23). Child brides also have double the pregnancy death rate of women in their twenties. Throughout the world, more than 51 million girls younger than 18 are already married, even though it is outlawed in many developing countries, and a series of international agreements and conventions also forbid the practice. It's estimated that in the next decade, 100 million more girls—or roughly twenty-five thousand girls a day—will marry before they turn 18.

Top left:
An 11-year-old girl is married to a 23-year-old priest in a traditional Ethiopian Orthodox wedding in a rural area outside the city of Gondar, Ethiopia.

Bottom left:
Three young brides 11, 12, and 13, are married to three brothers during a combined ceremony in the rural areas outside Hajjah, Yemen.

SEXUAL VIOLENCE
IN THE DEMOCRATIC REPUBLIC OF CONGO

Photographs by Marcus Bleasdale/VII

As Anneke Van Wouldenberg explains in her chapter, sexual violence has reached "extraordinary levels" in the Democratic Republic of Congo. While the most recent war in this country officially ended in 2003, conflict has continued in eastern regions. There are no exact statistics on sexual violence since collecting data in a war zone is exceedingly difficult, but the United Nations estimates that at least two hundred thousand women and girls have been raped since 1998, though most UN officials say they believe the number is much higher. In April 2010, the UN Special Representative on Sexual Violence in Conflict labeled Congo as "the rape capital of the world."

Top left:
A 27-year-old victim of sexual violence at a support group in Bunia, the capital of Ituri district in the eastern region of the Democratic Republic of Congo.

Bottom left:
This 35-year-old woman is a victim of sexual violence by government soldiers in the Democratic Republic of Congo.

US **RAPE** KITS

Photographs by Lorena Ros and Patricia Williams

Los Angeles County has the largest known rape kit backlog in the United States. More than twelve thousand untested sexual assault kits ("rape kits"), which potentially contain DNA and other evidence collected from rape victims' bodies and clothes immediately after the crime, are sitting in police storage facilities in the Los Angeles Police Department, the Los Angeles County Sheriff's Department, and dozens of independent police departments in Los Angeles County. As Sarah Tofte explains in her chapter, the untested rape kits in Los Angeles County represent lost justice for the victims who reported their rape to the police, and consented to the four-to-six-hour rape kit collection process. This problem occurs in the US beyond California: a 2010 Human Rights Watch report found that an estimated 80 percent of rape kits in Illinois have not been tested.

Julie, a young woman from Illinois, was raped by a friend of a friend on June 24, 2007, in the city of Bloomington. Her attacker had waited until he got her alone. Julie's rape kit is one of thousands in Illinois that remain untested.

"If the rape kit was tested, I feel like I, in some part, would have internal justice. It's hard and it's difficult to think that you could potentially be setting someone free to do it to someone else, and the reason is not testing a kit."

© 2010 Lorena Ros

Above:
Untested sexual assault kits at the Los Angeles
Police Department storage facility. © 2009 Patricia
Williams

Above right:
A rape kit photographed at the Santa Monica-UCLA
Rape Treatment Center. © 2009 Patricia Williams

LOS ANGELES COUNTY/CITY
SEXUAL ASSAULT EVIDENCE

FOR POLICE DEPARTMENT USE ONLY	FOR LAB USE ONLY
Booked To	Lab Receipt No.
	Date Received
	Criminalist
Item No.	

LAW ENFORCEMENT AGENCY INFORMATION

DEPARTMENT	STATION/DIVISION	FILE/DR#
Los Angeles Police Department		
Los Angeles Sheriff's Department		

HOSPITAL INFORMATION

Patient	Medical Record Number
Hospital	Date/Time of Examination
Examiner	Witness of Examination

Examiner: Follow appropriate Office of Criminal Justice Planning (OCJP) form for collection of evidence.

1. Please refer to each enclosed envelope for step by step instructions.

2. Return all envelopes with enclosed materials to this outer envelope. Secure with the enclosed evidence seal. Date and initial seal, so that the initials extend across the edge of the seal onto the envelope.

MATERNAL MORTALITY
IN INDIA

Photographs by Susan Meiselas/Magnum Photos

Bidyawati, sister-in-law of Kiran Yadav, holds Kiran's newborn son. Kiran died because she did not get the emergency care she needed. Gopalpur, Uttar Pradesh.

Above:
Relatives mourn the loss of Kiran Yadav, who died after giving birth. Gopalpur, Uttar Pradesh.

Above right:
Komal holds the ID of her mother, Kiran Yadav, who died after childbirth in Gopalpur, Uttar Pradesh.

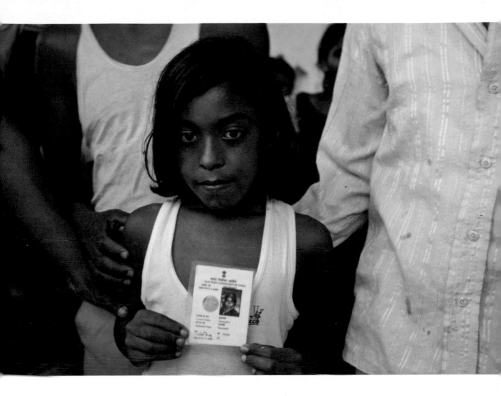

India is an emerging global superpower, but far too many women and girls continue to face severe barriers while trying to access lifesaving health care. Tens of thousands of Indian women needlessly die every year because of preventable health complications during pregnancy, childbirth, and unsafe abortions. Families accept these deaths as destiny or fate, unaware that most maternal deaths can be prevented with access to appropriate health care.

Aruna Kashyap writes in her chapter: "Childbirth should evoke images of joy and celebration, not death or disability." Yet, every year, more than 350,000 women and girls die needlessly from childbirth-related causes. Kashyap describes the severity of the problem in the Indian state of Uttar Pradesh, but also notes how another Indian state, Tamil Nadu, is seeking to reduce its high maternal mortality rates through an expanded use of mobile technology, training programs designed to help more doctors and nurses learn blood transfusion techniques, and more transparent reporting of fatality statistics.

PHOTOGRAPHERS

For more than eight years, British photojournalist **Marcus Bleasdale** has collaborated with Human Rights Watch in documenting the brutal conflict in the Democratic Republic of Congo. His images were published in *The Rape of a Nation* (Schilt, 2010).

Susan Meiselas has worked extensively around the globe, from Nicaragua to the highlands of Papua in Indonesia. Her work has earned her numerous prizes including the 1982 Leica Award for Excellence and the 2005 Cornell Capa Infinity Award.

Samer Muscati, a researcher for Human Rights Watch, contributed the chapter "Women in Iraq: Losing Ground" to this anthology. A former journalist, Muscati also photographed Iraqi women demonstrators for the cover of this book.

Platon, a staff photographer at *The New Yorker*, has worked with Human Rights Watch to celebrate human rights activists, including Burmese monks and Egyptian protest leaders. His Human Rights Watch portfolios have been published in dozens of international outlets.

Lorena Ros, a native of Barcelona, worked with Human Rights Watch on documenting the rape kits backlog in Illinois. In 2008 she was awarded a Getty Grant for Editorial Photography and a World Press Photo Award for her body of work on survivors of child sexual abuse.

American photojournalist **Stephanie Sinclair** contributes to publications including *National Geographic* and *Newsweek*. She received the Lumix Festival for Young Photojournalism FreeLens Award for her extensive work on child marriage.

Photojournalist and fine art photographer **Patricia Williams** has been documenting social justice issues for Human Rights Watch since 1996. Her work has been published in the *Los Angeles Times*, the *New York Times*, and various national magazines.

CHAPTER 22

Lasting Wounds
Female Genital Mutilation

Nadya Khalife

Dalya, an eighteen-year-old student from Halabja, was cut by her neighbor. "I remember that there was a lot of blood and a large fear," she told me. "This has consequences now during my period. I have emotional and physical pain and fear from the time when I saw the blood. I don't even go to school when I have my periods because there's too much pain. . . . My family supports me but sometimes I feel like killing myself because of the [menstrual] pain."

Dalya told me that she is to this day still fearful of her neighbor. Her mother never wants to discuss this with her. "When she sees me this way, my mother feels regret because she circumcised me," Dalya told me.

Dalya's story represents the experiences of countless young girls and women whose families still force them to undergo female genital mutilation (FGM), an unnecessary procedure that is harmful to their health in many ways. To me, one of the most astonishing aspects of my research in Iraqi Kurdistan on this subject was the vivid detail with which adult women described their pain and trauma years and even decades after being subjected to FGM. The more I listened to them,

Nadya Khalife, women's rights researcher for the Middle East and North Africa for Human Rights Watch, is the author of Human Rights Watch's 2010 report on female genital mutilation in Iraqi Kurdistan titled "They Took Me and Told Me Nothing." Prior to joining Human Rights Watch, she worked on a number of development projects following the 2006 Lebanon war. She has also conducted research for a European Union project on economic opportunities for women, contributed to work of human rights groups in the Great Lakes region of Africa, and worked on US-sponsored post-9/11 projects.

the more it became clear how confused they still were about the reasons for this practice.

In 2009, I met seventeen-year-old Gola in Sarkapkan, a small village in the rural area of Ranya in Iraqi Kurdistan. Dressed in a long blue gown, Gola came to a neighbor's house with her mother and younger sisters to speak to me. Before meeting her, I believed that women would have a difficult time speaking frankly about female genital mutilation, especially because of Iraqi Kurdistan's socially conservative culture. But much to my surprise, Gola was confident and adamant about sharing her experience with this painful procedure as a young girl.

Gola told me, "I remember my mom and her sister-in-law took us two girls, and there were four other girls. We went to Sarkapkan for the procedure. They put us in the bathroom and held our legs open, and cut something. They did it one by one with no anesthetics. I was afraid but endured the pain. There was nothing they did for us to soothe the pain."

Some of the women and girls I interviewed thought FGM was a religious duty, while others saw it as a traditional practice, performed because it is the norm in the community. Regardless of the reasons, girls and women felt especially betrayed by the women who made the decision to cut them, most often their mothers.

The World Health Organization (WHO) defines FGM as the partial or total removal of external female genitalia for non-medical purposes. The WHO classifies four types of FGM ranging from least to most severe. Type I, also known as clitoridectomy, refers to the partial or total removal of the clitoris, prepuce, or both. This is the least severe procedure, and the most common type of FGM practiced in Iraqi Kurdistan. Other types of FGM are more invasive and include the partial or total removal of the clitoris and the labia minora, or cutting and then stitching the labia minora, majora, or both with or without excision of the clitoris, otherwise known as infibulation.

100 Million Cuts

Globally, FGM is typically carried out on young girls, from infants to adolescents as old as fifteen. Occasionally, it is carried out on adult women. While it is difficult to obtain accurate data on the magnitude of this practice, the WHO estimates that between 100 and 140 million girls and women around the world have undergone some form of the procedure. More than 3 million girls in Africa alone are annually at risk of FGM.

In Kurdistan, there are no official statistics on the prevalence of this practice. Government ministers I met in Arbil, the capital of Iraqi Kurdistan, assured me that "there are a few cases, here and there . . . but the issue is not that big." After Human Rights Watch issued its report on the human rights abuses of FGM in 2010,[1] though, the Kurdistan Ministry of Health undertook a statistical study and found that 48 percent of their sample study of five thousand girls and women had undergone the practice.

FGM is practiced for various sociocultural reasons. The simplest is that it is rooted in local culture, and has often been passed from one generation to another. The practice serves as a means of preserving cultural identity by requiring girls and women to undergo this procedure to be accepted socially in Kurdish society.

Another factor is the gender inequality within some societies that view women as the gatekeepers of family honor. Such cultures believe that girls' sexual desires must be controlled early on to preserve their virginity and prevent immorality. In some communities, this practice is seen as necessary to ensure marital fidelity and to prevent deviant sexual behavior. Other societies practice FGM on young girls because they believe it can enhance sexual pleasure for men.

FGM is also performed ostensibly for hygienic and aesthetic reasons. In some cultures, as in Sudan, many believe that female genitalia are dirty and consider an "uncircumcised" girl to be unclean. This belief may reduce a girl's chances to get married if she is not circumcised. FGM is also considered to make girls more attractive. Infibulation, for instance, is thought to achieve smoothness—viewed as beautiful—around the genital area.

A Cloak of Religion

Other societies link FGM to religion, but the practice is not particular to any religious faith, and it predates both Christianity and Islam.

FGM has been practiced by adherents to Islam, Christianity, and Judaism. It is also practiced among animists.

The association of FGM with Islam has been refuted by many Muslim scholars and theologians, who say that FGM is not prescribed in the Koran, the Muslim holy text, and indeed is contradictory to the teachings of Islam. In 2006, the late Muhammad Sayyed Tantawi, Grand Sheikh of Al-Azhar University, the most respected Islamic university among Sunni Muslims, said that FGM is not an Islamic practice and it is not mentioned in "Sharia, in the Quran, in the prophetic *Sunnah* [an act performed to strengthen one's religion]." He stated that "circumcising girls is just a cultural tradition in some countries that has nothing to do with the traditions of Islam." In 2007, the Al-Azhar Supreme Council of Islamic Research issued a statement that FGM has "no basis in Islamic law or any of its partial provisions and that it is harmful and should not be practiced."

In Iraqi Kurdistan, I found that many women are perplexed about the reasons for this practice. Some women I spoke to insisted that FGM is a Kurdish tradition, a practice that has been around for generations. Other women said that FGM used to be a fad but is now less prevalent. Some referred to the practice as *sunnah*, giving FGM a religious significance. Most Iraqi Kurds are Sunni Muslims and adherents to the Shafi'i school of Islamic jurisprudence.

A mullah I interviewed in Germian, a rural area in Iraqi Kurdistan, contended that a girl goes through puberty faster in warmer climates and that therefore FGM is practiced to "allow girls not to show bad behavior." Other interviewees explained that if a girl does not undergo FGM, she may become very sexually active, and this will tarnish her reputation. Given the importance of chastity in Muslim societies, the reference to FGM as *sunnah* and a mandate by Islam strongly reinforces the justification for its continuation in the Muslim societies where it is practiced.

Nawal el-Saadawi, a well known Egyptian physician and feminist scholar, has pointed out that, "behind circumcision lies the belief that, by removing parts of girls' external genital organs, sexual desire is minimized." One can therefore argue that the ultimate reason for FGM in places like Iraqi Kurdistan is fear of women's sexuality. Regardless of its devastating health effects for women and girls, FGM continues to be referred to as *sunnah*, and remains shrouded under the cloak of religion.

Health Professionals Failing Women and Girls

One reason FGM proves intractable is that even doctors tasked with caring for the health of women and girls are not fighting to end the practice. "Circumcision is nothing," a respected gynecologist and obstetrician in Arbil, Dr. Atia al-Salihy, told Human Rights Watch. She added that the type of FGM practiced in Iraqi Kurdistan does not have any harmful health effects. Even after we issued our report extensively documenting serious harm to girls from FGM, female physicians at the Sulaimaniya Maternity Hospital claimed during a visit in November 2010 that Type I FGM doesn't have any adverse consequences—because, they said, only the tip of the clitoris is cut. They repudiated our findings and said that what we called FGM is what is practiced in places like Egypt and other parts of Africa, not in Iraqi Kurdistan.

According to the World Health Organization, though, all types of FGM have numerous acute and chronic physical health consequences, including implications for reproductive health. The most immediate consequences include death and the risk of death from hemorrhaging and shock from the pain and level of violence that may accompany the procedure. Heavy bleeding can be life threatening in a context of limited access to emergency health care. Serious sepsis may also occur, especially when unsterile cutting instruments such as razor blades are used. The risk of infection may increase when the same instrument is used to cut several girls. Acute urinary retention may also result from swelling and inflammation around the wound.

Long-term complications also include anemia, the formation of cysts, painful sexual intercourse, sexual dysfunction, and hypersensitivity to the genital area. Infibulation or Type III, the most severe form of FGM, may cause severe scarring, difficulty passing urine, menstrual disorders, recurrent urinary tract infections, fistula, prolonged labor, and infertility.

The World Health Organization confirms that women who have experienced any type of FGM, including clitoridectomy, run a greater risk of complications during childbirth. Pregnant women who have experienced FGM are more likely to need a Caesarean section or an episiotomy and may suffer from postpartum hemorrhage. All types of FGM also have detrimental health effects on fetuses and cause the risk of a stillbirth. Newborn babies may risk early neonatal death and may have lower birth weight. Obstetric complications may arise, depending on the extensiveness of the procedure.[2]

FGM also has severe consequences for a woman's sexual and psychosexual health. Both the clitoris and the labia minora include large sensory nerve receptors, which are often damaged in the course of a clitoridectomy or any other form of FGM, thereby impairing female sexual response.

Studies documenting the sexual health consequences of FGM show that when women undergo such a procedure, they may experience physical pain during intercourse and lack physical pleasure during sex. "The missing structures and tissue of a woman's sexual organs have negative effects on a woman's sexual desire, arousal, sexual pleasure and satisfaction," say Padmini Murthy and Clyde Lanford Smith in their book, *Women's Global Health and Human Rights.*[3] Cutting the glans clitoris makes it difficult for women to achieve orgasm. Such sexual difficulties may be more common in women who have undergone FGM either after a period of adolescent sexual activity or before childbirth. Nahid Toubia, a Sudanese surgeon and human rights activist, explains that "FGM removes the woman's sexual organ and leaves her reproductive organs intact."[4]

Infections and inadequate penetration during sexual intercourse may also affect the ability of a woman who has undergone FGM to become pregnant. In communities where fertility and childbirth constitute major roles for women, the failure to produce children is most often blamed on women and may lead to rejection by the husband and his family.

Regardless of the type of FGM performed in any given country, health care professionals should act as primary sources for reliable information about this practice. They should also exercise their ethical responsibility to ensure that women and girls have access to accurate information on the health consequences. And they should provide medical treatment to girls or women who have undergone the procedure, in addition to providing counseling, and making referrals for victims who experience emotional distress.

A Lasting Psychological Toll

While only a few studies have tackled the effects of FGM on girls' and women's mental and emotional health, psychological consequences may involve a loss of trust or a sense of betrayal by a close family member. Girls are often accompanied to the midwife's home by their mothers, aunts, or grandmothers—without any prior knowledge about where they are going and why. In other instances, close female relatives or neighbors, instead of traditional midwives, carry out the procedure on girls in their own families. Girls may grow to fear the female members of their families because of the experience, and sometimes mothers feel a sense of regret for forcing their daughters to undergo a harmful procedure. Halima Q., a twenty-eight-year-old mother told me, "My daughter is circumcised and I regret it. I feel pain for her because I saw blood coming out from cutting this part."

Mental health disorders associated with FGM may include depression, anxiety, phobias, post-traumatic stress disorder, psychosexual problems, and other mental health problems. The prevalence of post-traumatic stress is likely to be higher in girls and women who undergo more severe forms of FGM. The risk of post-traumatic stress may also increase if the girl or woman suffered severe complications as a result of the procedure or when she has flashbacks triggered by reminders of the procedure. These memory triggers may occur during sexual intercourse, during gynecological exams, and even during childbirth and delivery. A female obstetrics and gynecology specialist in Arbil who denied that Type I FGM has any health consequences, did concede that women who undergo FGM suffer psychologically. She said that when they marry, women may begin to remember the assault on their bodies when they were children, with severe consequences for sexual and mental health.

Chronic pain in women who undergo FGM is often the result of either trauma or physical complications they may have experienced while undergoing the procedure. Complications may include infections or painful menstrual periods. Chronic pain also causes girls and women to experience distress and feelings of sadness. Their social isolation, sense of worthlessness and feelings of guilt may also increase as a result.

A Road Map to Eradication

The recognition of FGM as a human rights violation has contributed to the development of global, rights-based strategies to combat the practice. International human rights frameworks have addressed FGM both as a health issue and as a form of violence against children and women. This has helped governments and institutions evaluate and map out strategies, including legislation and various programs, to address the issue at the national and local levels.

UN monitoring bodies have called on numerous countries to adopt laws to ban FGM. They have highlighted the importance of raising awareness and educating communities about harmful practices. These agencies have addressed the fact that FGM awareness campaigns need to address families, and entire communities, to convince them to abandon this practice. These agencies have also identified key stakeholders in elimination efforts such as religious leaders, health professionals, and traditional midwives.

While the elimination of any practice that has been entrenched as "cultural" or religious is complex, it is clear that the underlying factors perpetuating the practice must be addressed for eradication efforts to be effective. The criminalization of FGM alone is not an effective strategy to combat the practice and must be balanced with other protective measures. Unless accompanied by other measures, penalties on practitioners and family members who practice FGM may drive them underground and place the lives of girls and women at even greater risk. For instance, those who perform the cutting as a profession must be given information about the harmful consequences of FGM and be offered employable skills, and an alternative source of income. Above all, efforts must be made to integrate traditional midwives in FGM elimination efforts.

To succeed, FGM eradication programs must be implemented in institutions at all levels: national, regional, and local. A strong political commitment to abandon FGM through the development of policies and laws, adequately supported by resources, is essential. Coordination between governmental and nongovernmental agencies is equally critical.

An effective strategy also entails the mainstreaming of FGM prevention into policies and programs that seek to promote reproductive health and literacy. The medical community must play a primary role in disseminating accurate information on the health effects of the practice, while learning to manage complications resulting from FGM.

In Iraqi Kurdistan, efforts to curb FGM are under way. Awareness-raising programs, especially in rural areas, discuss the damaging health effects of this practice on girls and women. Some education programs even include participation by religious leaders, who travel to towns and villages to tell families about the health consequences of this practice and that it should not be carried out in the name of Islam. Similar efforts are being undertaken in certain African countries like Senegal, where the efforts of the NGO Tostan ("breakthrough" in the Wolof dialect) have successfully led to the abandonment of the practice in thousands of villages.[5]

A Fatwa Against FGM

Shortly after Human Rights Watch's report on FGM was published in July 2010, the High Committee for Issuing Fatwas at the Kurdistan Islamic Scholars Union, the highest Muslim religious authority in Iraqi Kurdistan, issued a fatwa, a religious edict or pronouncement, attesting that FGM is not an Islamic practice. This was a major step forward. Religious leaders in Iraqi Kurdistan, and especially in rural areas, have tremendous influence over people, and this fatwa was an exceptionally important pronouncement. The fatwa was not a complete solution, as it did not expressly denounce the practice, and left the decision to parents whether to mutilate their girls.

While the announcement of the fatwa in Iraqi Kurdistan was one vital piece of the puzzle of eradicating this harmful practice, the primary responsibility for protecting girls from FGM rests with the government. The Kurdistan parliament's adoption in June 2011 of a family violence bill, including two provisions on FGM, constituted another major milestone on the road to ending FGM. I and other rights activists had lobbied vigorously for the Kurdistan government to finally ban FGM as a show of political will that harmful traditional practices will no longer be tolerated in Kurdish society. For me, this was a deeply satisfying moment, as I recalled the harrowing testimonies of women and girls I interviewed in the course of my research.

What this teaches us is that FGM eradication efforts require a multifaceted approach—one that works with numerous key actors at the same time, including victims, their families, religious leaders, health care professionals, teachers, and community leaders. Debate and discussions are essential to encourage a community affirmation to stop the mutilation of girls. In every country where FGM exists, government authorities can follow the example of Iraqi Kurdistan and make a public commitment by sending out a clear message that this harmful practice has no place in their society. In fact, they should ban the practice. Any law to accomplish that goal should provide a clear definition of FGM, explicitly state that it is prohibited, and identify perpetrators and penalties—though sanctions alone will not suffice. Legal steps must always be paired with social outreach, otherwise criminalization could be counterproductive unless measures are taken to ensure the practice is not driven underground.

Global experience shows that a commitment to end FGM depends on a society's willingness and a government's commitment to safeguard the rights of girls and women. There are clear precedents for eradicating a harmful traditional or religious practice. At the beginning of the last century, girls across China had their feet bound to make them more attractive to men. Today, that harmful, traditional, and literally crippling practice is forever ended.

I hope that girls like Gola and Dalya, who so vividly recalled their own painful experiences and are still confused about the reasons for undergoing this harmful practice, will be at the forefront of the battle to end FGM. Parents and grandparents should learn more about the damage that this practice does to the health of their daughters and granddaughters. Above all, I hope that female genital mutilation and other harmful traditional practices will cease to be justified under the name of any religion, and that along with government leaders, religious figures will take the lead to eliminate it forever.

CHAPTER 23

Fistula
Giving Birth and Living Death in Africa

Agnes Odhiambo

At age thirteen while in primary school in a rural village in western Kenya, Kwamboka W. had sex for the first time. She had no information about contraception and used no protection during sex. Three months later, Kwamboka was shocked to discover that she was pregnant because, as she told me in an interview seven years later in 2009, "It was my first time and I did not think I would get pregnant." Kwamboka was more shocked when she later discovered, after laboring for close to three days and delivering a stillborn baby, that she could not control the flow of her urine and stool.

Years later, the pain—both physical and psychological—was still vividly seared in her memory. "My mother tells me, 'You can't get married; how can you go to someone's home when you are like this? They will despise you.' I was traumatized," she said. "I thought I should kill myself. You can't walk with people. They laugh at you. You can't travel;

Based in Nairobi, Agnes Odhiambo is the Africa researcher for the Women's Rights Division at Human Rights Watch. She is the author of the 2010 report "I Am Not Dead, but I Am Not Living": Barriers to Fistula Prevention and Treatment in Kenya. *Prior to joining Human Rights Watch in 2009, she worked as the HIV program manager for the South African NGO Gender Links. Dr. Odhiambo holds a Ph.D. from the University of the Witwatersrand in Johannesburg. In this chapter, she discusses the debilitating impact of fistula on African women, and the solutions needed to end the damages caused by this preventable childbirth injury.*

you are constantly in pain. It is so uncomfortable when you sleep. You go near people and they say urine smells and they are looking directly at you and talking in low tones. It hurt so much, I thought I should die."

Africa places a high premium on childbearing. However, for hundreds of thousands of women in the continent, giving birth can mean death or living death.

Kwamboka was just one of the more than fifty women and girls I interviewed in 2009 in Kenya who suffered obstetric fistula, an entirely preventable and treatable childbirth injury that leaves women and girls with urinary or fecal incontinence. It is caused by prolonged, obstructed labor—a condition that accounts for 8 percent of maternal deaths worldwide—without access to emergency obstetric care, usually a Caesarean section. During the prolonged obstructed labor, the soft tissues of the birth canal are compressed between the descending head of the fetus and the woman's pelvic bone. The lack of blood flow causes tissue to die, creating a hole (*fistula* in Latin) between the woman's vagina and bladder (vesico-vaginal fistula or VVF) or between the vagina and rectum (recto-vaginal fistula or RVF), or both. Many women live with fistula for several years or for the rest of their life, if unable to access treatment. Other direct causes of fistula include sexual abuse and rape, surgical trauma, and gynecological cancers and related radiotherapy treatment.

Most of the women and girls with fistula whom I interviewed while conducting research for the Human Right Watch report "*I Am Not Dead, but I Am Not Living*"[1] had little formal education, were poor, and lived in rural areas. They had poor knowledge of family planning and contraception. They married early, some as early as fourteen, and became pregnant young. Decisions on where they would deliver their babies were often made by their husbands, mothers-in-law, or other relatives. Many had no jobs, and struggled to pay for transport to reach a facility that could provide them adequate delivery care, usually a dispensary or health center. The facility usually had no capacity to handle obstructed labor and no ambulance to move them to a hospital where they could be helped.

Exactly how many women and girls suffer from fistula in Africa—and globally—is impossible to say with certainty because of poor data collection. Although there is widespread agreement that the existing data likely underestimate the problem, the World Health Organization (WHO) estimates that some two million women and girls currently live with fistula, and roughly fifty thousand to one hundred thousand are affected every year, mainly in sub-Saharan Africa and Asia. In Africa, Nigeria alone is estimated to have 1 million women living with fistula, while about six thousand to fifteen thousand fistulas occur annually in East Africa and nine thousand occur in Ethiopia. In Kenya, about three thousand women get fistula every year and there are some three hundred thousand existing cases. Fistula has been virtually eliminated in the developed world, according to the WHO.

Shame, Stigma, and Violence

The physical consequences of fistula are severe and can include a fetid odor, frequent pelvic or urinary infections, painful genital ulcerations, burning of thighs from the constant wetness, infertility, nerve damage to the legs, and sometimes early mortality. Many women suffering from obstetric fistula limit their intake of water and food because they do not want to leak. This can lead to dehydration and malnutrition. The majority of women and girls interviewed by Human Rights Watch who were married or in sexual relationships complained of pain and discomfort during sex.

Fistula has a huge psychological impact on women and girls, sometimes leading to depression and suicide. Most women we interviewed described feelings of hopelessness, self-hatred, guilt, and sadness, especially because their families or communities ostracized them.

Another young woman I interviewed in Nairobi in 2009, Kemunto S., told me, "You are always sad because every time you are washing clothes, you stain everything and you smell." Amolo A., who became pregnant after being raped, described how hopeless she felt before she had successful fistula repair in 2007: "I was raped, the baby was dead, I was leaking urine and I couldn't be treated. I felt so hopeless. My life was just useless. I was only nineteen. My age mates were getting married, and moving on with their lives and I was an outcast."

The social consequences of fistula are also dire. Women and girls living with fistula are often ostracized largely because of the foul odor they produce. They are often abused, beaten, abandoned, and divorced by their husbands. Women said they had been mocked and ridiculed for "smelling like a pit latrine," or "urinating everywhere." Nyasuguta J. told me about her cousin who was disowned by her family because she had fistula: "Her family said, 'She is just feces' and told her not go near visitors. When they see her approaching they say, 'The one with feces has returned.'" A midwife who works with community midwives on fistula in western Kenya said she found most married women living in their parental home: "They have been sent away from their marital homes. Even when they are not sent away, abuse and violence makes them to pack and leave."

Violence and stigma against women with fistula is also fueled by lack of information about what fistula is and the fact that it can be treated. Almost all the women and girls whom I interviewed had never heard about fistula before they developed it and thought they were the only ones with the problem. Some women thought that incontinence was normal after delivery, or that that they got fistula due to botched Caesarean sections. A man who used to beat his wife due to her incontinence told me, "If I knew that my wife had a medical condition that can be treated, I would not have beaten her. I used to think she is dirty and careless. I feel bad that I beat her."

Fistula survivors are also thought by some to be bewitched or cursed, or may be accused of being promiscuous. Fistula is more stigmatized when, due to misinformation, it is linked to other taboo conditions such as HIV/AIDS, abortion, and infertility. Wangui K. told me, "People say I have been aborting and are telling my husband to chase me away and marry another woman who can give birth." In addition to fueling stigma and violence, lack of information about fistula also contributes to delays in seeking treatment, and effectively adds to women's misery.

Fistula often leads to loss of social belonging and association. Some fistula sufferers live alone or in shacks outside their homes. Many women and girls with fistula lead isolated lives, confining themselves to their homes due to the stigma and shame attached to the illness. A large number of those we interviewed did not go to church, the market, or other social places. For example, Fatuma H. told me she did not leave her home because "When you have this problem you have a lot of worries. You don't have a lot of comfort. You can't mix freely with other people. You feel guilty to mix with them. You fear the thing [the cloths used to keep dry] will come out and embarrass you. You can't even go to church."

Exclusion from Education, Work, and Deepened Poverty

Some girls said they would have wanted to return to school after giving birth, but fistula made it impossible.

Fistula places a huge financial burden on poor families, leading to deepened poverty and vulnerability to repeat fistulas. Fistula victims need regular medical attention and an extra supply of soap to keep clean. Almost all the women I spoke to said they could not afford to buy sanitary pads and instead used rugs and pieces of old clothes to control the constant trickle of urine and feces. It is also expensive to keep the rags clean. Women and girls with fistula may also lose property when they are divorced or chased away by their husbands. Nyakiriro C., for example told me, "When I got the problem, my husband told me to go back to my mother. . . . I left with no property. He sold the land and the livestock after I left."

Fistula also decreases women's abilities to farm or do other economic activities. Although some women are able to work on their farms despite the pain and discomfort they suffer, others are unable to. Some lose jobs or are denied work when employers discover that they have fistula.

Nyaboke H. said, "My husband chased me away when I got this problem [fistula]. He used to beat me a lot. When I went back to my parents, my sister-in-law also became abusive saying she did not want a dirty smelly person in the home. I left, went to a nearby town, and rented a house. I started doing casual jobs like washing clothes and fetching water, but whenever it was discovered that I had a problem of [controlling] urine, I was chased away. Before long, everybody knew about my problem and I stopped getting work. I used to lock myself in the house and cry the whole night, and sleep hungry."

Some women also quit their jobs out of shame. Because of the shame and guilt women feel as a result of having fistula, they are reluctant to look for work or ask for financial support from their husbands and other family members.

Low-Cost Solutions That Empower Women

Treatment for obstetric fistula usually consists of surgical repair. For complex cases, repair may not be possible at all, or may fail to prevent incontinence. Some 90 percent of simple cases can be successfully repaired according to the United Nations Population Fund (UNFPA), which funds many procedures. The average cost of fistula repair for simple cases is around US$300-400. Some fistulas can be extremely complicated, involving damage to other bodily systems and requiring multiple, expensive surgeries to treat. Even for simple fistula repairs, most poor families in Africa cannot afford the cost, and women continue to suffer the consequences of fistula. UNFPA and various NGOs support free fistula repairs across Africa. However, although the number of fistula surgeons has increased over the past decade, there are few such surgeons in Africa. Also, in the case of Kenya for example, there is a general lack of interest in fistula training among doctors because the specialty brings little monetary gain. Furthermore, there are few hospitals equipped to handle fistula surgeries.

Yet women do not have to suffer the devastation of fistula, which is a preventable and treatable condition. Prevention requires providing universal access to adequate reproductive and maternal healthcare. Direct prevention measures include availability of emergency obstetric care, including access to a Caesarean section, and skilled birth attendance. Providing comprehensive sexuality education and family planning services to girls and women to enable them make informed choices about their sexual and reproductive lives are also important prevention strategies.

Equally important to fistula elimination are interventions to combat underlying social and economic inequities that contribute to the problem, including women's low status, lack of education for girls, early marriage and childbearing, malnutrition, poverty, and harmful traditional practices such as female genital mutilation (FGM). In some instances of FGM, unskilled traditional birth attendants perform a type of female circumcision called "infibulation" which may inadvertently extend to the bladder or rectum, causing a fistula. Although prevention is key to solving the problem, it has received less focus in current initiatives to address fistula, probably because, like other global health concerns, it is often the most difficult area in which to demonstrate success.

Years and sometimes decades of living with fistula leave women psychologically, socially, and financially unable to function in their families and communities. A comprehensive approach to fistula also means addressing the reintegration and rehabilitation needs of women and girls who have undergone repair. This can be through the provision of counseling, skills training, financial, and other support, to restore women's dignity, self-sufficiency, and to ensure future safe deliveries.

The WHO recommends national strategies to address obstetric fistula be integrated into existing programs on safe motherhood and those to improve maternal and neonatal health generally. According to the Campaign to End Fistula, about forty countries have conducted situation analyses on fistula prevention and treatment, and twenty-eight have integrated fistula into relevant national policies and plans. On the whole, an adequately resourced, equitable, and integrated health system is needed to improve maternal healthcare and to address fistula.

But the reality is different in Africa. Even when resources are limited, what is available is often mismanaged or misused, and monitoring of how resources are allocated and used or how the health system is performing is inadequate. These issues are not exclusive to Kenya, where the number of hospitals equipped to handle fistula surgeries is woefully insufficient. Most resource-poor countries, but especially those in Africa, are struggling with these problems. Even in the face these challenges, though, it is clear that many countries could do more to improve maternal healthcare and to restore lives of dignity to fistula sufferers. Countries must move from rhetoric to taking concrete measures to save women's lives.

Progress and Hope

Significant progress in addressing fistula has been made in the last decade, particularly since the launch of the UNFPA-led Campaign to End Fistula in 2003. The advocacy and awareness raising activities of the campaign and its partners have contributed to greater visibility and knowledge of the fistula problem at a global level. These efforts have also contributed to resource mobilization for fistula programs—addressing fistula prevention, treatment and care, and rehabilitation—and helped to strengthen health infrastructure.

African countries have pledged under the Millennium Development Goals (MDG) to reduce maternal deaths and to achieve universal access to reproductive health by 2015. Generally, there is more political will by African governments to improve maternal and reproductive health care, which is critical to addressing fistula. As reported by United Nations agencies in 2010, the maternal mortality ratio for sub-Saharan Africa declined 26 percent between 1990 and 2008, although the rate is insufficient to meet MDG criteria.

At the African regional level, there are many declarations and commitments to promoting maternal and reproductive health. These include the Protocol to the African Charter on Human and Peoples' Rights on the Rights of Women in Africa (Maputo Protocol), the African Road Map for Accelerating the Attainment of the MDGs related to maternal and newborn health (MNH Road Map) adopted by over forty countries, and the Maputo Plan of Action on sexual and reproductive health and rights. In 2009, the African Union began a campaign for accelerated reduction of maternal mortality in Africa (CARMMA), with the slogan "Africa Cares: No Woman Should Die While Giving Life." Some countries address fistula as part of the campaign. The African Union has also declared 2010-20 the African women's decade. This will require African governments to grant equal priority to health care for women as for men, and to allocate the necessary financial resources to this important objective.

Some countries have slowly begun to register notable advances in fistula prevention. A 2008 UNFPA report on its Campaign to End Fistula cites "steady treatment progress" in the Democratic Republic of

Congo, Mauritania and Niger, largely attributable to "increased human resources, upgraded facilities and the provision of equipment and supplies."[2] A pilot center established in Cote d'Ivoire's Region of Man successfully trained 12 ob-gyns and surgeons, 42 midwives and nurses, and 240 community health workers in fistula prevention, treatment, and reintegration.

Technology can also be used successfully in the fight to end fistula. Cell phones are an important tool in UNFPA-funded projects, as in Tanzania, where women affected by fistula can pay for their travel to a clinic through money transfers made via SMS text messages; or Mali, where mobile phones are increasingly used to transmit health statistics from the field into national databases.[3]

Yet despite the political will, and the progress made so far, many women and girls in Africa still lack access to adequate maternity care. The problem remains particularly acute in countries plagued by poverty or prone to violence, such as Ethiopia, Sudan, and Somalia. The Fistula Foundation notes that the number of obstetricians and gynecologists in Ethiopia is "abysmally low": just one for roughly every 530,000 people.[4] African women need action from their governments, not more words. African governments have to redouble their efforts. Words alone will not save the many women, particularly the poor, illiterate, and rural, who continue to die needlessly during pregnancy and childbirth or to live for years in pain due to fistula.

This can change if African governments invest in having strong health systems by ensuring that there are enough health care facilities providing emergency obstetric care, that they are equitably distributed and adequately stocked, and that there are adequate health professionals, including those with midwifery skills. Only then can we proudly say that "Africa Cares: No Woman Will Die While Giving Life."

CHAPTER 24

Fatal Consequences
Women, Abortion, and Power in Latin America

Marianne Mollmann

Lucila was twenty-two when I spoke with her in 2004 in the mud-floored office of a women's group on the outskirts of Buenos Aires, while conducting research for a report on reproductive rights in Argentina. During her first pregnancy two years earlier, the doctors at the local public hospital had diagnosed her with a rare heart condition, which converted her otherwise healthy pregnancy into a potentially lethal situation. Lucila was told, in no uncertain terms, that another pregnancy could kill her.

Nevertheless, when Lucila begged these same doctors to sterilize her, they refused the operation, telling her that she was "too young" to stop procreating. Lucila suffered regular beatings and rape at the hands of her husband and was unable to prevent another pregnancy—when

Marianne Mollmann is a senior policy adviser with Amnesty International's International Secretariat, having previously served as the advocacy director for the Women's Rights Division at Human Rights Watch. Her fields of expertise include reproductive rights and women's economic rights. She is the author of the 2005 Human Rights Watch report Decisions Denied: Women's Access to Contraceptives and Abortion in Argentina. *Before joining Human Rights Watch, she served as co-coordinator of the Women's Working Group of the International Network for Economic Social and Cultural Rights and as the executive director of the Network in Solidarity with the People of Guatemala. She holds a degree in International Human Rights Law from Essex University.*

I talked to her, she was already showing. And though she qualified for a legal abortion, even under the very strict Argentina law, she was barred from having one due to lack of proper regulation and the extreme stigma attached to abortion.

I later learned Lucila had managed to terminate her life-threatening pregnancy illegally. I did not hear under what conditions, though chances are they were not good. The Argentine health ministry admits that illegal abortions account for approximately one-third of maternal deaths in the country.

While Lucila's situation probably is extreme, it is by no means exceptional. Latin America is home to some of the world's most restrictive abortion laws. Three countries criminalize abortion in all circumstances, even when the pregnant woman's life can only be saved through terminating her pregnancy: Chile, El Salvador, and Nicaragua.

Across Latin America, most countries apply an "exceptions" model where abortion generally is outlawed but penalties are waived in specific circumstances, such as if the pregnancy threatens the life or health of the woman, if the pregnancy is the result of rape or incest, or if the fetus is so seriously damaged it is unlikely to survive birth. Only in Mexico City and Cuba is abortion freely available to all women and girls who need the intervention, as long as they seek an early termination.[1]

The restrictions placed on access to legal abortion have not made the practice scarce. In Argentina, an estimated 40 percent of all pregnancies terminate in induced abortions. In Peru, that proportion is 37 percent, and in Chile 35 percent. Most other countries in the region, including Mexico but also the United States, maintain a 20 percent ratio—one induced abortion for every 4 live births.

In fact, if you look at criminal law as only one of many potential policy instruments to affect the social phenomenon that is abortion, it would appear to be a very ineffectual choice: where abortion is illegal, it is equally—if not more—prevalent than in jurisdictions where it is legal. Also where abortion is illegal, it is much more likely to be unsafe. "You get overwhelmed by desperation," a thirty-five-year-old mother of ten children told me in Argentina. "You seek all the ways out, pills, anything. But if there is no way out, then you take a knife or a knitting needle."

Despite these facts, there are harsh criminal consequences for abortion in most Latin American countries. When it comes up in political or legislative debate, the criminalization of abortion is justified with reference to a need to protect the right to life of the unborn, and to a reluctance to "promote" abortion, which is considered a moral evil. In Peru, a prominent member of congress reportedly said it is better for a pregnant woman to die—and for her unborn child to die with her—than for her to have an abortion. This same argument was aired in Nicaragua when the parliament in 2007 decided to criminalize so-called therapeutic abortion (to save a woman's life and health), which had been legal since 1893.

Complex Notions of "Right" and "Wrong"

It is of course true that any government has a vested interest in promoting a civic sense of right and wrong. As human rights activists we routinely expect governments to promote laws that dictate certain morals, such as equality between men and women, the inappropriateness of corporal punishment, and the need to abolish the death penalty. The difference between these issues and abortion is not that abortion is too complicated. There is actually quite broad agreement in most Latin American countries that while abortion is "wrong," so are blanket bans of the practice.

The difference is that laws that promote equality and ban violence are generally effective in doing just that. Constitutional protections of equality, for example, have led to guarantees of equal pay for equal work. And the effective prosecution of domestic violence and even jay-walking has been proven to deter those practices, at least in part.

By contrast, the morals expressed through the stigmatization and criminalization of abortion are routinely set aside by women and girls who feel they need to terminate their pregnancies. In fact, of the hundreds of women I have interviewed over the years about pregnancy and choice, many have only a rudimentary or confused understanding of the law, but they have a clear sense of what is right. I have spoken to many women from various countries in Latin America who have expressed beliefs about the moral acceptability of abortion in specific circumstances, depending on the financial, marital, or emotional situation of the pregnant woman, and her ability to love the child if he or she were ever born.

"I don't think [abortion] is really all that criminal during the first month," Marienela, a thirty-seven-year-old mother of six, confided in me, as we were huddling in the corner of a dark old stable that functioned as a social hall in a slum quarter outside of Santa Fe, Argentina. "But if you already are seven months pregnant, then you have to have it."

"Sometimes abortion is the best option," a staunch pro-life activist said to me in 2006. The same woman declared not to believe in the need for modern contraception, but readily conceded the untenable nature of the current setup in her neighborhood, a muddy slum on the outskirts of Tucumán, Argentina: "The most usual form of contraception here is nothing: people either have children or badly done abortion. . . . It's still something I am thinking through, but I know we have to work on making sure that no one needs to get to that point." She then looked at me and said quietly, "You cannot even imagine what women end up putting in their uterus."

The sentiment that abortion is not a moral evil if you didn't want to be pregnant in the first place is both prevalent and pragmatic in the many women I have spoken to, and also surprisingly clear. "Abortion is necessary," said one woman in Nicaragua in 2007. "You can't just bring an undesired child into this world, especially when you didn't try to have one."

In fact, women and girls already know what they need in order not to need abortions. The vectors that influence real choice are neither fetal rights nor physical autonomy in the abstract. It's a very concrete sense of what is possible and what makes for a better life—mostly for the child.

Time and time again, women articulate concern about economic stability and the need to feed an existing family. They talk about apprehension with regard to bringing a child into an abusive relationship, often only commenting in passing on their own suffering and pain. They talk at length about difficulties in accessing affordable, easy-to-use, safe, and effective contraception of their choice.

And they always describe variations on a theme that sounds ideologically motivated but happens to be empirically true: that while women in Latin America are socially dependent on men, men are not held responsible for the reproductive disasters that ensue from the unprotected sex they often pressure women into having. "She got herself pregnant" is invariably the response I get from public officials to questions about why a particular woman should suffer through an unwanted pregnancy or unsafe birth. At times it is delivered with a dismissive shrug: "She is responsible for herself."

Why Legalize Abortion?

These very real experiences should make for excellent public policy: tackling the three issues of violence against women, access to contraception, and gender-based discrimination is what will make abortion less needed. The legalization of abortion will make the practice safe.

Most of these facts are undisputed. The real question is why none are adequately addressed in Latin America today.

The short answer is power. Everywhere in the region, proposals to legally limit access to abortion, and even absurd moves to extend the right to child support for all ova fertilized through rape, are used as political chips.

In Nicaragua, a 2006 vote to eliminate access to abortion for women whose life were threatened by their pregnancy was scheduled a mere ten days before the presidential elections, and most accounts suggest that this was no accident. The fact is that in all of Latin America, churches are powerful players in national politics—in particular the Catholic church—and few candidates want to be seen as "pro-abortion" and thereby lose the support of the church and other politically influential conservative groups. In this particular election, parliamentarians from the Sandinista party were reportedly ordered to vote for the penal code reform so that their candidate, Daniel Ortega, would win, but with an oral promise from the Sandinista party leadership that the issue would be "solved" after the elections. Meanwhile, Ortega went on record saying that "abortion is murder." More than five years after the blanket ban on abortion went into effect in Nicaragua, it is still in force with disastrous effects on women's health and lives.

In Mexico, after the Supreme Court in August 2008 upheld a Mexico City law to legalize abortion in the first trimester, several federal states in the country moved to amend their state constitutions to ban it.

Most of these constitutional changes have little effect on women's real access to legal abortion in those states: it was nearly impossible before and obviously not much better after. However, the fact that state legislatures were willing to spend time and energy on laws that are likely to have little effect on their stated objective is testament to how politically viable anti-choice arguments are, and how little power can be gained by raising the fact that women and girls continue to have abortions—some safe and most unsafe—regardless the legislative framework.

And during the presidential campaign in Brazil in 2010, the ruling left-wing party dropped the support of sexual and reproductive rights from its draft human rights plan, perhaps in the hopes that this would ensure the support of the Catholic church which had started publicly referring to then-President Lula as "Herod," an allusion to the king who, according to biblical accounts, ordered baby boys to be killed. During the Pope's 2007 visit to Brazil, Lula had already publicly pledged that his government would never propose the legalization of abortion, but this further step was thought necessary to appease the church.

The point is not that morality-based arguments for the criminalization of abortion are always a cheap veneer on actions that are motivated by political gain. In fact, my interaction with activists on both sides of the apparent abortion divide suggests to me that most people who profess to be either staunchly pro-life or staunchly pro-choice in fact are deeply attached to their beliefs and the morality on which they base them. With civility and mutual respect, these beliefs should be aired in public debate.

The point is that the morality of public policy depends on both its intention and its effect. The effect of abortion bans—in particular in the Latin American context of gender inequality and limited access to contraception—is death and suffering for the women who need abortions, with no discernable effect on lowering the number of abortions. As such, abortion bans are both ineffective and immoral.

Unfortunately, the bans continue. Six years after I talked with Lucila, I interviewed another woman in the same impossible situation. Silvia, who suffers from a serious kidney disease that could make another pregnancy near fatal for her, told me she received no help or even sympathy from the doctors who would tell her almost in the same breath, on the one hand, that she couldn't be pregnant and, on the other, that she had to carry the pregnancy to term: "I said, 'But you told me that I shouldn't have it! . . . I am close to needing dialysis as it is.' . . . I said, 'Are you going to guarantee that nothing will happen to my health?' . . . She said, 'I can't guarantee that.'"

Winds of Change

Despite this grim state of affairs, there are indications that things are slowly starting to change for the better. In April 2007, abortion was decriminalized in Mexico City, and this law was later upheld as constitutional by Mexico's Supreme Court. In 2008, Uruguay's congress approved a law to legalize abortion in the first trimester of the pregnancy. At the time, the law was immediately vetoed by the president, but a similar proposal is currently under consideration with much better prospects. In November 2010, the Argentine Congress also started a series of hearings on the legalization of abortion.

All of these developments are fueled by a growing empathy for the plight of poorer women, in particular. Most people know someone who has had an abortion, and it is increasingly an open secret that the criminalization of abortion mostly affects women who can't afford to go to the United States or to a private clinic for an illegal but safe intervention. The general rhetoric of the Latin America media on abortion has changed radically, even just over the past five years: questions and comments are now more about why women need abortions, not how to punish them for it.

Indeed, surveys confirm that most people in the region have a much more nuanced understanding of abortion than their elected officers: it must be legal, accessible, and rare. It is only a matter of time before policymakers catch on.

PART 7

POLITICAL CONSTRAINTS AND HARMFUL TRADITIONS

CHAPTER 25

Claiming Women's Rights in China

Sharon K. Hom

I n Xian in 1994, I conducted a workshop on legislative drafting with
more than a hundred women from various levels of women's federa-
tions, known as "fulians." To ground the discussion, we brainstormed a
list of top problems facing women in their communities. Most participants reported that violence against women and domestic violence were
leading concerns. But when we turned to examine draft legislation
aimed at providing greater protections for women, the group also
quickly identified the shortcomings of these draft laws: they lacked clear
definitions, lack of specificity about implementation mechanisms and
remedies, and no provisions for financing needed solutions. In a follow-
up exercise that identified common Chinese expression or sayings about
women, it became painfully clear that negative images and gender
stereotypes are embedded in the language, reinforcing cultural biases.

Although China has signed and ratified dozens of international
human rights treaties and passed many domestic laws to protect
women, the realization of rights for hundreds of millions of women

Sharon Hom is the executive director of Human Rights in China (HRIC), and professor of law
emerita, City University of New York School of Law. She is the coeditor of Challenging China:
Struggle and Hope in an Era of Change (New Press, 2007), and the editor of Chinese Women
Traversing Diaspora: Memoirs, Essays, and Poetry (Routledge, 1999). She contributed a chap-
ter to the anthology China's Great Leap: The Beijing Games and Olympian Human Rights
Challenges (Seven Stories, 2008). This essay draws on her chapter in the anthology Gender
Equality, Citizenship and Human Rights: Controversies and Challenges in China and the
Nordic Countries (Routledge, 2010).[1]

and girls remains an ongoing challenge that has domestic and international dimensions. In the fall of 1995, the United Nations convened the Fourth World Conference on Women. A parallel NGO event, Forum 95, was held along the same themes—equality, development, and peace—and attracted over 30,000 people. Slogans emerging from the conference included the now well-known "Women's rights are human rights," but also the Chinese slogan, "Connect the rails," calling for connecting (*jiegui*, to merge) with international women's movements, and promoting more women's activism in China. Anticipated or not, hosting a prominent international event such as the 1995 Women's Conference had positive spillover benefits for Chinese women and domestic women's groups. Through support and funding for numerous publications and new women's centers and programs, greater domestic awareness of women's issues and problems, as well as the role of NGOs in other countries, was advanced at different levels of government and among ordinary Chinese, the *laobaixing*.

Nearly two decades have passed since the 1995 Women's Conference and the adoption of the Beijing Declaration and the Platform of Action that called on all governments to take action on areas including education, health care, violence against women, media stereotypes, and the rights of girls. Then, as now, the future of women's rights in China is connected to overall progress in human rights, sustainable and equitable development, responsible stewardship of the environment, transparent and accountable governance, and greater openness and democratic reforms as called for by China's own citizens.

International Human Rights Obligations and Local Reality

Since the early 1980s, China has engaged in extensive efforts to rebuild a legal system, including passing numerous laws, policies, and programs aimed at eliminating discrimination against women and promoting gender equality. However, this domestic framework must be understood and implemented within the context of international human rights obligations that China has committed to, including the Convention on the Elimination of All Forms of Discrimination Against Women (CEDAW) and more than twenty other major rights conventions.[2] In addition to treaties and domestic legislative reforms, the PRC government also adopted the Program for the Development of Chinese Women (2001-10), which makes gender equality a basic state policy for the enhancement of national social progress.

As China has become increasingly active in the international human rights system over the past two decades, there have been challenges and opportunities presented by domestic efforts to implement these international obligations. As a state party to international human rights treaties on racial discrimination, torture, economic, social, and cultural rights, and rights of women and children, China has committed itself to their implementation, including participating in the international review and oversight of its implementation record, based upon international standards, principles, norms, and processes.

Over the past two decades, China has seen an unprecedented level of rapid economic growth, but the benefits and the costs of that growth have not been equally shared. Although the Chinese government calls for a "harmonious society," it continues to grapple with pervasive corruption; growing social inequalities; popular protests and unrest; and serious environmental, public health, and social welfare challenges.

Behind the glittery façades of Shanghai, Beijing, and the urban coastal areas, the vast majority of China's people are struggling to survive in the face of major social and economic dislocations; the collapse of social welfare safety nets; and lack of access to affordable and decent health care, housing, and education. Women—especially rural poor, migrant, or ethnic minority women and children—are disproportionately affected by these changes.[3] And rights defenders and activists investigating or reporting on these problems often find themselves the targets of harassment, surveillance, monitoring, or criminal prosecution.

Women's Rights Statistics a "State Secret"

Effective implementation of rights of women protected under Chinese and international law requires accurate, comprehensive and reliable data as the foundation for assessment of the issues and possible solutions. Yet, information such as statistics on kidnapping and trafficking of women and girls, forced abortions, infanticide are state secrets under Chinese law.

Thus, any assessment of the current human rights situation, including the status of women, presents a minefield. Accurate, reliable, and transparent information is the lifeblood of an independent media, health policy debates, responsible political participation, and human rights monitoring. The most serious obstacle to open access and distribution of information is the ongoing censorship and information control system in China. Information control is maintained by a comprehensive system of criminal, state security and state secrets laws, Internet and media laws, state-of-the-art technology, and a highly effective police and security apparatus.

In our report, *The State Secrets System: China's Legal Labyrinth* (2007), Human Rights in China provides a detailed examination of this system of information control, and its chilling effect on efforts to develop the rule of law and independent civil society inside China. A revised State Secrets Law went into effect October 1, 2010.[4] Its expanded scope addresses the rapid technological advances since the 1989 State Secrets Law was enacted, and places broader, tighter, and more rigorous control over information flow on the Internet and public information networks, in addition to traditional forms of communication.

This state secrets system controls the public dissemination of an all-encompassing universe of information as diverse as the total number of laid-off workers in state-owned enterprises, national statistics on the death penalty, statistics on unusual deaths in prisons; statistics on trafficking of women and children, and data on water and solid waste pollution in large and medium-size cities. The comprehensiveness of the information control system undermines review of China's human rights record by international expert bodies. It also undermines the development of an informed citizenry as well as the state and society's capacity to address complex social, legal, and environment issues

Rule of Law and Accountability

In order for women's rights in China to advance, there must be a functioning legal system that respects and protects rights, and a rule of law that is transparent, fair, and independent of the Communist Party of China. Although there has been significant progress since the 1980s toward rebuilding the legal system in China, including impressive legislative activity, training of legal personnel (lawyers, judges, law teachers), and development of legal and administrative institutions and processes, difficult challenges remain. Even China's own "White Paper on Human Rights" acknowledges that the development of the rule of law and democracy still falls short of the needs of economic and social growth. It specifically identifies the need for improvement of the legal framework; the lack of enforcement; the problems of bribery, corruption, and abuse of authority and power; and the need to educate the public about rule of law.[5]

Within a framework that maintains the supremacy of the Communist Party of China, the legal system being built continues to be plagued both by endemic corruption and influence of *guanxi* (relationships), as well as lack of independence from Party control. It remains essentially a rule "by" law rather than "of" law. The use of state security and state secrets law to restrict procedural due process protections exacerbates a politicized and secret decision-making process, especially in sensitive cases.

While the number of lawyers in China grew from about three thousand in the early 1980s to over one hundred thirty thousand in 2007,[6] there is only a small number willing to take on cases viewed as sensitive or political by the authorities. These include cases challenging problems such as official corruption, forced relocations, environmental degradation, health, and other pressing social and human rights issues. There has also been a major crackdown on rights defense lawyers, including prosecutions, violent attacks, and threats. These undermine the development of a professional and independent bar, and the integrity and fairness of the criminal justice system while contributing to an overall chilling effect on rights defense work.

When the authorities respond to individuals and grassroots groups that raise health issues—such as HIV/AIDS, sex workers, worker safety, or coercive population policies and practices—with repressive measures such as detentions, violence, and intimidation, they are also violating their rights of freedom of expression, and undermining the capacity of the government and society to address these problems. The economic, cultural, and social rights of women are related to their civil and political rights.

Abuse of Petitioners

In addition to the court system, there is also a vast administrative detention system that is outside the whole purview of judicial review and oversight, in which unlimited discretion is exercised by police and personnel in these camps. The avenues for citizens to present grievances to the authorities are ineffective at best. Numerous petitioners who travel to Beijing to petition the government for reasons ranging from official corruption, to land seizures, to withholding of payments, are detained and often sentenced to periods of "Reeducation Through Labor."

Mao Hengfeng is a Chinese woman who petitioned the authorities about abuses and coercive implementation of China's one-child population policy. In 1988, Mao was dismissed from her job at a soap factory after her refusal to abort a second pregnancy, which was ordered in accordance with the policy. Since that time, she has petitioned the government for redress on that dismissal and other subsequent abuses, including forcible eviction. As a result of her petitioning, she has been detained, forcibly admitted to a psychiatric hospital, sentenced to Reeducation Through Labor, and subjected to humiliating abuses while in prison. She was sentenced to two and a half years for having broken two table lamps and other objects while in detention for petitioning in 2006.

Although the Chinese government has discussed possible reforms to the Reeducation Through Labor system numerous times in recent years, the practice and its abuses, remain largely the same.

Finally, in order for there to be respect and protections of human rights and a rule of law with legitimacy and credibility, there needs to be accountability for past abuses. The past is not another country. Through the opportunities to host both the 1995 Women's Conference and the 2008 Olympics, China had hoped to create a different international image than the one broadcast live during and after the violent crackdown on democracy and labor activists on June 4, 1989.

The Tiananmen Mothers are a rights defense group that has worked to challenge the official accounts of the crackdown in China in June 1989, to document the deaths and those individuals still imprisoned, and present demands for full investigation, accountability, compensation, and dialogue with the authorities. Members of the group have been persecuted by the government, and their pleas for a reassessment of the 1989 events have been met with silence.

In order for China to make genuine progress toward a rule of law that protects and advances the rights of all of its people, these past abuses, this "forgotten history," must be addressed.

The Road Ahead

Several domestic and global drivers for change support a reasonable optimism. Despite the public rhetoric and toeing of the Party line, China's leadership is not monolithic. There are reform-minded allies in the government, think tanks, and throughout civil society, many of whom recognize the need to improve rights, health, and education prospects for women and girls. There is a growing civil society that is diverse and active, including feminist Chinese scholars and activists, and the development of women's legal centers and law school based clinics representing women's cases. However, the dramatic growth in numbers of registered and unregistered civil society organizations is also accompanied by a range of obstacles, including complex and confusing legal classifications and restrictive regulatory schemes.

At the end of the day, efforts to advance women's human rights in China must center on supporting Chinese women's voices, rights defense activists and lawyers, journalists, scholars, and grassroots groups, all of whom are working in extremely difficult conditions on the ground. To support these domestic forces more effectively, there need to be nuanced strategies that can exploit the role of new technologies and bridge the gap between international and domestic groups.

Technology is both opening greater civil space and providing increasingly sophisticated tools of censorship and social control. However, the extent to which the potential of the Internet can be exploited as tools for empowering rural, migrant, ethnic minority, or urban poor women and girls will depend on the extent to which the current digital divide will be addressed.

What is needed in China, as in other countries, are multipronged approaches that include domestic and international law, multilateral and national institutions, processes, cultural strategies, and diverse stakeholders.

The international community—foreign governments, rights organizations, corporations and other actors—needs to increasingly engage the Chinese government on issues central to human rights, and women's rights in particular. What is at stake is the human dignity, the well-being, and human rights of more than 600 million Chinese women, and the impact on the prospects of a sustainable and equitable future for all of China's almost 1.4 billion people. That future has environmental and human rights consequences for us all.

CHAPTER 26

A Long March for Women's Rights in China

Sheridan Prasso

When I was teaching at Guangdong University of Foreign Studies in China a few years ago, one of my students told me a shocking story about her childhood. With China's one-child policy in force since 1979, having more than one child was against the law, but my student, "Polly," five years old at the time, remembers her mother becoming pregnant. She also remembers her mother's screams as officials took her away to the hospital and ordered the forcible abortion of her fetus—three times. When Polly was eleven, her mother became pregnant again. This time, the mother did not wait for the authorities to take her away. As soon as she began to show visible signs of pregnancy, she fled to a faraway relative's home to hide and have her baby there. When she returned home months later with the newborn, the authorities showed up and demanded that the family pay a fine—equal to more than $1,000, which was a fortune to a family living in Sichuan province in those days.

Sheridan Prasso, the author of The Asian Mystique: Dragon Ladies, Geisha Girls & Our Fantasies of the Exotic Orient *(Public Affairs, 2005), is a longtime foreign correspondent in Asia, an Associate Fellow at the Asia Society, and an Adjunct Professor at the School of International and Public Affairs at Columbia University. In this chapter, she notes that China has made headway in improving basic human rights for women, but cautions that tremendous work remains in the areas of gender discrimination, particularly in the workplace, hiring practices, wage disparities—and in increasing the rights of rural women, particularly those in danger of trafficking.*

My student's story of her mother's forced abortions is one facet of China's approach to women in the last three decades. As a girl from rural Sichuan province who was able to go to university and later enter the workforce in one of China's "special economic zones," Polly can be seen as an emblem of progress women in China have made in education and employment, but also the challenges for women and girls that remain.

Women in China, it seems, are chronically engaged in a few-steps-forward-few-steps-back cycle. The Chinese government has improved women's health overall and raised its rank on UN measures of well-being. Consider how far the country has come in maternal mortality; from a rate of 110 deaths per 100,000 births in 1990, the rate has fallen to 38 today. In fact, China ranks only just behind the United States but ahead of Russia on the UN Development Program's (UNDP's) overall Gender Inequality Index of human development indicators measuring reproductive health, labor participation, and inequality between genders. Among Asian countries, only wealthier Japan, South Korea, and Singapore rank higher.

But gender inequality remains a problem and is most acute in rural areas, where women have unequal access to services and employment, are sometimes trafficked into prostitution, and suffer more domestic violence than women in China's cities.[1] Rural women also have less decision-making power at home and in their communities, and less chance of receiving education, nutrition, and health care, according to a survey by the China Agricultural University in Beijing. The survey also found that the prevalence of illness of rural women is 5 percent higher than among rural men. Long work hours, poor nutrition, and lack of care after childbirth were blamed.

The Gender Gap

The one-child policy has undoubtedly slowed down population growth, but it has often been implemented in abusive ways. Additionally, the lower birth rates have raised major new challenges including a significant gender imbalance. China's dependency ratio—the number of young and old people who have to be supported by the working-age population—is growing faster than even Europe's; as a direct result of both the one-child policy and a traditional preference for boys, by 2025 China will be home to 96 million men in their early twenties, but only 80 million women of the same age. In some provinces, according to recent government data, the gap between the sexes is 130 baby boys for every 100 girls. By some estimates, China will soon have 50 million more men than women.

The impact of these unequal numbers of men and women may be severe, with women more likely to be adversely affected. The lack of young women may lower the average age of marriage; in turn, early marriage, sex, and childbirth have grave, sometimes fatal consequences for young women: a literature review conducted for the World Health Organization (WHO) on making pregnancy safer shows that pregnant girls under age sixteen face four times the risk of maternal death than women in their twenties, and the infant mortality rate is about 50 percent higher. China has made progress in reducing maternal mortality, but increasing numbers of younger women having children may reverse these gains.

For both rural and urban women, increased competition among men may also increase sex trafficking and forced marriages, especially of women from the poorest provinces or less-well-off neighboring countries. Already, between 10,000 and 20,000 women and children are estimated to be trafficked in China; a large anti-trafficking campaign by Chinese police last year freed more than 7,300 women and 3,400 children. As China's population becomes increasingly male, these numbers of trafficked women are feared to increase.[2]

Early marriage undermines women and girls' ability to complete their education and establish financial independence. Marrying young can hold women back and leave them without skills they need later in life. The pressure to become a young mother displaces a career track and earning potential, with resulting implications for the economic stimulus that women normally contribute to an economy. Rural women are more likely to be married early in life and prematurely pregnant.

It may be that more Chinese women have access to education today than at any time in history, and laws guarantee equal access to education for girls and women. Children above the age of six receive compulsory education for nine years, regardless of sex, nationality, and race.[3]

The population age twenty-five and older that has attained an education level of secondary school or higher level, expressed as a female-male ratio, is .778—or around seventy-eight girls for every hundred boys, according to the UNDP. The numbers may appear low but they are impressive when considering they include older women, who were around since the days of almost complete female illiteracy pre-1949. While these are important gains, concerns about girls and women's access to education remain.[4]

The Committee on the Elimination of Discrimination Against Women (CEDAW) acknowledged in its 2006 report (the most recent report for China) that some progress had been made in increasing women and girls' access to education, but expressed concern that rural girls have disproportionate illiteracy and school dropout rates and continue to face discrimination in access to education, both at primary and secondary levels. The Committee recommended that China take immediate measures to ensure that rural girls are able to complete nine years of compulsory education.

China has made particular strides in addressing the gender imbalance in higher education, and increasing women's access to universities and colleges. Women today account for 49 percent of undergraduate students at Chinese universities, 44 percent of students studying for master's degrees, and 31 percent of those studying for PhDs. Back in 1995, just over 30 percent of master's degree students and 16 percent of doctoral students in China were women.

Access to education has clearly increased access to employment for women. Communist work units increased the number of women in the workforce from just 600,000 in 1949 to more than 50 million in the 1990s, when China began embracing capitalist-style market reforms and economic growth began to take off. That number was nearly 340 million by 2003. Today, more than 80 percent of working-age urban women in China have held jobs outside the home—among the highest rate of workforce participation in the region. China's growth statistics can be credited in large part to women's empowerment: according to authors Nicholas Kristof and Sheryl WuDunn, 8 out of 10 factory workers in coastal China are female.[5] And a recent Grant Thornton International Business Report cited in the *China Daily* reported that women in China these days hold 34 percent of senior management positions, up from 31 percent in 2009; and 19 percent of those hold the title of CEO, compared to 9 percent in the European Union, and 5 percent in the United States.[6]

Women's Work Challenges

But Chinese students are no longer assured employment. China has trouble providing jobs for all its college graduates—some 30 percent of the 6.6 million students who graduated in the last few years are still unemployed. Again, women bear a disproportionate burden: they are less likely to find employment and frequently find themselves as the second choice for male employees in many industries. The Chinese government has passed and updated laws making discriminatory practices illegal in the workplace, such as the 1995 Labor Law, which states that "[w]omen shall enjoy the right of employment equal to that of men," and that "women may not be refused employment" because of their gender. Despite this, women still face wide-ranging employment related discrimination.

"Industries and employers usually put the economy first and believe male employees can bring more production," Liang Jie and Shi Wangli at the School of Civil Engineering at Southwest Jiaotong University in Sichuan province found in another study. "Employment of female students would increase the operation cost of industries, and the limitation of female employment in turn reduces the opportunity in the job market for female students. Industries set job categories and limitations, and payment to female students is usually lower than payment to male graduates. In fact, many employers do not want to hire female students even if female students willingly accept lower pay, which greatly frustrates female employment."

My former student Polly's work experience confirms that women workers are seen as less valuable and treated differently. She graduated in 2006 with a job offer from a large, multinational accounting firm in

Guangdong province, and immediately found the hours long and the work frustrating. (She did not say whether she was being paid less than male colleagues, and perhaps she did not know). Her male supervisors would promise clients that tight deadlines could be met, forcing Polly and her female colleagues to work around the clock. On a blog she kept on sina.com, Polly complained of fatigue and no time to eat—and lamented that her male bosses seemed to have it easy, even finding time for napping on the job. Many of her female coworkers quit as soon as they married or left for another reason.

But Polly was among the lucky ones. The researchers Liang and Shi point out that of the college graduates they studied around the same time Polly entered the workforce, female employment was just 63 percent, nearly 9 percent lower than for male students. They cited another study showing that out of seventy-five employers, forty-two preferred to hire males when equivalent-pay policies were in force. A study released last year by Beijing human resources consulting company MyCOS HR Digital Information, quoted in the *China Daily*, found that of the 2010 crop of graduating college students, 30 percent of males had job offers by graduation, compared to 21 percent of female students.

Women who do find work face other forms of discrimination. Female grads in IT and telecommunications were offered 420 yuan ($62) less than male students; in transportation and logistics they were offered 523 yuan ($77) less. Statistics from the state-run All-China Women's Federation, for example, show that the income of female migrant workers is 20 percent lower than that of their male counterparts. One state-owned real estate and development company which employs 70 percent males on its staff was quoted as saying that women were considered only for secretarial jobs. "Females are never considered for other positions, including construction supervisors," an official said, "even though some of the female applicants were equally excellent as male counterparts."[7]

The CEDAW Committee identified gender discrimination in employment as an important concern, highlighting the lack of legal provisions guaranteeing equal pay for equal work, persistent wage gaps between men and women, the high concentration of women in informal employment and gender related income reduction in a very competitive job market, as issues for China to address.

In addition to discrimination in education and employment, women in China also face pressing human rights issues related to lack of freedom of expression, assembly, and worship, and a lack of legal due process and protections under law. Since 2008, the Chinese government has tightened controls on lawyers, human rights defenders, and nongovernmental organizations, including those doing important work for women and girls. In March 2010, China's leading independent women's rights organization, the Women's Legal Research and Services Center, was notified that its affiliation with Beijing University had been terminated, effectively shuttering the center.

Traditional Practices

Chinese people like to point out with pride that China has had five thousand years of civilization. What is often left unsaid is that only in the last sixty years or so has this civilization formally extended benefits to women in the form of measures to grant them human rights and legal protections equal to men. A combination of Confucian beliefs, Imperial practices, and feudal traditions were responsible for concubinage, footbinding, child marriage, infanticide, and violence against women, not to mention lack of equal access to education. While the Communist revolution formally abolished these practices, several millennia of repressive traditions are difficult to expunge in just a generation or two.

Confucian beliefs, developed around 500 B.C., held women to be lower in status than men and dictated obedience. A virtuous woman was supposed to uphold the "three subordinates": to her father before marriage, to her husband after marriage, and to her son after her husband's death. A woman's greatest duty was to produce a son. Because many Chinese families believe that only male heirs can carry on the family lineage, the preference for male children has long been strong in Chinese tradition—and its remnants endure today. There are also economic reasons. A girl child upon marriage was sent to join the household of her husband. Upon the old age of her husband's parents, she became the primary caregiver to her in-laws. So in order to ensure that parents would be cared for in their old age, having a son—who would marry and bring a woman into the home—was essential.

In Imperial China, women were not deemed worthy of the same level of education granted to men. Men of high social class were taught to read and write Chinese characters and the Confucian classics so that they could sit for the imperial examination system—the basis of the Mandarin civil service that ruled the country. The result of leaving women out was almost complete female illiteracy, except at the very highest levels of society.

In the 1920s, when Western colonialism brought modernization to Chinese cities under Qing Dynasty rule, Chinese women began cutting their hair short, wearing the *qipao*—a traditional tunic of Mandarin men that, when fitted to a woman's form, became the embodiment of Chinese femininity—and demanding more rights in line with the women's movement around the world. Foot-binding, which had been a mark of high social status for over a thousand years (peasant women who needed to work in the fields did not practice it), was banned in 1911 and began to decline. More girls began to go to school. But it was not until the post-1949 era that the Chinese government began enforcing more rights for women, and adopting global laws and standards.

In 1995, China was chosen to host the Fourth World Conference on Women in Beijing, and Chinese leaders used the major international meeting featuring Hillary Clinton as a coming-out party to trumpet the country's progress, for example, having just the year before passed a Mother and Child Health Act to outlaw the practice of fetus gender identification and sex-selective abortions.

Today, the Chinese government continues to pass and update laws making discriminatory practices illegal, but the problem remains of enforcement, and ending engrained traditions that devalue girls. The central government now subsidizes girl-only rural families, employing financial incentives to correct gender imbalance rather than the types of punitive measures Polly's mother endured. A government "Care for Girls" advocacy program seeks to demonstrate the value of girls and women in underdeveloped areas. While male preference is not expected to end any time soon, giving families clear reasons to raise girls and changing perceptions about their burden of care can go a long way.

Polly, my student, ultimately married. Returning from her honeymoon in Europe, she discovered she was pregnant. Expressing "bittersweet" emotion over the prospect of child raising, and fearing that pregnancy might interfere with her job, she made arrangements for her parents back in Sichuan province to care for the infant for its first few years of life. She had little choice. Despite her treatment in the workplace, she had worked hard to have a career and wanted to keep it. But young mothers are particularly susceptible to involuntary termination. The risk was made even riskier by the timing. It was 2008 when the baby was due, just as layoffs began decimating the manufacturing sector in Guangdong province due to the global economic downturn, affecting the accounting firms that do work for it. Polly's mother readily agreed to raise the child.

Polly had a boy. Full of spunk, he looks healthy and strong in the photos sent by Polly's mother, which she regularly posts on her blog. As for gender, Polly never expressed a preference. In twenty or thirty years, when he grows up and starts looking to have his own family, women will be scarcer than back in the era when his mother was born. Perhaps, despite the weight of tradition, they will be more treasured as well.

CHAPTER 27

Girls Not Brides

Graça Machel and Mary Robinson

Northern Ethiopia's Amhara region has a landscape of red soil, small farms, and rolling green hills. Amhara's 19 million people are poor and rely almost entirely on agriculture. The region is served by few roads, children rarely get more than a few years of education, and they often walk many miles to school.

It also has one of the highest rates of child marriage on earth. Eighty percent of girls in Amhara are married by the time they are eighteen; half by the age of fifteen. This harmful traditional practice affects an estimated 10 million girls around the world every year[1]—that's more than twenty-five thousand girls every day.

In Amhara, we met many young women in their late teens and early twenties, some of whom had married as young as eight or ten and had their first children at thirteen or fourteen. Archbishop Tutu admitted frankly that he found the experience "devastating." In one tiny village, sitting in the shade of tall trees, these women and girls explained that, for them, marriage was not a day of happiness. It was the day they stopped going to school, began living with a man they had never met, and started having sex, whether they wanted to or not.

Graça Machel and Mary Robinson are members of The Elders, the independent group of global leaders formed by Nelson Mandela in 2007, who work together in support of peace and human rights. Graça Machel is former education minister of Mozambique and an international advocate for women's and children's rights. Mary Robinson is former president of Ireland and former United Nations High Commissioner for Human Rights. With their fellow Elders, they initiated "Girls Not Brides: The Global Partnership to End Child Marriage" in 2011.

Child marriage is deeply embedded in the social customs of Amhara, as it is in many countries in Asia, Africa, the Middle East, and some communities in Europe and the Americas. For thousands of years, families have married girls young. There are many reasons for this: to protect her and the family's honor, as sex before marriage is seen as shameful; to reduce the economic burden on the family; or to gain a bride price. In close, traditional communities, social pressure to marry is considerable, and a girl not married by eighteen often risks being viewed with suspicion—along with her entire family.

While we acknowledge the value of tradition in all our lives, we believe that child marriage is a harmful traditional practice—it is a violation of human rights and a major hindrance to development.

A Violation of Human Rights and a Hindrance to Development

Child marriage, whether an official marriage under the law or a customary union, is without doubt a fundamental violation of human rights. Article 16 of the Universal Declaration of Human Rights sets out that "[m]arriage shall be entered into only with the free and full consent of the intending spouses." However, few child brides have any choice about when or whom they marry.

Is there a suitable minimum age of marriage? The widely ratified United Nations Convention on the Rights of the Child defines eighteen as the age of adulthood—a standard to which we should all aspire. So, although we acknowledge that a number of countries have set the minimum age of marriage below eighteen, we refer to UNICEF's definition of child marriage as a legal or customary union in which at least one spouse is under eighteen.

Child marriage affects millions of children, predominantly girls. It is important to remember that boys are also affected by the practice, albeit in far smaller numbers, and with a generally less destructive impact on their health and opportunities. The reality of life for most child brides is forced marriage, forced sex, an end to education, and few choices about the future. Early pregnancy and childbirth bring additional risks, with girls under fifteen five times more likely to die in pregnancy and childbirth than women age twenty and older.

Child brides are therefore among the most vulnerable people on earth. Rarely accorded any rights, yet expected to assume adult responsibilities at a very young age, they are disempowered, often abused, and frequently isolated. Child brides are also out of the reach of many development programmes that target girls, as they are often confined to their homes.

The voices of these girls are seldom heard, but the impact of child marriage is felt throughout their communities—and that impact is overwhelmingly negative. Poverty and child marriage often go hand in hand. Without education or other skills, girls have little chance to lift themselves out of poverty. Their children are also more likely to be poor; lack education; and suffer higher risks of illness, malnutrition, and death in infancy. For generations, their rights to health, nutrition, and education are consistently denied.

In short, child marriage perpetuates the cycle of poverty, illiteracy, and ill health. Indeed, it hinders realization of six of the eight Millennium Development Goals, the UN-agreed global targets: eradicating extreme poverty and hunger; achieving universal primary education; promoting gender equality and empowering women; reducing child mortality; improving maternal health; and combating HIV/AIDS, malaria, and other diseases.[2] Ending child marriage is an essential step in advancing both development and respect for basic human rights.

Child Marriage, in Numbers and Lives

It is difficult to get accurate figures on the extent of child marriage, in part because data collection mechanisms in a large number of countries are so weak. Many countries do not collect data on sexual and reproductive topics from girls under the age of fifteen. Birth registration systems are often inadequate, making it difficult to gather comprehensive data on ages of educational attainment, marriage, and childbearing. An even more important reason is that marriages involving children are often not registered with civil authorities.

However, on the basis of data available, we can see that the prevalence of child marriage varies starkly between regions and even within countries.

In Africa, for example, countries with very high rates of child marriage such as Niger (76 percent), Chad (71 percent) and Mali (65 percent) exist alongside others with lower rates, such as Togo (31 percent) and South Africa (8 percent). Similarly, in South Asia the rate is very high in Bangladesh (65 percent), lower in Sri Lanka (14 percent),[3] and moderately high in India (48 percent). However, India is home to more than one-third of all child brides worldwide, and in the state of Madhya Pradesh, some 73 percent of young women are married by age eighteen. In Ethiopia, most child marriages occur in the north, where, in Amhara for example, the proportion of young women married by age eighteen (around 80 percent) greatly exceeds the national rate (49 percent).

One positive trend is the apparent decline in the practice of child marriage. Girls are getting married later in most sub-Saharan countries, as well as North Africa, South Asia, and Southeast Asia. Yet the pace of change is slow, and even in places where the median age of marriage is increasing, it has remained under eighteen. At current rates it will still take hundreds of years to eradicate child marriage completely.

It is the lack of choice and the waste of talent that is the terrible legacy of child marriage. These vast numbers of girls who continue to marry as children—as many as 100 million in the next decade alone—will become women whose opportunities to fulfil their potential will be curtailed at an early age.

Sacrificing Education, Risking Health

The education gap between boys and girls in the developing world, especially at the secondary school level, is often greater in communities where child marriage is common.[4] Many parents question the value of sending their daughters to school—particularly secondary school—because they intend to marry them off before they complete their education. Other reasons parents fail to send girls to secondary school include poor access to secondary schools for girls, risks of sexual violence en route and at school, inadequate transport, employment discrimination that diminishes the returns on education for girls, and high school fees and related costs that force parents to choose among children. For child brides who do remain in school, domestic chores often compete with their studies and dropout rates are high. In very few settings are there opportunities for married girls to continue their studies. The curtailment of girls' education leaves them ill prepared for any sort of employment they might hope to have in the future.

In the course of our research, we spoke with child brides whose testimony deeply moved us. In Ethiopia, we met a girl of sixteen who had married at fifteen. When asked about her wedding day (sitting next to her husband, a man well into his twenties), she shyly replied: "It was the day I left school." We asked if she could return to school now that she was married. "No chance," she replied. "I have to look after him."

Child marriage and early pregnancy vastly increase a girl's risk of death or injury in pregnancy and childbirth. Girls are often under pressure to prove their fertility soon after marrying, and many are thus exposed to risk of illness, birth-related injury such as obstetric fistula, and death during childbirth. In 2007, UNICEF reported that a girl under the age of fifteen is five times more likely to die during pregnancy and childbirth than a woman in her twenties.[5] A girl age fifteen to nineteen is twice as likely to die. Child brides living in poor communities suffer from lack of access to health services, and usually have limited access to information on reproductive health, making them even more vulnerable to family and cultural pressures.

Child brides are at greater risk of contracting HIV than their counterparts who marry later. They are often married to older, more sexually experienced men with whom it is difficult to negotiate safe sexual behavior, including wearing condoms to protect against HIV/AIDS. A study conducted in Kenya and Zambia in 2004 found that married girls ages fifteen to nineteen were 75 percent more likely to contract HIV than sexually active, unmarried girls of the same age.[6] Similar figures have been found in twenty-nine countries across Africa and Latin America.[7]

Girls who are married early are more likely to experience domestic violence and sexual abuse as well as isolation from their family and their communities. In 2005, a survey conducted in India revealed that girls who married before age eighteen reported experiencing physical violence twice as often as girls who married at a later age; younger married girls reported experiencing sexual violence by their husbands three times more often.[8]

And the risks extend to their babies; if a mother is under eighteen, her baby's chance of dying in the first year of life is 60 percent greater than that of a baby born to a mother older than nineteen.[9]

A Harmful Tradition—and a Message to Men

Child marriage reflects a set of social norms that typically also include early childbearing and relatively high fertility; changing these norms is difficult and touches on sensitive areas of tradition, family, and sometimes religion.

Traditions behind child marriage may serve to consolidate family, caste and tribal ties, or to maintain ethnic or community relations. Child brides may also be used to settle family feuds, as in certain regions of Pakistan, where the Pashtun *swara* custom consists of giving a girl in marriage as compensation for a murder perpetrated by her family, or to settle other inter-clan or family disputes.[10] Early marriage is particularly encouraged by the widespread cultural values surrounding the virginity and chastity of a girl. In many societies a woman's premarital sexual activity brings dishonor to her family and community, so parents are under tremendous pressure to marry off their daughters as early as possible. Protection from rape is also offered as a reason for early marriage as a married girl has a husband to defend her, while an unmarried girl does not.

Does religion play any role in perpetuating child marriage? In fact, no major religion explicitly promotes child marriage, nor is it the preserve of any particular faith. We have encountered child marriage in Orthodox Christian, Muslim, and Hindu communities in Africa, Asia and the Middle East. We have also been encouraged to meet senior religious leaders who have openly spoken against the practice. However at local level, marriages involving children are often blessed by religious leaders who perpetuate the norms and traditions of that community.

In most of the world, a woman's most important role is still to be a wife, mother, and homemaker, and a girl's adolescence is perceived to be the time when she prepares to take on such roles. As a consequence, girls' schooling and preparation for economic roles—and their right to play and socialize with their peers—may be viewed as being in competition with preparation for a lifetime of caregiving.

As Archbishop Tutu has pointed out, child marriage is rooted in a way of thinking which men have endorsed for far too long: "Child marriage occurs because we men allow it. Village chiefs, religious leaders, decision makers—most are male. In order for this harmful practice to end, we need to enlist the support of all the men who know this is wrong, and work together to persuade all those who don't."

Traditions Can Change

Child marriage has long been a hidden, unspoken, and largely unaddressed crisis. It sits on the margins of other development challenges: girls' education, maternal and child mortality, gender based violence, and the empowerment of girls and women. We can only speculate about why it has remained on the sidelines, despite the vast numbers of girls and women affected. Perhaps there has been a reluctance to take on a practice that is so bound up in family traditions and cultural practices. But this is not an adequate response to something that has such a major impact on development challenges and the lives of millions of girls.

We are not against tradition. We know that tradition and culture are essential for social cohesion and can represent the very best of humanity's achievements. But traditions that are misused to perpetuate harmful and discriminatory practices are not acceptable. And as man-made things, traditions can change. We must be respectful, but have the courage to say that change is necessary.

Like foot-binding in China, female genital mutilation, and slavery, child marriage is a practice that we believe has had its day, and must end—not only for the sake of the millions of girls affected, but for their families and communities.

Strategies That Work

Ending child marriage is not a challenge that can be met in a two-year funding cycle. Shouting from the sidelines will also achieve nothing, and so will trying to change behavior one girl or one family at a time. It will require sustained effort, first to raise awareness, then begin dialogue, and gradually change social norms and traditions.

Our partners have shown us that there are effective methods to reduce the practice of early marriage and speed up the pace of change. These cover three broad areas: enforcement of the law, investment in girls, and community-level engagement.

First of all, legal frameworks need to be in place that reflect international conventions and human rights standards, and most important, are publicized and enforced. Most countries with high rates of child marriage have laws against it, but these laws are not implemented. We have heard of situations where police officers themselves believe that marrying their daughters young is the best way to protect them. Educating police and judicial officials, communities, and girls themselves about the law is an important start to ending child marriage.

A second component of any change strategy is the empowerment of girls. Supporting girls' education, providing incentives to parents, and books and uniforms to girls boosts their status and may encourage their families to delay marriage and see their daughters as an asset rather than a burden. Girls' clubs—places where girls can meet and talk in safety—have also been shown to be effective in empowering girls, especially if they provide a place to turn if they are to be married against their will.

Third and perhaps most important is the need to facilitate discussion within communities about harmful customs such as child marriage. When the whole community collectively decides to end the practice, change becomes sustainable. Any strategy that simply condemns the practice, without engaging the men and women who determine the community's behavior, is doomed to fail. Respectful discussion, initiated with trusted leaders and based on factual information about the risks of injury and death in childbirth, of contracting HIV, and encouraging respect for human rights has already delivered results.

As our partners have repeatedly told us, these interventions cannot succeed in isolation. Efforts must be holistic, multifaceted, and rights-based to have lasting impact in curbing child marriage. That is why we, with our fellow Elders, have initiated Girls Not Brides: The Global Partnership to End Child Marriage as a space for activists to combine their efforts more effectively.

Girls Not Brides: a New Global Partnership

Some governments are beginning to recognize that ending child marriage must be part of their poverty-reduction, human-rights, and development plans, and there are a number of courageous organizations and individuals who have been working to change traditions, but these activities are taking place on a relatively small scale.

In order to focus greater attention on the issue of child marriage, The Elders have created Girls Not Brides: The Global Partnership to End Child Marriage, a new platform and mechanism for all organizations addressing the issue of child marriage to share information; learn from one another; and develop effective strategies to drive change at the local, national, and global level.[11]

Girls Not Brides was born at a meeting of some fifty organizations in Addis Ababa in June 2011. We believe it is the first time that there has been such a gathering of experts and activists on child marriage from all over the world, and we take great encouragement from them. At the same time, the emphasis must be on encouraging change at the local and community level, while sharing approaches that have been tested and proven successful.

Once that change is made, it is irreversible. Those who have had the chance to go to school and marry later are highly unlikely to impose early marriage on their daughters. For that reason alone we say that we can indeed end child marriage in a single generation.

CHAPTER 28

Damned If You Do, Damned if You Don't
Religious Dress and Women's Rights

Judith Sunderland

O n April 11, 2011, Kenza Drider, a thirty-two-year-old mother of
four, broke the law in Paris: she wore the niqab in public. She had
traveled by train from her home in Avignon to protest a new law banning the full-face Muslim veil in all public spaces throughout France.
In June 2010 twenty-five-year-old Louiza (not her real name) was shot
at close range with a paintball gun as she walked down the street in
Grozny because she wasn't wearing a headscarf. That summer many
women in the Russian republic of Chechnya fell victim to attacks and
harassment during a "virtue campaign" to force women to cover themselves.

What these two incidents have in common is interference—sometimes brutal, always wrong—with the fundamental human rights of
women in the name of religion, tradition, or misguided protectionism.
In Indonesia's Aceh province, Saudi Arabia, Iran, and Afghanistan
under the Taliban, as well as parts of Somalia, Gaza, and Chechnya,

*Judith Sunderland is a senior researcher on Western Europe in Human Rights Watch's Europe
and Central Asia Division, covering issues including counterterrorist measures, immigration
policy, and religious freedom. Before joining Human Rights Watch, she worked as a human
rights observer for the United Nations Mission in Guatemala, and as a journalist covering Central America. In this chapter she argues why rules on religious dress for women violate their
rights to freedom from discrimination, religious expression, and personal autonomy.*

women are forced to cover up. At the same time, local and national governments in Europe have moved to prohibit women and girls from wearing the veil in schools and public service. In April 2011, France enacted a national law banning the wearing of full-face veils anywhere in public; Belgium is poised to adopt a similar law, and comparable nationwide bans have been proposed in a number of other European countries. Several cities in Belgium, Spain, and Italy already have local bans in place.

The sad irony is that whether they are being forced to cover up or to uncover, these women are being discriminated against. Banned from wearing the *hijab*—a traditional Muslim headscarf—or forced to veil themselves, women around the world are being stripped of their basic rights to personal autonomy; to freedom of expression; and to freedom of religion, thought, and conscience.

Though men are also subject to religious and traditional practices, including dress codes that impinge on their freedoms, women around the world are far more likely to see their decisions dictated, their options curtailed, even their physical integrity and lives threatened, by official and societal norms about propriety.

Women's rights activists, both within and outside Muslim communities, have long argued that veiling, and full veiling of the face and body in particular, is a powerful symbol of the oppression and subjugation of women. The *burqa*, a full face and body covering, is commonly associated with the Taliban, who systematically violate the fundamental rights and freedoms of women in Afghanistan, a country with the lowest life expectancy in the region and some of the highest rates of maternal death.

"Virtue" Campaigns to Enforce Veiling

Authorities often justify enforcement of dress codes on grounds of tradition, virtue, or decency. In Gaza, for example, Hamas officials administering this Palestinian territory initiated in July 2009 their own "virtue" campaign. When the school year began in August of that year, we heard about schools turning away girls for not wearing the headscarf and traditional gown called the *jilbab,* on the basis of unofficial orders from Hamas authorities.[1] The paintball attacks against women in Chechnya came several years into a quasi-official, though extra-legal "virtue campaign" initiated by Chechen President Ramzan Kadyrov in 2006.[2] As part of this campaign, local authorities prohibit women from working in the public sector if they do not wear head-scarves, and female students are required to wear headscarves in schools and universities. Gradually, throughout 2009 and 2010, the authorities broadened their enforcement of this de facto "headscarf rule" to other public places, including entertainment venues, cinemas, and even outdoor areas. In addition to the pelting with paintball guns, Chechen women told us they are threatened with more "persuasive" measures if they do not cover their hair. Though such measures do not have any basis in the written laws applicable in the Chechen Republic, they are strictly enforced.

Promoters of such codes argue that policies of forced veiling are expressions of a shared societal concept of decency analogous to laws prohibiting public nudity. But decency laws prohibiting public nudity are virtually universal, are not associated with and do not lead to other limitations on rights, and are not the subject of significant dissent. In contrast, forced veiling—and in particular, forced wearing of the *niqab* and the *burqa*—are associated with serious human rights violations. And, of course, the purpose, meaning, and nature of veils vary widely among communities and nations, and are hotly contested issues within Muslim communities. Many of the rules requiring certain kinds of dress for women, as in Gaza and Chechnya, are relatively new.

Forced veiling and other dress codes often have dire consequences for women's physical integrity, freedom of movement, and economic opportunities. In areas of Somalia controlled by the Islamist militant group al-Shabaab, authorities have imposed strict dress codes for women, requiring they wear an *abaya* made of particularly thick cloth that touches the ground and hides all physical contours.[3] Women who wouldn't comply shared with us their stories of being beaten, whipped, and jailed. The *abaya* decrees have severely hampered freedom of movement for women who simply cannot afford these expensive, imported garments. Many poor women have had to share one *abaya* across an entire family or group of households, meaning that only one of them can leave the home at any time. These dress codes have been accompanied by rules barring women from working in public and strict segregation between men and women, even family members, in public places.

Given the evidence that forced veiling constitutes a serious women's rights issue in so many parts of the world, it is perhaps not surprising that proponents of bans on veils in Europe see them as a way to liberate women and protect women and girls from societal pressure to veil themselves. Bans on students and teachers wearing headscarves in schools, on civil servants wearing any kind of religious symbol, and on full-face coverings are also variously justified by the need to ensure secularism in state institutions, as well as on security grounds. Though some (but not all) bans are crafted in neutral terms, the political debate around them in Europe is infused with discomfort with an increasingly visible Muslim minority population, and concerns about integrating newer Europeans while preserving so-called European values.

Pro-ban arguments relating to women's rights have the greatest resonance. Yet denying women the right to cover themselves is as wrong as forcing them to do so. Muslim women, like all women, should have the right to dress as they choose, and to make decisions about their lives and how to express their faith, identity, and moral values. And they should not be forced to choose between their beliefs and their chosen profession.

Generalizations about women's oppression do a disservice to one of the basic tenets of gender equality: the right to self-determination and autonomy, the right a woman has to make decisions about her life and her body without interference from the state or others. There are undoubtedly women who are forced to wear the veil or feel tremendous pressure to do so against their own convictions. But there are also Muslim women in Europe, some of them converts, who have spoken out to say that veiling was their own decision, citing motivations such as an expression of their faith and a desire to assert their identity. As alien as it may to seem to some Europeans, veiling can be a choice, in the same way that other convictions or conduct that have been shaped by societal, family, or religious influences are experienced by the individual as an expression of their identity.

Freedom from Coercion

The right to autonomy, a core principle of women's rights, is a part of the right to a private life guaranteed under international human rights law. The right to autonomy encompasses the right to make decisions freely in accordance with one's values, beliefs, personal circumstances, and needs. Exercise of this right presupposes freedom from coercion and from illegitimate restrictions. It also includes the right to adopt a lifestyle of which others in society disapprove, or deem harmful to the person who pursues it.

At a practical level, it is hard to see how proscriptive laws targeting women wearing veils serve the cause of women's equality. Local laws and the nationwide French ban enacted in April 2011 banning the full-face veil provide for a variety of sanctions on women who violate the terms of the ban, including fines, "good citizenship" courses, and community social work. The law also makes it a crime to coerce women and girls into wearing such veils, punishable by up to one year in prison and a €30,000 fine. A similar ban soon to enter into effect in Belgium envisions up to seven days in prison. In essence, bans like these are a lose-lose proposition: they violate the rights of those who choose to wear the veil, and do nothing to help those who are forced to do so.

For those who cover themselves by choice, such bans force them to choose between the ability to participate fully in society and the manifestation of their religious faith. They make commonplace activities—taking the bus, attending a parent-teacher conference in a public school, filing documents at a municipal office, even getting medical attention in a hospital—impossible while following their religious beliefs.

For those women who are compelled by family members to cover themselves, a ban on full-face covering veils in all public spaces may mean they trade what critics call an "ambulatory prison" for one made of brick and mortar: their homes. The women themselves or their male relatives may decide they cannot go out of the house without their veils, or at least severely restrict how much they go out in public. Many of the women interviewed by the Open Society Foundation in the lead-up to the ban imposed in France on full-face veils said they would avoid going outside once the ban entered into force. As Karima, a twenty-one-year-old living in Rennes, put it, "They say that it's our husbands who are locking us away but it's actually they who are locking us away. . . . We shouldn't delude ourselves. . . . I would end up taking it off. But what is clear is that I'm really going to restrict the number of times I go out to the bare minimum. I'll go out only when I need to do necessary things."[4]

Strong social censure within Muslim communities against the wearing of full-face veils, and against forced veiling generally, will likely do more to empower women than laws and fines. State coercion and punishing the victims will not uproot oppression. What is needed is further education on these issues, access to support and economic possibilities, as well as effective means to seek justice against those who are oppressing them.

Restrictions on teachers and other public servants wearing the headscarf are for the most part unjustifiable and harmful. While it may be legitimate to prohibit teachers from wearing the full-face veil when that impedes communication, it's hard to see how wearing the headscarf interferes with essential requirements of a teacher's job. The ban on teachers wearing headscarves in parts of Germany has led observant Muslim women to abandon their chosen career, resulting in a loss of independence, social standing, and financial well-being. For women who are coerced by family members into wearing a headscarf, blocking access to these professions will not protect them from oppression. Moreover, this type of state regulation appears to aggravate discrimination against women who wear the headscarf in the private employment sector. Far from empowering them, the bans may lead to a deterioration in their social position. A woman in Cologne remarked to a colleague of mine, "As long as we were cleaning in schools, nobody had a problem with the headscarf."

Observant Muslim women in Belgium also face obstacles in pursuing their chosen careers. Several cities, including Antwerp and Brussels, have introduced bans on civil servants in contact with the public wearing religious (or political or ideological) symbols, and semipublic hospitals and caring institutions are increasingly copying this example. Students who wear the headscarf are discouraged from pursuing careers as teachers, nurses, or doctors.

Both forced veiling and bans on veils raise questions about the appropriate role of the state in matters of religion and traditional practices, including how, when, and where the state can legitimately impose or restrict the wearing of religious dress and the display of religious symbols. From a human rights perspective, less is more. Human rights law requires the state and state authorities to refrain from discriminating on the basis of religious beliefs. This means the state should be neutral in matters of religion—an important guarantor of religious freedom. Human rights law also guarantees the right to a private life, including the right to autonomy—for example, the freedom to choose what to wear, in private and in public. These are not absolute rights; governments can impose limits, but only when they can demonstrate convincingly that restrictions are necessary to protect public safety, public order, health, or morals, or the fundamental rights and freedoms of others. This is a high threshold.

That's why Asma Jahangir, former United Nations special rapporteur on freedom of religion or belief, and her predecessor, Abdelfattah Amor, have both criticized rules that require the wearing of religious dress in public. In particular, Amor has urged that dress should not be the subject of political regulation. Jahangir has said that the "use of coercive methods and sanctions applied to individuals who do not wish to wear religious dress or a specific symbol seen as sanctioned by religion" indicates "legislative and administrative actions which typically are incompatible with international human rights law."[5] Thomas Hammarberg, the human rights commissioner for the Council of Europe, has expressed concerns that bans violate the rights to privacy and to freedom of religion and belief guaranteed in the European Convention on Human Rights. He warned that prohibiting the *burqa* and the *niqab* in Europe could alienate the women who wear them in European societies.[6]

Colleagues at Human Rights Watch and I have been criticized as anti-Muslim when we denounce forced veiling, and as anti-women when we denounce bans on the veil. Of course, we are neither. We believe that Muslim women, like all women, should enjoy the right to dress as they choose, and to make decisions about their lives and how to express their faith, identity, and moral values. No woman should be forced to cover her hair or her face. Victims of coercion and violence in the name of religion, tradition, or "virtue" deserve protection and assistance, not censure. No woman should be forced to remove her veil without a legitimate reason. The convictions of those who choose to wear the veil deserve consideration.

PART 8

THE NEXT FRONTIER

A ROAD MAP TO RIGHTS

CHAPTER 29

Funding an Unfinished Revolution

Gara LaMarche

Thirty-five years ago, I was a young staffer at the American Civil Liberties Union (ACLU), with a ringside seat on its board meetings since I took the minutes. A female board member ran for the organization's presidency as a symbolic gesture and got all of five votes, which may have represented most of the other women then on the eighty-three-member board. Not too long before that, it was hard to get the (mostly male) staff and board members of the organization to see women's rights as an issue sufficiently serious to warrant a place on the agenda of the leading rights watchdog in the US.

I joined the staff of Human Rights Watch at the same time as Dorothy Thomas, the founding director of what was then called the Women's Rights Project, and a fellow contributor to this anthology. That was barely twenty years ago, but it's easy to forget that there was considerable skepticism about the effort in many quarters of the organization, from staff and board members (including some of its female leaders), who feared that an emphasis on women's rights would dilute the organization's focus and cost it credibility with key partners

Gara LaMarche is a senior fellow at New York University's Robert F. Wagner School of Public Service, where he teaches a course on philanthropy and public policy. He has served as president of the Atlantic Philanthropies, vice president of the Open Society Foundations, and associate director of Human Rights Watch, and also held high-level positions at the New York and Texas branches of the American Civil Liberties Union. He is the editor of Speech and Equality: Do We Really Have to Choose? *(New York University Press, 1996).*

in Africa, Asia, and Latin America. (As I learned a few years later when working to expand Human Rights Watch's mandate to include lesbian and gay rights issues, it was often the case that our traditional local "partners" were themselves unaware of the strong and vibrant work by women's and LGBT groups in their own countries.)

Thomas and her women's rights staff had to earn their credibility just as the parent organization had to a dozen years earlier—with painstakingly researched reports (such as early ones on honor killings in Pakistan and impunity for rape in Brazil) based on airtight documentation and concluding with pointed and achievable policy recommendations.

In short, even in progressive rights organizations, those working on women's issues had to be twice as good—constantly fending off internal challenges, just to survive. And of course, they were, aided by the star quality of founding leaders such as Ruth Bader Ginsburg in the ACLU and Dorothy Thomas at Human Rights Watch. The vision and backing of one man, Aryeh Neier, were of critical importance in both institutions (he led ACLU from 1970 to 1978 and Human Rights Watch from 1978 to 1991), as well as at the Open Society Foundations, a third institution in which he also launched a women's rights program.

I provide this bit of history, drawn from my personal involvement in rights organizations and therefore necessarily impressionistic, because the revolution that began to take place in the last few decades is far from finished.

In their 2010 book, *Half the Sky*, Pulitzer Prize winners Nicholas Kristof and Sheryl WuDunn reinforce the arguments that women's rights activists have been making for making years, that there can be no social or economic justice, or human rights progress around the world, that does not have women and girls at the core. It's a compelling case, and the other essays in this book demonstrate just how much work is being done—and how much remains to be done—to assure the political empowerment and equal treatment of women, and to achieve their full access to justice when their rights are violated.

Yet to what extent is this insight represented today in the work of human rights organizations and the foundations that support them? The short answer, of course, is "not enough"—though recent years have seen some improvement. The weakness or absence of a gender lens is an all-too-common omission among social justice advocates and organizations, as Linda Burnham writes compellingly in her 2008 working paper "The Absence of a Gender Justice Framework in Social Justice Organizing," growing out of the Ford and Ms. Foundation's New Women's Movement Initiative.[1] Burnham found that gender is often absent from social justice and human rights work because sexism is frequently viewed as a subordinate concern to racism and other forms of bias, where entire communities are vulnerable. Women are often disproportionately affected by inequalities related to race, economic status, or ethnicity, but the connections between gender and other inequalities are regularly overlooked.

However, if you take a closer look at populations subject to disadvantage and human rights abuses, it is evident that they are often largely women and girls, and that to try to address these issues without considering gender is to hobble the response from the outset. To use an example from the economic realm, on poverty and aging, Joan Kuriansky, executive director of Wider Opportunities for Women, which works to build pathways to economic independence for women, girls and families, points out: "Women tend to live longer than men and are often the caregivers for men who die earlier, leaving women with fewer resources to care for themselves." In fact, it is not far-fetched to suggest that in many ways, aging itself can be seen as a women's rights issue.

Outlining the demographics of elder poverty in the US in a 2008 report, the Center for American Progress noted that, as in other age groups, poverty does not affect older men and women equally. A lifetime of lower earnings due to wage discrimination, intermittent absence from the labor market due to pregnancy and childbirth, caregiving for the young and old, and jobs that are less likely to have employer-sponsored retirement plans take a toll. For instance, nearly one in five single, divorced, or widowed women over the age of sixty-five are poor (the poverty rate for a single person over sixty-five was $10,326 in 2008), and the risk of poverty for older women only increases as they age. US women age seventy-five and older are more than three times as likely to be living in poverty as men in the same age range.

Given these realities, Atlantic Philanthropies, which I headed until 2011, worked to identify organizations pursuing policies and programs to meet the needs of aging women. For example, we provided support to the Women's Foundation of California to replicate a successful older women's advocacy leadership training program in which groups of women decide what issues are important in their communities and then learn and practice the skills needed to be effective advocates for needed policy change. Our grant to Wider Opportunities for Women provided women and their advocates concrete information about the true costs of aging and the impact of a life-long pattern of gender inequity that is being used to develop programs and policies to increase resources for all low-income and disadvantaged community members.

Gender and the Human Rights Movement

The centrality of gender to a broader human rights agenda is even more critical. I've spent the last thirty years working in two frontline rights organizations—the ACLU, the leading US domestic rights advocacy group, and Human Rights Watch, which plays the same role on the global level. I've also worked in senior positions with two of the leading global human rights funders, the Open Society Foundations and the Atlantic Philanthropies. And I've found myself on many occasions the only man on the boards or advisory committees of the OSF Network Women's Program, the Women's Rights Division Advisory Committee at Human Rights Watch, and the White House Project, a US NGO promoting women's political leadership. These experiences have given me an unusual perspective, for a man, on the trajectory of change, and on the many institutional obstacles we face in eliminating abuses and empowering women and girls.

By 1995, ahead of the landmark UN Women's Conference in Beijing, Human Rights Watch produced its first Global Report on Women's Human Rights, with chapters reporting on rape as a weapon of war and repression in Bosnia-Herzegovina, Haiti, Somalia, Kashmir, and Peru; the sexual assault of refugee and displaced women in Bangladesh and Kenya; abuses of women in custody in Pakistan, the United States, and Egypt; the trafficking of women and girls in Thailand, Nepal, and

Bangladesh; discrimination against female workers in Kuwait, Russia, and Poland; domestic violence enforcement in Brazil, Russia, and South Africa; forced virginity exams in Turkey; and abortion policy in Ireland and Poland.

A few years before Human Rights Watch launched women's rights research, two influential rights-focused funds had been created to mobilize the power of women donors and their allies: Mama Cash, in the Netherlands, in 1983, and the Global Fund for Women, based in San Francisco, in 1987. These groups, which work closely together, have been instrumental in steering funds to many of the indigenous grassroots women's organizations, particularly in the global South, that Human Rights Watch partnered with in reporting over the years.

As recently as twenty years ago, few of the other "mainstream" international human rights organizations had women's human rights on their agenda. Today the picture is very different. Both Human Rights Watch and Amnesty International devote resources to women's rights issues, including campaigns against violence against women and for improved maternal health care, and promoting the ratification by the United States of the Convention on the Elimination of All Forms of Discrimination Against Women (CEDAW). Human Rights First, long a leader in protecting the rights of asylum seekers and refugees, has a special focus on women among those groups.

This just scratches the surface of organizations, mostly based in the West, that are global in scope. Regionally and nationally, NGOs closer to the ground are in many ways leading their international counterparts. The efforts of two grantees of the Global Fund for Human Rights, which has been a leader in supporting local human rights work, illustrate this point. The Association of Female Lawyers of Liberia led a successful campaign to secure legal recognition of women's inheritance rights in that country, and the Mexican group Elige helped lead a campaign that secured a major victory for reproductive rights when that nation's highest court upheld a law decriminalizing abortion.

The Funding World

The philanthropic sector on which these NGOs depend has been much slower to catch up. Marie Wilson, the founding director of the Ms. Foundation for Women, used to joke that "the women's movement is one foundation away from welfare" (she was referring to the Ford Foundation), but it was always a joke with an edge. If it was somewhat true then, it is still too close to the truth now. A 2006 report for the Foundation Center by the Women's Funding Network found that while growing slightly, funding for women and girls had remained below 7.5 percent of all foundation funding for fifteen years. A Mama Cash report for the Foundation Center earlier this year, "Untapped Potential: European Foundation Funding for Women and Girls," found the level in Europe even lower, at 4.8 percent, though 37 percent of European foundations made some grants designed to benefit women and girls in the year studied, 2009.

You can search the mission and programs of many of the leading global funders and find little that focuses on women. The Ford Foundation, with both a dedicated women's rights unit and a strong cross-program emphasis on reproductive health and rights, remains a shining exception. OSF's International Women's Program now focuses on access to justice, political participation and discrimination, and violence against women—broad and important areas, but now limited to working in Nepal, Colombia, Guatemala, Kenya, Uganda, Sudan, Liberia, Sierra Leone, Palestine, Iraq, and Bosnia-Herzegovina, with some work in Tajikistan, Burma, Cambodia, and Lebanon at a lower scale.

A tremendously encouraging recent development in the funding world is the emergence of the NoVo Foundation, focused not only on women and girls—and already a leading funder of work to combat trafficking and other forms of gender violence and exploitation—but also on leadership development and networking. Along with the strong emphasis on gender-based violence and related issues shown in recent years by the Sigrid Rausing Trust, based in the United Kingdom, there is both critical mass and growing momentum on an international level.

One of the largest human rights funders, Atlantic Philanthropies, has never had a dedicated women's rights program. But as may have been apparent from the aging work described above, the foundation sought to "mainstream" a women's rights lens into all its funding. This represents an approach that could be effective for other philanthropic groups as well.

Atlantic supported a consortium of advocacy organizations working to restore civil liberties that have been eroded since the September 2001 attacks as a result of the "war on terror," but we had not paid enough attention to the rarely acknowledged way in which the war on terror has had a uniquely negative impact on women. For example, women not suspected of terrorism-related offenses have been unlawfully detained and ill treated, either to obtain information about male family members or to compel male suspects to turn themselves in, provide information, or make confessions. Militarized counterterrorism activities in countries like Iraq and Afghanistan have also served to decrease dramatically the security of civilians, intensify the trafficking of women and girls, and increase insecurity and poverty. Atlantic made a grant to the New York University Center for Human Rights and Global Justice to report on and extensively disseminate the findings of the extensive research on gender and counterterrorism being conducted as part of its Gender, National Security, and Counterterrorism Project.

Women, we came to realize, are disproportionately affected by global migration through exposure to violence and economic exploitation. In Ireland, a traditionally insular society that has experienced a wave of temporary workers and newcomers in recent years, Atlantic supported AkiDwa, a national network of migrant women living in the country. Originally created as an African women's network, the organization has grown substantially and today it provides an array of services to, and advocates on behalf of, women of all minority and ethnic backgrounds. Its activities include leadership and capacity building training, research, advocacy, networking, and the provision of information and advice on a myriad of issues from immigration status to education, employment, and health. The organization focuses on issues of gender, racial discrimination, gender-based violence, and access to employment. Another grantee, the Immigrant Council of Ireland, has been working in partnership with other NGOs and various government departments to deliver quality services to women in Ireland who are victims of sex trafficking.

In Northern Ireland, as in all conflict zones, while men during the Troubles did much of the fighting and many ended up dead, imprisoned, or physically and psychologically damaged, women have played a significant role in peace building and community development work. Two of the women leading our grantee, the Suffolk Lenadoon Interface Group—Jean Brown from the loyalist Suffolk estate in West Belfast and Renee Crawford from the neighboring nationalist Lenadoon estate—were presented with the Northern Ireland Community Relations Award in 2009 for bringing polarized communities together to reduce violence and improve relations.

In South Africa, Atlantic has funded organizations like the Equality Project, the Joint Working Group, and the Forum for the Empowerment of Women, MASK, and People Opposing Women Abuse to address gender-based abuse and hate crimes against lesbians. To advocate for the legal rights of rural women, we have funded the Legal Resources Centre to challenge legislative efforts to deprive rural women of their property rights.

In Vietnam, as elsewhere, local health care does not respond adequately to the special needs of the rural poor, and rural older women in particular. The Vietnam Women's Union is the leading organization promoting awareness and actions on gender equity and advocating for gender equality related laws. Atlantic supports them to initiate innovative approaches contributing to the alleviation of rural poverty and improving health care services for older adults, build the capacity of community-based older people's groups to respond to their own needs and provide support to each other, and conduct public awareness campaigns for policymakers and the public about the health needs of rural older people.

In the United States, health care reform measures moving through Congress—aided by grants from Atlantic to Health Care for America Now! and to Planned Parenthood Federation of America—could dramatically transform women's health care, guaranteeing maternity coverage, ending the practice of discriminatory higher premiums for women, and barring the treatment of everything from Caesarean sections to the health consequences of domestic violence as "pre-existing conditions" cited to turn down coverage. So health care turns out to be a "women's issue" as well as a key element of the social compact.

We can hardly expect human rights organizations to model that approach if few funders see the issues that way. So despite the gains that have taken place in the last twenty to thirty years, we are still looking at a landscape in which women's human rights work is either segregated in institutional silos, or worse, absent from the agendas of key foundations and NGOs—a recipe for failure and frustration in a world in which no path to social change can be successful without the central engagement and involvement of women.

Looking at philanthropy though the gender lens is more challenging than a more traditional approach of in effect segregating the work in a dedicated program, since the issue is multidimensional. In some instances, women and girls experience discrimination because they are female, as in the case of reproductive rights or domestic violence. In others, they suffer disproportionately from a range of problems that don't expressly target women, but that affect them more than men, such as lack of access to health care, low wage work, and poverty. This means that in order to address gender, it will always be necessary to dig a bit beneath the surface in order to find out what the real story is.

It will be necessary, as with the national security and immigration agenda, to look not just at traditional "women's issues," but at all issues and ask the question of how gender plays out—how the failure to see that and deal with it stands in the way of justice. A full menu of creative strategies will be necessary to address the challenges of the twenty-first century.

CHAPTER 30

The Challenge of Changing the World for Women

Liesl Gerntholtz

I interviewed Gentile in an empty tent in one of the enormous camps that had sprung up in Port-au-Prince immediately after the Haiti earthquake in February 2010. The quake devastated much of the city, the economic hub of the country and the seat of government, killing some 200,000 men, women, and children and leaving 1.2 million people without food, water, shelter, and sanitation. Gentile was just sixteen, alone in the city, clearly still traumatized and frightened as she recounted how she had been gang raped a few nights before. Like thousands of other women and girls, she was homeless and vulnerable, an easy prey for the gang of men who dragged her into the darkness and assaulted her amid the rubble. Later, I wrote about that interview and my trip to Haiti to investigate sexual violence. Many people contacted me, having read the piece, to express surprise that violence against women could still take place during a massive humanitarian crisis.

Liesl Gerntholtz is the director of the Women's Rights Division at Human Rights Watch, with particular expertise on women's rights in Africa. She has worked and written extensively on violence against women and HIV/AIDS in Southern Africa. Before joining Human Rights Watch, she worked for some of the key constitutional institutions promoting human rights and democracy in post-apartheid South Africa, including the South African Human Rights Commission and the Commission on Gender Equality. A lawyer by training, she was involved in human rights litigation to promote women and children's rights, including a case that changed the definition of rape in South Africa.

317

Human Rights Watch has documented violence against women in different contexts in many countries over the past two decades. We have reported on domestic violence in Brazil and Turkey, sexual violence in conflict in the Democratic Republic of Congo, Bosnia, and Côte d'Ivoire, trafficking of women and girls in Nepal and India, honor killings in Jordan, and female genital mutilation in Iraq. We have documented violence against migrant domestic workers in Saudi Arabia and Lebanon, women in immigration detention in the United States, schoolgirls in South Africa and women living with HIV in Zambia and Kenya. Most recently, we investigated the use of sexual violence against both women and men during the Libyan revolution. We have released numerous reports and made hundreds of recommendations to governments, international donors, the United Nations, and civil society about their obligations and responsibilities to protect women from violence and to respond to their needs in its aftermath. In this endeavor, we are not alone, and every day, all over the world, individuals and organizations work to protect and support victims and survivors of all forms of violence against women.

Violence has a direct and detrimental impact on women's human rights. Women may be evicted from their homes by abusive partners, leaving them—and often their children—homeless. Violence may limit women and girls' access to education and employment and hinder their ability to participate in public life. In addition to the impact on individual woman's economic empowerment, it also costs countries millions of dollars every year to deal with the consequences of violence.

According to the Committee on the Elimination of Discrimination Against Women, "[V]iolence against women puts their health and life at risk."[1] The World Health Organization's ten-country study of the health consequences of domestic and intimate partner violence concludes that violence against women "is a major contributor to the ill health of women."[2] Women are at risk of death through femicide, suicide, HIV, and maternal mortality. Violence can precipitate fractures, chronic pain, disability, fibromyalgia, and gastrointestinal disorders. Women with violent partners are at risk of sexual and reproductive health issues that include unwanted and unplanned pregnancy, abortions, and fistulas. Psychological and behavioral results can manifest in depression, drug and alcohol abuse, eating and sleeping disorders, poor self-esteem, post-traumatic stress disorder, and self-harm.

"Perhaps the Most Shameful" Violation

Kofi Annan, during his term as secretary-general of the United Nations, described violence against women in a 1999 speech as the most pervasive violation of human rights. He also named it as "perhaps the most shameful."[3] His recognition of violence against women as a global phenomenon is confirmed, if indeed we need it to be, in the 2010 United Nations Report on the Status of Women in the World. The conclusions in the chapter on violence against women are a stark reminder that the daily reality for millions of women all over the world is about pain, fear, and disempowerment. The chapter concludes that "women are subjected to both moderate and severe physical violence from their intimate partners," "young women are more exposed to intimate partner violence," and "many women are sexually molested during their lifetimes."[4] Research conducted by the Centers for Disease Control and Prevention in the United States in 2010, confirms the widespread nature of sexual violence, stating that it is endemic in US and that nearly one in five women surveyed had been raped or were subject to an attempted rape.[5]

The international community has only relatively recently begun to grapple with violence against women. The so-called Women's Convention, the Convention on the Elimination of All Forms of Violence Against Women (CEDAW), which came into effect in 1981, does not explicitly mention violence against women, and the first meaningful engagement by the world on violence came at the Third World Conference on Human Rights in Vienna in June 1993. Initially the conference program did not include any references to women's rights, an omission that galvanized a hugely effective global campaign led by women, including women from grassroots groups and organizations worldwide, who demanded that violence against women be recognized as a violation of human rights and that women's rights be included on the conference agenda. The campaign included a global petition that garnered more than 1 million signatures.

The Declaration on the Elimination of Violence Against Women was then adopted by the General Assembly of the United Nations in December 1993, a special rapporteur on violence against women was appointed by the UN Commission for Human Rights, and the Security Council has since adopted several landmark resolutions on violence against women, including on sexual violence in conflict. In 2006, Kofi Annan released a major report on violence against women containing key recommendations for member states. His successor as UN secretary-general, Ban Ki-moon, has reinforced the commitment of the UN to ending violence against women by launching a global campaign against violence in 2008. At an event marking the International Day for the Elimination of Violence against Women, on November 23, 2011, he noted that "violence—and in many cases the mere threat of it—is one of the most significant barriers to women's full equality."[6]

In addition to international instruments, there are also regional treaties in Africa, Latin America, and, most recently, Europe that contain progressive and useful provisions to combat violence against women and girls.

These advancements at international and regional levels have been accompanied by improvements in national responses to violence against women. Activism and advocacy, led by committed women and women's groups, have encouraged many countries to develop responses to violence, including adopting legislation criminalizing sexual and domestic violence, establishing shelters for abused women, appointing more female police officers, providing specialized training for law enforcement officers, and developing victim support programs.

While women's rights activists, human rights practitioners, and lawmakers all acknowledge that there are often problems with the implementation of many of these initiatives, they are still a clear step forward.

A Continuing Challenge

But we must also acknowledge that they are not enough. The 2010 United Nations Report on the Status of the Women in the World highlights the continuing lack of reliable global statistics on the incidence and prevalence of violence against women, and the consequent need to collect more and better information about the various forms of violence. Despite its limitations, the data we do have illustrates that the struggle to end violence against women is far from won. National statistics, where these exist, show that in many countries extraordinarily high numbers of women continue to experience violence in their daily lives, and in some countries there have been increases in the numbers of women who suffer violence. These numbers and stories told by the women my colleagues and I have interviewed all over the world suggest that while much needed progress has been made in responding to violence, we need to do more, much more, to prevent it in the first place.

The critical issue of prevention has not been ignored internationally. The 1995 Beijing Platform for Action, for example, urges states to take integrated measures to "prevent and eliminate" violence against women. This includes a comprehensive set of actions intended to assist states in preventing violence and recommends, among other things, that states condemn violence against women; ensure due diligence in preventing, investigating, and punishing acts of violence against women (both those committed by the state and private persons); adopt legislation that emphasizes preventing violence; and undertake education programs that "modify the social and cultural patterns of conduct of men and women" and that seek to eliminate gender stereotypes and the notion that women are inferior. The Platform also recommends that states and civil society "provide, fund, and encourage" counseling and rehabilitation programs for perpetrators of violence; and provide information and education programs for boys and girls, men and women, about the detrimental effects of violence against women and the need for communication without violence. Both the state and civil society are encouraged to raise awareness about the role of the media in promoting progressive images of women, and eliminating patterns of media representations of women that generate and promote violence.[7]

A 2010 manual developed by the UN agency for the advancement of women, on legislating violence against women,[8] recognizes that prevention remains a major challenge and notes that many countries continue to fail to live up to their international commitments to prevent violence. The handbook does however contain a small section on national laws that have sought to include provisions on prevention. There are other innovative initiatives, some still in their infancy, that are being developed to prevent violence against women, including linking micro-credit to information and community awareness about domestic violence, and education programs that target adolescent boys. We are slowly learning what works, and what may not, but there is still a long way to go.

Real progress in preventing violence requires changing deeply entrenched social norms and challenging cultural, traditional, and religious stereotypes about women, their role in society and their relationships with men. Effecting real change will not be easy, and will require a high level of political leadership and commitment, both internationally and nationally, if it is to be successful. Governments will need to commit themselves to achieving a genuine reduction in the numbers of women who experience violence. They must invest in research that deepens our understanding of the causes and consequences of violence against women. And they must put in place rigorous monitoring and evaluation systems to measure progress and determine effectiveness. Governments will also need to engage with civil society, and develop deep and lasting partnerships with them to prevent violence against women.

Not so long ago, I met up with a woman I had worked with in South Africa several years ago. She had come to the center where I worked to seek help in leaving a violent relationship. At the time she was unemployed and had two small daughters to care for. She was traumatized by years of physical abuse and deeply afraid that her husband would kill her if she left him, but she told me, with quiet dignity, that she wanted a better life for her daughters. Today, she has a job and she recently moved out of a shelter into her own apartment. When I asked her how she was doing, she grinned at me and said, "Life is good, but I still check the locks every night."

Although her story has a happy ending, I am sometimes haunted by those words, because they remind me of how much she suffered and how close she came to staying with her husband. I remember how she was trembling when she left my office to return to the shelter. I remember the hundreds of other women I met whose stories did not end as happily and know that we must redouble our efforts to ensure they can live lives of dignity and freedom, able to achieve their full potential, without needing to check the locks at night.

The Revolution Continues

Dorothy Q. Thomas

Everything that rises must converge.

—Flannery O'Connor

In the fall of 1989 the Women's Rights Project, as it was then called, had just been established at Human Rights Watch and I had recently returned from a year monitoring Namibia's transition to independence from South Africa. By a rare stroke of luck, I got the job as the Project's founding director. I was exactly thirty years old.

I am now fifty-one and can only marvel at all that the Women's Rights Division, as it is now known, has achieved. In our first full year of operation, we had one and a half full-time employees, including me, and a small budget from generous donors who believed in the cause of women's human rights. Today, the division is vastly expanded and it has a full-time staff of a dozen highly qualified women's rights advocates and researchers covering all the continents of the world.

The journey from 1989 to 2011 was arduous for the Women's Rights Division and for the women's human rights movement as a whole. The former was in many ways a microcosm of the latter; the movement's

A pioneering human rights activist, Dorothy Q. Thomas served as the founding director of the Women's Rights Division at Human Rights Watch from 1990 to 1998. In 1998 she was the recipient of both the Eleanor Roosevelt Human Rights Award and a MacArthur Fellowship. She is the author of numerous reports and articles on human rights, and the coauthor and editor of Close to Home: Case Studies of Human Rights Work in the United States *(Ford Foundation, 2004). She is a member of the Board of Directors of the British Institute of Human Rights and the Ms. Foundation for Women.*

fortunes quite often shaped our own. In 1990, especially if you lived in the United States or Western Europe, you could be forgiven for thinking that no global women's human rights movement existed. In fact, as Charlotte Bunch's landmark 1981 essay, "Copenhagen and Beyond: Prospects for Global Feminism," made clear, its foundations were already well laid by the anti-dictatorship feminists of Latin America; the anti-colonial ones of the Americas, Africa, and Asia; the anti-Communist ones in Central and Eastern Europe; the anti-fundamentalist ones in North Africa, South and Southeast Asia, and the Middle East; and indigenous women's movements throughout the world. Those of us working in the West and the North, with the exception of indigenous women and some pioneering civil and economic rights activists, were among the last to make the women's-rights-to-human-rights connect. Indeed, Human Rights Watch, then fifteen years old and one of the world's premier international human rights organizations, had never done any systematic reporting on the rights of women.

The belated uptake of women's human rights by Western activists and groups initially made my position as a North American woman working at the largest US-based human rights organization extremely awkward. We were Janey-come-latelies to the whole women's human rights struggle, yet we were fast becoming one of its designated experts. The press constantly asked us to comment on women's rights issues that neither we, nor our sister regional divisions, knew anything about. "When in doubt, shut up," Human Rights Watch's straight-talking then Communications Director Susan Osnos used to say. Sound advice that the Division follows to this day.

The Central Challenge

The challenge that all women's—and human—rights advocates face, then as now, is how to expose abuse in a very specific context without either diminishing or aggrandizing it. With governments looking to dismiss Human Rights Watch's women's rights reports as Western propaganda and the media looking for their shock value, accuracy was both a basic necessity and a constant discipline. Human Rights Watch's founder and then executive director, Aryeh Neier taught me to stick to the facts and he set and upheld that standard for the organization as a whole.

The truth is that with respect to the state of women in the world the facts were and—as these pages attest, still are—shocking enough. When a man engaged in the premeditated murder of his estranged wife and her lover and was exculpated by a country's highest court on the grounds that he was defending his offended honor, the facts pretty much spoke for themselves. When a woman found that courts used medical evidence she submitted in proof of rape to convict her of extramarital sex, we saw no need to elaborate. When women and girls were herded into camps and raped en masse by men who sought to exterminate in whole or in part their and their community's very existence, the truth seemed self-evident. As these early findings and so many subsequent Women's Rights Division reports make plain, we need neither underestimate nor exaggerate the abuse of women's human rights to be heard: its specificity and its prevalence, once recognized, speak volumes.

So, you could be forgiven in 1990 for thinking that no global women's human rights movement existed—not because one didn't but because so few relevant state and nonstate actors recognized it, including the mainstream human rights organizations ourselves. Every fight that outside feminist groups were having to get local and international human rights groups to cover women's rights was being fought inside those organizations as well. Is domestic violence a human rights abuse? Do equal rights trump religious law? Does a virginity control exam differ from a dentist appointment? Is sex between an officer and a prisoner always rape? Does trafficking in women equal sex slavery? Is the denial of reproductive health care sex discrimination? Can unremedied violence against women be grounds for asylum? Do the day-to-day indignities that women suffer in the home or on the job rise to the level of human rights violations?

These and many others issues raised by early Human Rights Watch publications prompted legitimate and often thorny conceptual, strategic, legal, and methodological debates for both human and women's rights organizations and governments and intergovernmental bodies. Women's rights issues had never before been systematically examined through a human rights lens and the implications of this reframing needed—and still need—to be skillfully and painstakingly worked out.

Under the leadership of Ken Roth, Aryeh Neier's successor as Human Rights Watch's executive director, the Women's Rights Division has honed its ability, strikingly evident in these pages, to classify what aspect of a given pattern or practice with respect to the treatment of women, often one that was previously deemed perfectly acceptable, actually amounts to an abuse of human rights for which the perpetrators could and should be held to account under national and international law. The Division has been further guided through this complicated theoretical and practical labyrinth by a succession of exemplary divisional directors, Regan Ralph, LaShawn Jefferson, and now Liesl Gerntholtz, and a diverse troupe of Advisory Committee members that include some of the most rigorous, experienced (and opinionated) women's and human rights activists in the world. We remember in particular our late colleagues Rhonda Copelon and Jeanne Sindab.

Progress In Recent Decades

So much progress has been made in linking women's rights to human rights since 1989 that you might now be forgiven for wondering what all the fuss was about.

Hillary Clinton's official declaration at the 1995 Beijing World Conference that "women's rights are human rights," which felt like a bombshell then, today seems commonplace. Human rights organizations at both the local and international level routinely address women's human rights concerns, feminist groups see themselves as part of the human rights struggle, governments and intergovernmental agencies and experts take up the protection and promotion of women's human rights as an integral part of their obligations and mandates, the press routinely investigates these issues, and donors see such work as fulfilling rather than diluting the human rights idea. Most important, women's dignity, equality, and power, once often consigned to the margins of public policy and civil society, now constitute central pillars of any effective strategy to secure the development and survival not only of this or that household or community or country, but also of the human race itself. Women's rights are human rights indeed.

Given this remarkable level of success, do we still need a Human Rights Watch division or a governmental department or a United Nations agency that focuses exclusively on the human rights of women? Haven't we, as an organization, or a society or a world community, finally outgrown the tendency to see women's oppression as acceptable or defensible or marginal or to not see it at all? Isn't it time we took up the human rights of *all people* as one, rather than dividing our attention, and our resources, between this and that issue, or this and that group?

Readers of this volume can be left in little doubt: the need for concerted, expert, rigorous, and impassioned attention to women's human rights remains as vital today as it was more than twenty years ago.

Regressive Forces

Yes, enormous progress has been made, and, yes, we have cause to celebrate. But one thing remains unchanged: the palpable rage, evident the world over, to put women back in our place, to reverse our gains, and to resort to violence and discrimination against us and against other specific groups—as way to maintain or restore outmoded means of social and political control. These forces are behind the total lack of domestic violence laws in approximately 100 countries, behind the highly restrictive laws on basic reproductive health services in almost all countries, and behind the policies that deny women their right to act as autonomous adults, like male guardianship policies or those that restrict women's inheritance, land ownership or economic and civic engagement. Human and women's rights groups, governments and intergovernmental bodies, men and women, must fight these regressive forces as one, but we cannot do so effectively without the dedicated experts who keep track of women's human rights abuse as it retrenches or resurges and, all too often, takes on new and virulent forms.

Dedicated attention to the violation of women's rights and other identity or locality specific abuse, however necessary, raises new conceptual, strategic, legal, and methodological challenges of its own. How do we focus on abuse targeted at women and other groups, and attributed to certain states or regions, for example, without losing sight of how such practices relate to one another and require an integrated rather than isolated response? Human Rights Watch has made some headway in tackling this problem: women's rights, for example, are now taken up by the organization as a whole rather than the Women's Rights Division alone. Nonetheless, the benefit of attending to thematic or region-specific problems carries a considerable risk: it can limit our understanding not only of the scope of a given human rights abuse but also of its most effective remedy.

With women's rights, for example, there's often a risk that you focus so mightily on the victim that you forget that she herself often acts to remedy the problem at a later date. We so want the world to recognize what is happening to women that we may reinforce the public perception of women as victims to the exclusion of our role as actors in remedying the very violations that we suffer. One of the most important human rights strategies advanced by women's rights work is to show that often those very communities most affected by abuse— whether trafficking, rape in war, workplace bias, or domestic violence—are also the ones who turn around and fight to remedy injustice themselves. Take, for example, the Asian migrant domestic workers who leave abusive employers and go on to demand better labor laws and international standards, resulting last year in a landmark treaty on domestic workers.

The Need for Systemic Reform

Sadly, we may have to attend a lot more women's human rights meetings that raise only "gender-related" questions, or many more human rights ones that never mention women, before we ever fully recognize that no human rights violation occurs in a vacuum; they always have both generic elements and specific manifestations and require both targeted and systemic reforms. Laws on administrative detention in Jordan, for example, are not just a generic abuse of due process rights, they also implicate women's rights in very specific ways. Governors have invoked administrative detention laws to jail women threatened with family violence, in at least one case for more than 10 years. The challenge for the human rights movement going forward is to understand how such seemingly discrete practices intersect both with one another and with more general human rights concerns, and to craft equally integrated remedies. A remedy to Jordan's abusive administrative detention laws is not just to improve due process procedures, but also to push for more non-custodial domestic violence shelters and to challenge the inappropriate use of detention in general.

As a result of decades of very specific women's human rights work, for example, we now know more than ever before about how rape and other sexual violence functions in conflict. But we will never remedy such egregious abuse unless we also understand and address its connection with women's fundamental inequality in society and to the conduct of war overall. That's why when Human Rights Watch investigated, for example, how armed combatants in Côte d'Ivoire subjected women and girls to individual and gang rape, sexual slavery, forced incest and other sexual assaults, the investigation also covered women's low status in law and in custom, and how that subordination is linked to wartime violence designed to subjugate both women and an entire opposing group. We need a both/and, rather than either/or, approach to the relationship between the human rights of specific groups and those of all people.

As the American author Flannery O'Connor wrote, "Everything that rises must converge." Yet today's human rights movement, for all its astonishing growth over the past sixty years or more, remains remarkably disconnected. This partly reflects the sheer enormity of the task at hand and the perennial disparities of geography, capacity, and money. But something even more worrisome is also at work: the tendency of those of us who concern ourselves with human rights, whether in government, in intergovernmental bodies, in philanthropic institutions, or in NGOs, to work in isolation from one another. International human rights organizations don't always work in their own backyards; human rights donors under-resource local work; friendly governments often disregard their own misconduct; and the United Nations human rights mechanisms disaggregate by region, by country, by issue, and by group. Each of us moves our own human rights ball forward, but we lack a strategy for the field overall.

No one expects (or expected) the women's rights movement to solve all the human rights movement's problems or vice versa. But we have learned something that may yet help to save us all from ourselves: how integrally related we are to one another and how deeply the fulfillment of both women's *and* human rights depends on our working together. This mutual recognition of both difference and interdependence holds the key to continued progress for the global human rights movement writ large. At a time when the human rights movement faces staunch opposition even from some of its supposed supporters, including in the United States and Western Europe, human rights officials, organizations, and activists need to strengthen our relationships to one another—at all levels and across every regional and thematic divide—in order for the human rights idea not only to survive, but also to flourish.

When I began work as the director of Human Rights Watch's Women's Rights Division, I often said that our goal was to put ourselves out of business. Now I recognize that the fight for the human rights of women and girls, like that for the human rights of us all, may always be, as this book's title points out, "unfinished."

But the story of women's human rights over the past two decades gives anyone concerned about the unfinished business of human rights in general great hope. In the face of little support, less resources, considerable opposition, and outright bias, it gradually took hold. In the process, it helped to change not only itself and the larger human rights movement, but also the world. The revolution continues.

Notes

INTRODUCTION (Minky Worden)

1. Kwame Anthony Appiah, *The Honor Code: How Moral Revolutions Happen* (Norton, 2010).
2. Nicholas D. Kristof and Sheryl WuDunn, *Half the Sky: Turning Oppression into Opportunity for Women Worldwide* (Vintage Books, 2010), p. 207.

CHAPTER 1 (Ellen Chesler)

1. This chapter on the historical foundations of women's human rights, including the role of Eleanor Roosevelt, is adapted from Ellen Chesler's introduction to Wendy Chavkin and Ellen Chesler, *Where Human Rights Begin: Health, Sexuality, and Women in the New Millennium* (New Brunswick, NJ: Rutgers University Press, 2005), pp. 1-34.
2. Eleanor Roosevelt, "Where Do Human Rights Begin?" Remarks at the United Nations, March 27, 1958, in Allida Black, *Courage in a Dangerous World: The Political Writings of Eleanor Roosevelt* (New York: Columbia University Press, 1999), p. 190.
3. "Universal Declaration of Human Rights," December 10, 1948, in Carol Elizabeth Lockwood, Daniel Barstow Magraw, Margaret Faith Spring, and S. I. Strong, eds., *The International Human Rights of Women: Instruments of Change* (New York: American Bar Association, 1998), p. 138.
4. Eleanor Roosevelt, "Eisenhower Administration Rejects Treaty," *My Day*, April 8, 1953, in Black, *Courage in a Dangerous World*, pp. 187-188.
5. Paul Gordon Lauren, *The Evolution of International Human Rights: Visions Seen* (Philadelphia: University of Pennsylvania Press, 2003), p. 303.
6. Felice D. Gaer, "And Never the Twain Shall Meet? The Struggle to Establish Women's Rights as International Human Rights," in Lockwood et al., *The International Human Rights of Women*, p. 8.
7. Eleanor Roosevelt, "Making Human Rights Come Alive," Speech to the Second National Conference on UNESCO, 1949, http://www.udhr.org/history/114.htm.
8. Arvonne S. Fraser, "Becoming Human: The Origins and Development of Women's Human Rights," *Human Rights Quarterly* Vol. 21, No. 4 (November 1999), p. 891.
9. "Convention on the Elimination of All Forms of Discrimination Against Women (CEDAW), December 18, 1979, in Lockwood et al., pp. 269-280.

10. Rebecca J. Cook, "Women's International Human Rights Law: The Way Forward," in Rebecca Cook, ed., *Human Rights of Women: National and International Perspectives* (Philadelphia: University of Philadelphia Press, 1994), p. 11.

11. "Committee on the Elimination of Discrimination Against Women: General Recommendation Number 19," January 29, 1992, in Lockwood et al., pp. 352-58.

12. Charlotte Bunch, "Women's Rights as Human Rights: Toward a Re-Vision of Human Rights," *Human Rights Quarterly* Vol. 12, No. 4 (November 1990), p. 486.

CHAPTER 2 (Charlotte Bunch)

1. The petition was launched as the first action of the "16 Days of Activism Against Gender Violence" annual campaign (November 25–December 10), which came out of the Women's Global Leadership Institute organized by Rutgers University's Center for Women's Global Leadership in 1991.

2. The Women Human Rights Defenders International Coalition, formed in 2005, has produced a number of useful publications addressing this issue available at the websites www.defendingwomen-defendingrights.org and http://awid.org.

CHAPTER 3 (Isobel Coleman)

1. International Center for Research on Women. "Bridging the Gender Divide: How Technology Can Advance Women Economically" (ICRW Publications, 2010), p. 2.

2. GSMA Development Fund and the Cherie Blair Foundation for Women, "Women & Mobile: A Global Opportunity" (Cherie Blair Foundation, 2010), p. 6.

3. *Ibid.*

4. Isobel Coleman, "Saudi Arabia's Social Media Battles" (Democracy in Development Blog @CFR, July 11, 2011), available at http://blogs.cfr.org/coleman/2011/07/11/saudi-arabias-social-media-battles/.

5. "Women & Mobile: A Global Opportunity," p. 7.

6. Karim Khoja, "Engaging Boys and Men as Allies for Long-Term Change," The Clinton Global Initiative, September 22, 2011.

7. *Ibid.*

CHAPTER 5 (Sussan Tahmasebi)

1. The text of this petition is available at the Million Signatures Campaign website: http://www.1millionchange.info/english/spip.php?article19.

2. For an analysis on the election results, see Issandr El Amrani and Ursula Lindsey, *Tunisia Moves to the Next Stage, Middle East Research and Information Project*, November 8, 2011, available at http://www.merip.org/mero/mero110811.

3. Ibid.

4. Kouichi Shiryanagi, *Ennahda Spokeswoman Souad Abderrahim: Single Mothers Are a Disgrace to Tunisia*, Tunisia-Live, November 2, 2011, http://www

.tunisia-live.net/2011/11/09/ennahda-spokeswoman-souad-abderrahim-single-mothers-are-a-disgrace-to-tunisia.

CHAPTER 6 (Esraa Abdel Fattah)

1. See Mara Revkin, "Has Egypt's Revolution left women behind?" available at http://mideast.foreignpolicy.com/posts/2011/12/08/has_egypts_revolution_left_women_behind. The November 2011 elections are also discussed in Manar Amar, "Egypt women call for parallel parliament, greater rights," available at http://bikyamasr.com/50600/egypt-women-call-for-parallel-parliament-greater-rights.

CHAPTER 8 (Christoph Wilcke)

1. Human Rights Watch, *Looser Rein, Uncertain Gain: A Human Rights Assessment of Five Years of King Abdullah's Reforms in Saudi Arabia* (September 2010), p. 17. Available at http://www.hrw.org/en/reports/2010/09/27/looser-rein-uncertain-gain-0.

2. Human Rights Watch, *Perpetual Minors: Human Rights Abuses Stemming from Male Guardianship and Sex Segregation in Saudi Arabia* (April 2008), p. 13. Available at http://www.hrw.org/en/reports/2008/04/19/perpetual-minors-0.

CHAPTER 9 (Jody Williams)

1. For more details, please see the "Refugee Women" page of the United Nations High Commissioner for Refugees's website, www.unhcr.org/pages/49c3646c1d9.html.

CHAPTER 10 (Hawa Abdi with Sarah Robbins)

1. Internal Displacement Monitoring Centre and Norwegian Refugee Council, *Internal Displacement: Global Overview of Trends and Developments in 2010* (IDMC Publications, March 2011), available at www.internal-displacement.org/publications/global-overview-2010.pdf.

2. See Rachel Mayanja, "Armed Conflict and Women – Ten Years of Security Council Resolution 1325," *UN Chronicle*, February 25, 2010, available at https://www.un.org/wcm/content/site/chronicle/cache/bypass/home/archive/issues2010/empoweringwomen/armedconflictandwomenscr1325.

3. Save the Children, *Champions for Children: Sate of the World's Mothers 2011*, available at www.savethechildren.org/site/c.8rKLIXMGIpI4E/b.6743707/k.219/State_of_the_Worlds_Mothers_2011.htm.

4. *Ibid.*

CHAPTER 11 (Anneke Van Woudenberg)

1. Not her real name.

2. In this chapter "Congo" refers to the Democratic Republic of Congo, not the neighboring Republic of the Congo.

3. "UN official calls DR Congo 'rape capital of the world,'" *BBC News*, April 28, 2010, available at http://news.bbc.co.uk/2/hi/africa/8650112.stm.

4. Katrina Manson, "Congo colonel gets 20 years for rape," *Financial Times*, February 21, 2011. Available at http://www.ft.com/cms/s/0/04b7bb36-3dc4-11e0-ae2a-00144feabdc0.html#axzz1RHiRdnPC.

CHAPTER 12 (Georgette Gagnon)

1. Georgette Gagnon gratefully acknowledges the contribution of Madoka Saji to this article in addition to the efforts of the UNAMA Human Rights Unit.
2. The UN's Committee on the Elimination of Discrimination against Women (CEDAW) describes harmful traditional practices as: "traditional attitudes by which women are regarded as subordinate to men or as having stereotyped roles" and perpetuate "widespread practices involving violence or coercion, such as family violence and abuse, forced marriage. . . . Such prejudices and practices may justify gender-based violence as a form of protection or control of women. The effect of such violence on the physical and mental integrity of women is to deprive them of the equal enjoyment, exercise and knowledge of human rights and fundamental freedoms." CEDAW Committee General Recommendation No. 19, 1992.
3. United Nations Assistance Mission in Afghanistan, *Harmful Traditional Practices and Implementation of the Law on Elimination of Violence Against Women in Afghanistan* (UNAMA, December 2010).
4. World Health Organization, UNICEF et al., *Trends in Maternal Mortality, 1990 to 2008* (WHO Publications, 2010), available at http://whqlibdoc.who .int/publications/2010/9789241500265_eng.pdf.
5. Human Rights Watch, *"We Have the Promises of the World": Women's Rights in Afghanistan* (December 2009), available at http://www.hrw.org/reports/ 2009/12/03/we-have-promises-world-0.
6. Human Rights Watch, *The "Ten-Dollar Talib" and Women's Rights: Afghan Women and the Risks of Reintegration and Reconciliation* (July 2010), available at http://www.hrw.org/reports/2010/07/13/ten-dollar-talib-and-women-s-rights-0.

CHAPTER 13 (Rachel Reid)

1. "Nadia" is a pseudonym, as are the other names of Afghan women cited in this chapter, who were the recipients of threats by the Taliban.
2. USAID, "Afghanistan Gender Fact Sheet" (December 2010), available at http://afghanistan.usaid.gov/documents/document/Document/1266/Gender_Fact_Sheet2142011.
3. Lynne O'Donnell, "Afghan women dice with death to work," *AFP*, March 8, 2010, available at http://www.google.com/hostednews/afp/article/ALeqM5i VHKkrE5S8KNekzWKhwJ9eVAhurg.

CHAPTER 15 (Nisha Varia)

1. "Oda a la mujer invisible," poem written by Cristina Michaus of the Mexican NGO *Centro de apoyo y capacitación para empleadas del hogar* (Support and Training Center for Domestic Workers, known as CACEH), March 30, 2011.
2. Human Rights Watch interview with Sandra C., Filipina domestic worker, Jeddah, Saudi Arabia, December 9, 2006. Excerpts published in Human Rights Watch's report *"As if I Am Not Human": Abuses Against Asian Domestic Workers in Saudi Arabia* (July 2008). Available at http://www.hrw.org/reports/2008/07/07/if-i-am-not-human-0.
3. Human Rights Watch interview with Siti Mujiati W., Indonesian domestic worker, Jeddah, Saudi Arabia, December 11, 2006. Published in Human Rights Watch's report *"As if I Am Not Human": Abuses Against Asian Domestic Workers in Saudi Arabia* (July 2008), p. 52. Available at http://www.hrw.org/reports/2008/07/07/if-i-am-not-human-0.
4. "Oda a la mujer invisible," by Cristina Michaus/CACEH, March 30, 2011.

CHAPTER 16 (Mark Lagon)

1. Donna M. Hughes, "The Demand: Where Sex Trafficking Begins," Address at "A Call to Action: Joining the Fight Against Trafficking in Persons," conference at the Pontifical Gregorian University, Rome, Italy, June 17, 2004. See http://www.uri.edu/artsci/wms/hughes/demand_rome_june04.pdf.
2. See Catharine A. MacKinnon, "Trafficking, Prostitution, and Inequality," *Harvard Civil Rights-Civil Liberties Law Review*, Vol. 46, No. 2 (Summer 2011), pp. 271-309.
3. US Department of State, *Trafficking in Persons Report* (June 2011), p. 38. See http://www.state.gov/documents/organization/164453.pdf.
4. *Ibid.*, pp. 97-98.
5. US Department of State, *Trafficking in Persons Report* (June 2008), pp. 182-184. See http://www.state.gov/documents/organization/105658.pdf.
6. Lydia Cacho, *Esclavas Del Poder: Un Viaje Al Corazon De La Trata Sexual De Mujeres Y Ninas En El Mundo* (Barcelona: Grijalbo, 2011)

CHAPTER 17 (Elaine Pearson)

1. All names of victims of trafficking in this chapter, except for one who has voluntarily publicized her case, have been changed to protect their identity.
2. Article 3 of the UN Trafficking Protocol states (a) "Trafficking in persons" shall mean the recruitment, transportation, transfer, harbouring or receipt of persons, by means of the threat or use of force or other forms of coercion, of abduction, of fraud, of deception, of the abuse of power or of a position of vulnerability or of the giving or receiving of payments or benefits to achieve the consent of a person having control over another person, for the purpose of exploitation. Exploitation shall include, at a minimum, the exploitation of the prostitution of others or other forms of sexual exploitation, forced labour or services, slavery or practices similar to slavery, servitude or the removal

of organs; (b) The consent of a victim of trafficking in persons to the intended exploitation set forth in subparagraph (a) of this article shall be irrelevant where any of the means set forth in subparagraph (a) have been used; (c) The recruitment, transportation, transfer, harbouring or receipt of a child for the purpose of exploitation shall be considered "trafficking in persons" even if this does not involve any of the means set forth in subparagraph (a) of this article; (d) "Child" shall mean any person under eighteen years of age. Article 3 of the UN Trafficking Protocol, available at http://www2.ohchr .org/english/law/protocoltraffic.htm.

3. Mende Nazer with Damien Lewis, *Slave: My True Story* (PublicAffairs, 2004).

4. Louise Shelley, *Human Trafficking: A Global Perspective* (Cambridge University Press, 2010), p. 16.

5. ILO, *A Global Alliance Against Forced Labour*, 2005, available at http://www.ilo.org/public/english/standards/relm/ilc/ilc93/pdf/rep-i-b.pdf.

6. Men who are trafficked are often not identified as such. For instance, Thai authorities were slow to provide support to Cambodian and Burmese men trafficked onto fishing boats, as noted by the UN Special Rapporteur on Trafficking Joy Ezeilo after her August 2011 visit to Thailand.

7. Principle 3 of the UN Office of the High Commissioner on Human Rights Recommended Principles and Guidelines on Human Rights and Human Trafficking, May 2002. See http://www.ohchr.org/Documents/Publications/Traffickingen.pdf. A detailed commentary to the Principles and Guidelines was released in 2010 and is available at http://www.ohchr.org/Documents/Publications/Commentary_Human_Trafficking_en.pdf.

8. US Department of State, Trafficking in Persons report, Thailand, 2011, available at http://www.state.gov/g/tip/rls/tiprpt/2011/index.htm.

9. This discussion on shelter detention is based on the author's previous research with Dr. Anne Gallagher for the Asia Regional Trafficking in Persons project. The findings of the research were published in Anne Gallagher and Elaine Pearson, "The High Cost of Freedom: A Legal and Policy Analysis of Shelter Detention for Victims of Trafficking," *Human Rights Quarterly*, Vol. 32, 2010, pp. 73-114.

10. OHCHR Press Statement "Thailand must do more to combat human trafficking effectively and protect the rights of migrant workers who are increasingly vulnerable to forced and exploitative labor," dated August 19, 2011, available at http://www.ohchr.org/en/NewsEvents/Pages/DisplayNews.aspx?NewsID=11319&LangID=E.

11. For instance, see US Government Accountability Office, Report to the Chairman, Committee on the Judiciary and the Chairman, Committee on International Relations, House of Representatives. Human Trafficking Better Data, Strategy and Reporting Needed to Enhance US Anti-trafficking Efforts Abroad, 2006.

12. Global Alliance Against Traffic in Women, *Collateral Damage: The Impact of Anti-Trafficking Measures on Human Rights Around the World*, Bangkok, 2007, p. 21.

13. As an example, see Home Office (United Kingdom), *Human Trafficking: The Government's Strategy*, 2011, available at http://www.homeoffice.gov.uk/publications/crime/human-trafficking-strategy.

14. Elaine Pearson, *Human Traffic, Human Rights: Redefining Victim Protection*, Anti-Slavery International, 2002, p. 151 at http://www.antislavery.org/includes/documents/cm_docs/2009/h/hum_traff_hum_rights_redef_vic_protec_final_full.pdf.

CHAPTER 19 (Meghan Rhoad)

1. United Nations, Department of Economic and Social Affairs, Population Division (2009). *Trends in International Migrant Stock: The 2008 Revision* (United Nations database, POP/DB/MIG/Stock/Rev.2008).

2. Human Rights Council, "Report of the Special Rapporteur on Violence Against Women, Its Causes and Consequences, Ms. Rashida Manjoo: Mission to the United States of America" (June 2011) A/HRC/17/26/Add.5, para. 98, available at http://www2.ohchr.org/english/bodies/hrcouncil/docs/17session/A.HRC.17.26.Add.5_AEV.pdf.

3. Michael Hennessey, "Secure Communities destroys public trust," *San Francisco Chronicle*, May 1, 2011.

4. Tessie Borden, "INS: Border policy failed Sherrie Buzby," *The Arizona Republic*, August 10, 2000.

5. Anna Ochoa O'Leary, "Close Encounters of the Deadly Kind: Gender, Migration, and Border (In)Security," *Migration Letters*, October 2008, Vol. 15, No. 2, pp. 111-122.

6. Human Rights Watch interview with Lydia N., Nogales, Mexico, April 2011.

7. Navi Pillay, "Migration, Conflict and Xenophobia," opening address at the SANPAD Conference in The Hague, May 10, 2011.

8. Suzanne Gamboa, "ICE investigating alleged sexual assault of detainees," *Associated Press*, May 28, 2010.

9. Mayra Soto, testimony before the National Prison Rape Elimination Commission Testimony, Los Angeles, December 13, 2006, accessed July 15, 2010, at http://www.justdetention.org/en/NPREC/esmeraldasoto.aspx.

10. Alfonso Chardy and Jay Weaver, "Agent charged with raping woman," *The Miami Herald*, November 17, 2007.

11. Jay Weaver, "Ex-ICE agent: I had sex with immigration detainee," *The Miami Herald*, April 4, 2008, accessed July 15, 2010, at http://www.detentionwatchnetwork.org/node/808.

12. Department of Justice, Office of Public Affairs, "Detention Officer Sentenced for Repeated Sexual Abuse of Detainees," April 7, 2010, accessed July 15, 2010, at http://www.justice.gov/opa/pr/2010/April/10-crt-380.html.

13. Parliamentary Assembly of the Council of Europe, "Migrant Women: At Particular Risk from Domestic Violence," July 15, 2009, available at http://assembly.coe.int/Documents/WorkingDocs/Doc09/EDOC11991.pdf.

14. International Organization for Migration, "Women Migrants in South Africa Suffer Violence Long After 2008 Xenophobic Attacks," December 18, 2009, available at http://www.iom.int/jahia/Jahia/media/feature-stories/featureArticleAF/cache/offonce?entryId=26722.

CHAPTER 21 (Aruna Kashyap)

1. World Health Organization et al, *Trends in Maternal Mortality: 1990 to 2008* (WHO Publications, 2010), p. 1. Available at http://whqlibdoc.who.int/publications/2010/9789241500265_eng.pdf.

CHAPTER 22 (Nadya Khalife)

1. Human Rights Watch, *"They Took Me and Told Me Nothing": Female Genital Mutilation in Iraqi Kurdistan* (June 2010), available at http://www.hrw.org/reports/2010/06/16/they-took-me-and-told-me-nothing-0.

2. World Health Organization, "Progress in Sexual and Reproductive Health Research: Female Genital Mutilation—New Knowledge Spurs Optimism," Vol. 72 (2006), p. 7.

3. Padmini Murthy and Clyde Lanford Smith, *Women's Global Health and Human Rights* (Massachusetts: Jones and Bartlett Publishers, 2010), p. 465.

4. Nahid Toubia, "Female Genital Mutilation," in Julie Peters and Andrea Wolper, eds., *Women's Rights Human Rights: International Feminist Perspectives* (New York: Routledge, 1995), p. 229.

5. Celia Dugger, "Senegal curbs a bloody rite for girls and women," *New York Times*, October 16, 2011, available at http://www.nytimes.com/2011/10/16/world/africa/movement-to-end-genital-cutting-spreads-in-senegal.html.

CHAPTER 23 (Agnes Odhiambo)

1. Human Rights Watch, *"I Am Not Dead, But I Am Not Living": Barriers to Fistula Prevention and Treatment in Kenya* (July 2010), available at http://www.hrw.org/reports/2010/07/15/i-am-not-dead-i-am-not-living.

2. United Nations Population Fund, *Campaign to End Fistula—2008 Annual Report* (UNFPA, 2008), p. 16.

3. Campaign to End Fistula, "When new technology saves lives," September 7, 2011, available at http://www.endfistula.org/public/pid/7441?feedEntryId=15412.

4. The Fistula Foundation is a major donor to fistula treatment centers in Ethiopia, such as the Hamlin Fistula Hospitals in Addis Ababa. See http://www.fistulafoundation.org/wherewehelp/ethiopia/.

CHAPTER 24 (Marianne Mollmann)

1. Due to Mexico's federal structure, access to abortion is governed by state law. Except for Mexico City, all jurisdictions in Mexico criminalize abortion both

for the pregnant woman who procures the abortion and for the health professional who provides it. Mexico City's law criminalizes abortion, but defines it as the termination of a pregnancy after twelve weeks of gestation. As a result, a pregnancy termination during the first trimester of the pregnancy is legal because it is not technically defined as an abortion. In Cuba, abortion is available upon request in the public health system up to the tenth week of the pregnancy.

CHAPTER 25 (Sharon Hom)

1. Sharon Hom, "Advancing Women's International Human Rights in China." in Pauline Stoltz, Marina Svensson, Sun Zhongxin, and Qi Wang, eds., *Gender Equality, Citizenship and Human Rights: Controversies and Challenges in China and the Nordic Countries* (Routledge, 2010), pp. 59-73.

2. China has signed and even ratified key international treaties for human rights, including the Convention on the Elimination of All Forms of Discrimination Against Women (signed July 17, 1980, ratified November 4, 1980); International Convention For Elimination of Racial Discrimination (CERD) (acceded December 29,1981); UN Convention Against Torture and Other Cruel, Inhuman or Degrading Treatment (1988); The Convention on the Rights of the Child (CRC) (signed August 29, 1990, ratified March 2, 1992); and International Covenant on Economic, Social, and Cultural Rights (ICESCR) (signed October 27, 1997, ratified March 27, 2001, with reservations regarding independent unions).

3. Committee on the Elimination of Discrimination against Women, 2006; HRIC CEDAW Report, 2006; Human Rights in China (HRIC) and Minority Rights Group International (MRG), *China: Minority Exclusion, Marginalization and Rising Tensions* (HRIC & MRG, 2007); Sharon Hom and Stacy Mosher, *Challenging China: Struggle and Hope in an Era of Change* (New Press, 2007).

4. Law of the People's Republic of China on Guarding State Secrets [中华人民共和国保守国家秘密法], issued by the Standing Committee of the National People's Congress [全国人民代表大会常务委员会], promulgated September 5, 1988, effective May 1, 1989; revised April 29, 2010, effective October 1, 2010; an unofficial English translation is available in Human Rights in China, "Nationwide State Secrets Education Campaign Launched as New Law Goes into Effect," October 1, 2010, http://www.hrichina.org/content/842.

5. Information Office of the State Council of the People's Republic of China, 2008. *White Paper: China's Efforts and Achievements in Promoting the Rule of Law*. Beijing: Information Office of the State Council of the People's Republic of China, February 28, 2008.

6. *People's Daily*, April 22, 2007.

CHAPTER 26 (Sheridan Prasso)

1. This was one of the findings of a national survey conducted in 2010 by the All-China Women's Federation (ACWF), the largest women's non-government organization in China. See Mitch Moxley, "For Too Many, Domestic Violence Part of Family Life," IPSNews.net, October 5, 2010, available at http://ipsnews.net/news.asp?idnews=53071.

2. Chen Jia. "Traffickers Target Young Females," *China Daily*, March 18, 2010. See: http://www.chinadaily.com.cn/usa/2010-03/18/content_11016991.htm. See also "China National Plan of Action on Combating Trafficking in Women and Children (2008-2012)," Academy for Educational Development. See: http://www.humantrafficking.org/countries/china.

3. Compulsory Education Law, art. 5.

4. See for example Implementation of the Convention on the Elimination of All Forms of Discrimination Against Women, A Parallel NGO Report by Human Rights in China, New York, 2006.

5. Nicholas D. Kristof and Sheryl WuDunn. *Half the Sky: Turning Oppression into Opportunity for Women Worldwide* (New York: Vintage Books, 2009), p. xix.

6. Hu Yuanyuan. "China Ranks High in Women CEOs," *China Daily*, March 8, 2011, p. 3. See: http://www.chinadaily.com.cn/cndy/2011-03/08/content_12132579.htm.

7. Wang Wei. "Male Grads Given Edge in Job Recruitment," *China Daily*, March 12, 2010. See: http://www.chinadaily.com.cn/bizchina/2010-03/02/content_9525192.htm.

CHAPTER 27 (Graça Machel and Mary Robinson)

1. Population Council, 2004 analysis of UN country data on marriage.

2. The Millennium Development Goals set UN-agreed targets on: poverty and hunger, universal education, gender equality, child health, maternal health, HIV/AIDS, environmental sustainability, and global partnership. The goals are set out in detail at http://www.un.org/millenniumgoals/.

3. L. Levine, C. Lloyd, C. M. Greene, and C. Grown. "Child Marriage, Risk of HIV, and Sexual Violence: How Girls Are Affected and What Can Be Done," in *Girls Count: A Global Investment and Action Agenda* (Center for Global Development, 2009), available at http://www.cgdev.org/content/publications/detail/15154.

4. Cynthia B. Lloyd with Juliet Young. *New Lessons: The Power of Educating Adolescent Girls* (Population Council, 2009), available at http://www.popcouncil.org/pdfs/2009PGY_NewLessons.pdf.

5. UNICEF. *The State of the World's Children 2007* (New York: UNICEF, 2007). Available at http://www.unicef.org/sowc07/docs/sowc07.pdf.

6. S. Clark. "Early Marriage and HIV Risks in Sub-Saharan Africa," *Studies in Family Planning* (2004), Vol. 35(3): 149-160, http://www.ncbi.nlm.nih.gov/pubmed/15511059.

7. S. Clark, J. Bruce, & A. Dude. "Protecting Young Women from HIV/AIDS: The Case Against Child and Adolescent Marriage," *International Family Perspectives* (2006), 32(2): 79-99. http://www.guttmacher.org/pubs/journals/3207906.html .

8. International Center for Research on Women, "Development initiative on supporting healthy adolescents (DISHA) project" (ICRW, 2005).

9. *Ibid.*

10. See "Pakistan: Tribal custom forces girls into compensation marriages," IRIN, August 20, 2003, http://www.irinnews.org/PrintReport.aspx?ReportId=20618.

11. A complete description of *Girls Not Brides*' agenda and activities is available on the organization's website: http://girlsnotbrides.org/. Other initiatives undertaken by The Elders are described here: www.TheElders.com.

CHAPTER 28 (Judith Sunderland)

1. See Human Rights Watch press release, "Gaza: Rescind Religious Dress Code for Girls," September 4, 2009.

2. See Human Rights Watch report, "You Dress According to Their Rules": Enforcement of an Islamic Dress Code for Women in Chechnya, March 2011.

3. See Human Rights Watch report, Harsh War, Harsh Peace: Abuses by al-Shabaab, the Transitional Federal Government and AMISOM in Somalia, April 2010.

4. Open Society Foundations At Home in Europe Project, "Unveiling the Truth: Why 32 Muslim Women Wear the Full-face Veil in France, p. 74.

5. "Report of the Special Rapporteur Asma Jahangir on freedom of religion or belief on Civil and Political Rights, including the question of religious intolerance, E/CN.4/2006/5, UN Commission on Human Rights, January 9, 2006, para. 55.

6. Thomas Hammarberg. "Europe must not ban the burka," *The Guardian*, March 8, 2010, http://www.guardian.co.uk/commentisfree/2010/mar/08/europe-ban-burqa-veil.

CHAPTER 29 (Gara LaMarche)

1. Linda Burnham. "The Absence of a Gender Justice Framework in Social Justice Organizing" (Center for the Education of Women, University of Michigan, 2008), available at http://www.cew.umich.edu/sites/default/files/BurnhamFinalProject.pdf.

CHAPTER 30 (Liesl Gerntholtz)

1. Committee on Discrimination Against Women, General Recommendation 19: Violence Against Women, 1992.

2. Claudia García-Moreno et al, *WHO Multi-country Study on Women's Health and Domestic Violence against Women* (WHO Press, World Health Organization, 2005), Preface, p. vi. Available at http://www.who.int/gender/violence/who_multicountry_study/en/.

3. Kofi Annan, Remarks on International Women's Day, March 8, 1999.

4. United Nations, *The World's Women 2010: Trends and Statistics* (United Nations, Department of Economic and Social Affairs, October 2010), pp. 127-139. Available at http://unstats.un.org/unsd/demographic/products/Worldswomen/WW_full%20report_color.pdf.

5. Roni Caryn Rabin, "Nearly 1 in 5 Women in U.S. Survey Say They Have Been Sexually Assaulted," New York Times, December 14, 2011, available at http://www.nytimes.com/2011/12/15/health/nearly-1-in-5-women-in-us-survey-report-sexual-assault.html.

6. United Nations press release, "Secretary-General's Remarks at Event to Commemorate the International Day for the Elimination of Violence Against Women," November 23, 2011, available at http://www.un.org/apps/sg/sgstats.asp?nid=5705.

7. "Beijing Declaration and Platform for Action" (1995), available at http://www.un.org/womenwatch/daw/beijing/platform/.

8. United Nations Department of Economic and Social Affairs, Division for the Advancement of Women, *Handbook for Legislation on Violence against Women* (United Nations, 2010), available at http://www.un.org/womenwatch/daw/vaw/handbook/Handbook%20for%20legislation%20on%20violence%20against%20women.pdf.

Suggestions for Fur

HISTORY OF THE MOVEMENT FOR WOMEN'S HUMAN
GENERAL BACKGROUND

Brooke Ackerly, *Universal Human Rights in a World of Differ*
University Press, 2008)

Marjorie Agosín, ed., *Women, Gender, and Human Rights: A Glo*
(Rutgers University Press, 2001)

Kwame Anthony Appiah, *The Honor Code: How Moral Revolutions Happen*
(W.W. Norton, 2010)

Jennifer Baumgardner, Amy Richards, *Manifesta: Young Women, Feminism and the Future* (Macmillan, 2000)

Charlotte Bunch, *Passionate Politics: Feminist Theory in Action* (St. Martin's Griffin, 1987)

Ellen Chesler, *Woman of Valor: Margaret Sanger and the Birth Control Movement in America* (Simon and Schuster, 2007)

Rebecca Cook, ed., *Human Rights of Women: National and International Perspectives* (University of Philadelphia Press, 1994)

Angela Davis, *Women, Race and Class* (Random House, 1981)

Carolyn Heilbrun and Katha Politt, *Writing a Woman's Life* (W.W. Norton, 2008)

Nicholas Kristof and Sheryl WuDunn, *Half the Sky: Turning Oppression into Opportunity for Women Worldwide* (Vintage Books, 2009)

Jeri Laber, *The Courage of Strangers: Coming of Age with the Human Rights Movement,* (Public Affairs, 2005)

Liz McQuiston, *Suffragettes to She-Devils* (Phaidon, 1997)

Chandra Mohanty, *Feminism without Borders: Decolonizing Theory, Practicing Solidarity* (Duke University Press, 2003)

Susan Deller Ross, *Women's Human Rights: The International and Comparative Law Casebook* (University of Pennsylvania Press, 2009)

Hanna Beate Schopp-Schilling, ed., *The Circle of Empowerment: Twenty-Five Years of the UN Committee on the Elimination of Discrimination Against Women* (Feminist Press, 2007)

...sic Books, 2009)

...ion (SAGE, 1997)

TRAFFICKING

...rvice and Servitude (Columbia University Press, 1998)

...or the Family? How Class and Gender Shape Women's Work ...sity Press, 2011)

...renreich and Arlie Russell Hochschild, Global Woman: Nannies, Sex Workers in the New Economy (Henry Holt & Co., 2002)

...el Lloyd, Girls Like Us: Fighting for a World Where Girls Are Not for Sale, an ...ctivist Finds Her Calling and Heals Herself (HarperCollins, 2011)

Somaly Mam, The Road of Lost Innocence (Random House, 2008)

Mende Nazer, with Damien Lewis, Slave: My True Story (Public Affairs, 2004)

Jesse Sage, Liora Kasten & Gloria Steinem, Enslaved: True Stories of Modern Day Slavery (Macmillan, 2008)

Benjamin Skinner, A Crime So Monstrous (Simon & Schuster, 2009)

VIOLENCE AGAINST WOMEN

Nujood Ali with Delphine Minoui, I Am Nujood, Age 10 and Divorced (Random House, 2010)

Maya Angelou, I Know Why the Caged Bird Sings (Random House, 1970)

Andrea Ashworth, Once in a House on Fire (Macmillan Children's Books, 2004)

Claudia García-Moreno et al, WHO Multi-country Study on Women's Health and Domestic Violence against Women (WHO Press, World Health Organization, 2005)

Joshua Goldstein, War and Gender (Cambridge University Press, 2003)

Ann Jones, War Is Not Over When It's Over (Macmillan, 2010)

Mmatshilo Motsei, The Kanga and the Kangaroo Trial: Reflections of the Trial of Jacob Zuma (Jacana Media, 2007)

Zainab Salbi et al, The Other Side of War (National Geographic Books, 2006)

Lisa Shannon, A Thousand Sisters: My Journey into the Worst Place on Earth to Be a Woman (Seal Press, 2010)

MATERNAL MORTALITY, REPRODUCTIVE RIGHTS, AND OTHER HEALTH ISSUES

Wendy Chavkin and Ellen Chesler, eds., Where Human Rights Begin: Health, Sexuality and Women in the New Millennium (Rutgers University Press, 2005)

Rebecca Cook, Bernard Dickens & Mahmoud Fathalla, Reproductive Health and Human Rights: Integrating Medicine, Ethics, and Law (Oxford University Press, 2003)

Padmini Murthy and Clyde Lanford Smith, *Women's Global Health and Human Rights* (Jones & Bartlett Publishers, 2010)

Rosalind Pollack Petchesky, *Global Prescriptions: Gendering Health and Human Rights* (Zed Books, 2003)

Laura Reichenbach and Mindy Jane Roseman, *Reproductive Health and Human Rights: The Way Forward* (University of Pennsylvania Press, 2009)

Gita Sen, Adrienne Germain & Lincoln Chen, eds., *Population Policies Reconsidered: Health, Empowerment and Rights* (Harvard University Press, 1994)

Cecilia Van Hollen, *Birth on the Threshold: Childbirth and Modernity in South India* (University of California Press, 2003)

WOMEN AND DEVELOPMENT

Arvonne S. Fraser and Irene Tiner, eds., *Developing Power: How Women Transformed International Development* (Feminist Press, 2004)

Martha C. Nussbaum, *Women and Human Development: The Capabilities Approach* (Cambridge University Press, 2000)

Amartya Kumar Sen, *Development as Freedom* (Random House Digital, Inc., 1999)

TRENDS AND STATISTICS

International Center for Research on Women, *Bridging the Gender Divide: How Technology can Advance Women Economically* (ICRW Publications, 2010)

United Nations, *The World's Women 2010: Trends and Statistics* (United Nations, Department of Economic and Social Affairs, October 2010)

World Health Organization et al, *Trends in Maternal Mortality, 1990 to 2008* (WHO Publications, 2010)

WOMEN'S RIGHTS IN THE MIDDLE EAST

Leila Ahmad, *Women & Gender in Islam* (Yale University Press, 1992)

Qanta Ahmed, *In the Land of Invisible Women* (Sourcebooks, Inc., 2008)

Hanan Al-Shaykh, *Women of Sand and Myrrh* (Bloomsbury, 2010)

Geraldine Brooks, *Nine Parts of Desire: The Hidden World of Islamic Women* (Random House, 1995)

Isobel Coleman, *Paradise Beneath Her Feet: How Women Are Transforming the Middle East* (Random House, 2010)

Shirin Ebadi and Azadeh Moaveni, *Iran Awakening: A Memoir of Revolution and Hope* (Random House, 2006)

Nawal El Saadawi, *The Hidden face of Eve: Women in the Arab World* (Zed Books, 1981)

Erika Friedl, *The Women of De Koh: Lives in an Iranian Village* (Penguin Books, 1991)

Rana Husseini, *Murder in the Name of Honor* (Oneworld Publications, 2007)

Fatima Mernissi, *Dreams of Trespass: Tales of a Harem Girl Child* (Basic Books, 1995)

Azar Nafisi, *Things I've Been Silent About* (Random House, 2008)

Roxana Saberi, *Between Two Worlds: My Life and Captivity in Iran* (HarperCollins, 2010)

Nadje Sadig Al-Ali and Nicola Christine Pratt, *What Kind of Liberation? Women and the Occupation of Iraq* (University of California Press, 2009)

Zainab Salbi and Laurie Becklund, *Between Two Worlds: Escape from Tyranny: Growing Up in the Shadow of Saddam* (Penguin, 2006)

Haifa Zangana, *City of Widows: An Iraqi Woman's Account of War and Resistance* (Seven Stories Press, 2007)

ON ASIA AND AFRICA

Bina Agarwal, *A Field of One's Own: Gender and Land Rights in South Asia* (Cambridge University Press, 1994)

Jung Chang, *Wild Swans: Three Women of China* (Simon & Schuster, 1991)

Ellen Kuzwayo, *Call Me Woman* (Picador Africa, 2004)

Mukhtar Mai, *In the Name of Honor* (Simon & Schuster, 2007)

Sheridan Prasso, *The Asian Mystique: Dragon Ladies, Geisha Girls and Our Fantasies of the Exotic Orient* (Public Affairs, 2005)

Aung San Suu Kyi, *Freedom from Fear: And other Writings* (Penguin Books, 2010)

FICTION

Chimamanda Ngozi Adichie, *Half of a Yellow Sun* (Random House, 2007).

Daisy Al-Amir, *The Waiting List: An Iraqi Woman's Tales of Alienation* (University of Texas Press, 1994).

Ama Ata Aidoo, *No Sweetness Here: A Collection of Short Stories* (Longman, 1970)

Hanan al-Shaykh, *The Story of Zahra: A Novel* (Pustaka Alvabet, 1987)

Margaret Atwood, *The Handmaid's Tale* (Doubleday, 1998)

Tahar Ben Jelloun, *The Sacred Night* (Johns Hopkins University Press, 2000), originally published in French as *La Nuit Sacrée* in 1987

Ismat Chugtai, *Lifting the Veil* (Penguin Books, 2001)

Sandra Cisneros, *Woman Hollering Creek* (Bloomsbury, 2004)

Chris Cleave, *Little Bee* (Random House, 2009)

Edwidge Danticat, *The Farming of Bones* (Soho Press, 1998)

Chitra Banerjee Divakaruni, *Arranged Marriage* (Black Swan, 1997)

Assia Djebar, *So Vast the Prison* (Seven Stories Press, 1999)

Unity Dow, *Far and Beyon'* (Spinifex Press, 2001)

Nawal El Saadawi, *Woman at Point Zero* (Zed Books, 2007)

Buchi Emecheta, *The Joys of Motherhood* (Heinemann, 1994)

Eve Ensler, *The Vagina Monologues* (Random House Digital, Inc., 2001).

Marilyn French, *The Women's Room* (Virago Press Ltd., 1997; first published 1977).

Ursula K. Le Guin, *The Left Hand of Darkness* (Little, Brown, 2009)

Naguib Mahfouz, *Palace Walk* (Anchor, 1990)

Toni Morrison, *Beloved* (Random House Digital, Inc., 2004)

Lynn Nottage, *Ruined* (Theatre Communications Group, 2008)

Orhan Pamuk, *Snow* (Random House Digital, Inc., 2005)

Marge Piercy, *Gone to Soldiers* (Fawcett Crest, 1988)

Joanna Russ, *The Female Man* (Beacon Press, 2000)

Raja Abd Allah Sani, Rajaa Alsanea & Marilyn Booth, *Girls of Riyadh* (Penguin, 2008)

Thrity Umrigar, *The Space Between Us* (HarperCollins, 2007)

Alice Walker, *The Color Purple* (Houghton Mifflin Harcourt, 2006)

Jeanette Winterson, *Sexing the Cherry* (Grove Press, 1998)

Virginia Woolf, *A Room of One's Own* (Penguin Books, 2000; first published in 1928)

Acknowledgments

When I proposed the idea of a book on the rights of women and girls to my fearless publisher Dan Simon, he immediately proved the correct choice because the first thing he had to do was ignore the fact I was visibly pregnant and trust I could deliver both manuscript and baby on time. In addition to green-lighting the project, Dan provided inspiration for our title, writing that he once heard Nicaraguan author Gioconda Belli call women's rights "the one great unfinished revolution of our time."

Indeed, this book's title was chosen just before uprisings rippled across the Arab world in 2011. It turned out to be prophetic, as the euphoria of overthrowing dictatorships faded, and women, who in some cases risked their lives for change, found themselves without seats at the governing table. The Arab Spring has not been centrally about women's rights, but if we do not seize this moment to assess and address long-standing abuses of women and girls, the changes in the Middle East could well end up as only partial revolutions.

As Archbishop Desmond Tutu says, for women's rights to be achieved, men are key. For this book on women's rights to reach fruition, one man made a big difference: Peter Huvos of Human Rights Watch, our dedicated taskmaster, project manager, and supporter from concept to publication.

This book was conceived to celebrate the twentieth anniversary of the Women's Rights Division (WRD) at Human Rights Watch; special thanks go to Liesl Gerntholtz, director of WRD and my chief partner in crime; Janet Walsh, Miriam Wells, Matthew Rullo, Rumbidzai Chidoori, Daniela Ramirez, and all our other colleagues in the Women's

Rights Division, especially those who contributed chapters. The vision of past WRD leaders—founding director Dorothy Thomas, Regan Ralph, and LaShawn Jefferson—shaped the work that is reflected in the book. They all deserve much credit for the book's content and inspiration, and no responsibility for any errors. Legal eagle Dinah PoKempner thought the chapters would never stop arriving in her inbox, yet cheerfully edited and improved them anyway.

Facebook Chief Operating Officer Sheryl Sandberg has called gender equality "this generation's central moral problem." I am fortunate to work at Human Rights Watch, an organization that not only researches human rights abuses against women globally, but counts more than 60 percent of its staff and much of its leadership as women.

The Human Rights Watch communications team—especially Emma Daly, Carroll Bogert, Kathy Rose, Pierre Bairin, Veronica Matushaj, Jessie Graham, Kathryn Semogas, Drake Lucas, Francisco Fagan, Ivy Shen, Mariam Dwedar, Amanda Bailly, Elena Testi, Xabay Spinka, Jim Murphy, Enrique Piraces, Amr Khairy, and Hannah Taylor—all provided invaluable editing, transcribing, and translating assistance, as well as moral support.

Other colleagues vetted, edited, and headed off embarrassing errors. They include Tom Porteous, Joe Saunders, Tom Malinowski, Sarah Leah Whitson, Joe Stork, Heba Morayef, Faraz Sanei, Nadim Houry, Sahr MuhammedAlly, Brad Adams, Sophie Richardson, Phil Robertson, Meenakshi Ganguly, Alison Parker, Jamie Fellner, Daniel Wilkinson, Letta Tayler, Joe Amon, Jo Becker, Zama Coursen-Neff, Ben Ward, Rona Peligal, Corinne Dufka, Sara Darehshori, Elizabeth Seuling, Nisha Varia, Marianne Mollmann, Clive Baldwin, and Aisling Reidy. Liba Beyer, Miriam Mahlow, Tara Golden, Michele Alexander, Jasmine Herlt, Andrea Dew Steele, and Jobi Peterson advised on strategy and outreach.

Thanks to Platon, because he keeps getting on planes with me, and to Benedict Evans, Steven Laxton, Nagwa Hassaan, and Siobhan Bonhacker for making our Tahrir teamwork so amazing. New mother Anna Lopriore helped create our photo essay and gave guidance at every stage. I'm deeply grateful to Samer Muscati for not only writing a chapter, but shooting the cover photo in Iraq. Graphic designers Wai

Hung Young and Martin Bell of Fruitmachine Design created a dynamite book cover and photo essay design.

Katy Cronin of The Elders let me ruin her summer, but I hope that the chapter on early marriage made it worth her while. Essential brainstorming, editing, and publishing assistance came from Sarah Robbins, Tunku Varadarajan, Peggy Kerry, Laura Silber, Hadi Ghaemi, Maggie Thomas, Annie Sparrow, and Abigail Pesta. Susan Osnos never pours water on my crazy ideas, even though I'm sure she's been tempted over the years.

Special thanks to Dan Simon's talented team at Seven Stories Press, including Ruth Weiner, Jon Gilbert, Eva Fortes, Elizabeth DeLong, and Phoebe Hwang, and copy editor Jamie McNeely Quirk.

Thanks to the loyal donors of the Women's Rights Division—you know who you are—who have supported our work from the beginning, and who continue to help us respond to ongoing abuses and emergencies.

Sheryl WuDunn and Nick Kristof have been an inspiration for the nearly two decades I've known them. Their intrepid reporting and book *Half the Sky* bring statistics alive by giving women and girls a voice.

As I was, er, conceiving this book, I was also conceiving a baby, Thomas Worden Crovitz. I took off a few days in the hospital, but otherwise Tom put up with my editing for months without complaint while nursing. I expect that what he and his older brothers, Jack and James, have overheard in the process will cause them to grow up as very enlightened and women's rights-respecting men. Above all, my husband, Gordon Crovitz, has set a good example by doing dishes and caring for the boys. He was looking after the baby so didn't have much time to help with this book. But, as he points out, "I let you go to Egypt when you were eight months pregnant, didn't I?"

Finally, we salute the courage of the many women who shared their stories with us, without whom this book could not have been written.

Minky Worden
January 2012

Index

ABOUT SEVEN STORIES PRESS

Seven Stories Press is an independent book publisher based in New York City. We publish works of the imagination by such writers as Nelson Algren, Russell Banks, Octavia E. Butler, Ani DiFranco, Assia Djebar, Ariel Dorfman, Coco Fusco, Barry Gifford, Hwang Sok-yong, Lee Stringer, and Kurt Vonnegut, to name a few, together with political titles by voices of conscience, including the Boston Women's Health Collective, Noam Chomsky, Angela Y. Davis, Human Rights Watch, Derrick Jensen, Ralph Nader, Loretta Napoleoni, Gary Null, Project Censored, Barbara Seaman, Alice Walker, Gary Webb, and Howard Zinn, among many others. Seven Stories Press believes publishers have a special responsibility to defend free speech and human rights, and to celebrate the gifts of the human imagination, wherever we can. For additional information, visit www.sevenstories.com.